Gender, Culture and Politics in England, 1560–1640

Cultures of Early Modern Europe

Series Editors: Beat Kümin, Professor of Early Modern European History, University of Warwick; and Brian Cowan, Associate Professor and Canada Research Chair in Early Modern British History, McGill University

Editorial Board:
Adam Fox, University of Edinburgh, UK
Robert Frost, University of Aberdeen, UK
Molly Greene, University of Princeton, USA
Ben Schmidt, University of Washington, USA
Gerd Schwerhoff, University of Dresden, Germany
Francsesca Trivellato, University of Yale, USA
Francisca Loetz, University of Zurich, Switzerland

The 'cultural turn' in the humanities has generated a wealth of new research topics and approaches. Focusing on the ways in which representations, perceptions and negotiations shaped people's lived experiences, the books in this series provide fascinating insights into the past. The series covers early modern culture in its broadest sense, inclusive of (but not restricted to) themes such as gender, identity, communities, mentalities, emotions, communication, ritual, space, food and drink, and material culture.

Published:
Food and Identity in England, 1540–1640, Paul S. Lloyd (2014)
The Birth of the English Kitchen, 1600–1850, Sara Pennell (2016)
Vagrancy in English Culture and Society, 1650–1750, David Hitchcock (2016)
Angelica's Book and the World of Reading in Late Renaissance Italy, Brendan Dooley (2016)

THE
World turn'd upſide down:

OR,

A briefe deſcription of the ridiculous Faſhions of theſe diſtracted Times.

By T. J. a well-willer to King, Parliament and Kingdom.

London : Printed for *John Smith*. 1647.

Title page of [John Taylor], *The World Turn'd Upside Down, or A briefe description of the ridiculous Fashions of these distracted Times.*

Gender, Culture and Politics in England, 1560–1640

Turning the World Upside Down

Susan D. Amussen and David E. Underdown

BLOOMSBURY ACADEMIC
LONDON • NEW YORK • OXFORD • NEW DELHI • SYDNEY

BLOOMSBURY ACADEMIC
Bloomsbury Publishing Plc
50 Bedford Square, London, WC1B 3DP, UK
1385 Broadway, New York, NY 10018, USA

BLOOMSBURY, BLOOMSBURY ACADEMIC and the Diana logo are
trademarks of Bloomsbury Publishing Plc

First published in Great Britain 2017
Paperback edition first published 2018

A catalogue record for this book is available from the British Library.

ISBN: HB: 978-1-3500-2067-2
PB: 978-1-3500-9005-7
ePDF: 978-1-3500-2068-9
ePub: 978-1-3500-2069-6

Names: Amussen, Susan Dwyer, author. | Underdown, David, co-author.
Title: Gender, culture and politics in England, 1560–1640: turning the world
upside down / Susan D. Amussen and David E. Underdown.
Description: London; New York: Bloomsbury Academic, an imprint
of Bloomsbury Publishing Plc, 2017. | Includes bibliographical references.
Identifiers: LCCN 2016043586 (print) | LCCN 2016044816 (ebook) |
ISBN 9781350020672 (hardback) | ISBN 9781350020689 (PDF) |
ISBN 9781350020696 (ePub) | ISBN 9781350020689 (Epdf) | ISBN 9781350020696 (EPub)
Subjects: LCSH: Sex role–England–History. | Role reversal–England–History. | Women–
England–History. | Patriarchy–England–History. | Politics and culture–England–History. |
Literature and society–England–History. | England–Social
conditions–16th century. | England–Social conditions–17th century. | Great Britain–Politics
and government–1558–1603. | Great
Britain–Politics and government–1603–1714.
Classification: LCC HQ1075.5.G7 A68 2017 (print) | LCC HQ1075.5.G7 (ebook) |
DDC 305.30942/09031–dc23
LC record available at https://lccn.loc.gov/2016043586

Series: Cultures of Early Modern Europe

Typeset by Newgen Knowledge Works Pvt Ltd., Chennai, India.

To find out more about our authors and books visit
www.bloomsbury.com and sign up for our newsletters.

To Simone, Sam, Sara and Christopher

Contents

Illustrations

Preface and Acknowledgements

I have been having a fantastic time pursuing popular culture ... Could it just possibly be that charivari becomes directed at women who defy patriarchal norms in the 16th and 17th centuries in these particular areas because these are precisely the ones in which women's economic role ... is becoming more important and hence threatening? ... There's so much I don't know – about the use of the cucking stool in punishing scolds, for instance.

David Underdown to Susan Amussen, 16 July 1979

David Underdown began to plan this book after he published *Start of Play: Cricket and Society in Eighteenth Century England* in 2000. He worked intensely on it during the first part of the year we spent at the Huntington Library in 2002–3. Yet, as any reader familiar with his work can see, it represents an attempt to bring together a series of ideas he had been working with – and talking about – since the late 1970s; the letters I received when I was a graduate student doing dissertation research were full of his thinking and discoveries. As he planned this book, he wanted to focus attention on the ways in which inversion worked as a cultural, political and social trope in the early seventeenth century. It was inversion, he believed, that connected his interest in politics, in skimmingtons and in early seventeenth-century drama. He saw this book as a way to pull these pieces together; he called it his 'mental world' book. It was harder than he expected, and the surgeries and chemotherapy he endured during the six and a half years he lived with stage four colon cancer made it more difficult for him to concentrate and write. But the challenges were more basic: all of his other books follow a chronological structure, and this project did not lend itself to that. By the time of his death in 2009, however, David had an outline, and had written about 40,000 words; he had drafted some part of each chapter. (Chapter 4 was empty, but he had written its core, the 'Wells May Games', and refined that for publication.) In the summer of 2009, he went through his drafts and made notes about what he wanted to do with the chapters. We also agreed at that time that I would become his co-author, though his health deteriorated so rapidly that we never worked together on it. Although we had been talking about the project over almost thirty years in one way or another, I did not read the manuscript while he was alive. The draft as he left it, he would have been the first to admit, was his standard first draft, a bit conversational, too often descriptive or narrative, and with big gaps.

After he died, I debated whether to finish the book. I decided to do so because it offered an opportunity to think in fresh ways about old questions. It also enabled me to bridge gaps between the social history tradition which had shaped David's thinking, one often allied with structural models of historical change, and the cultural history prevalent today, which engages with a range of post-structural theoretical traditions. It seemed to me that these were conversations that could benefit from being brought together, and this project provided a vehicle for doing so.

This is not the book he would have written: while our intellectual interests overlapped, they did not coincide, and we did not always agree. When I first read the manuscript, I realized that I was going to need to push the theoretical framework in ways that he had not yet done. Thus, although most of the material he had was about gender, he had not defined this as a book about gender. I also realized in reading his draft that we needed to think about failed patriarchs as a complement to the unruly women he had written about. Even more, I have tried to anchor this in a set of contemporary intellectual preoccupations. I have tried to draw links to humour theory as a resource. I have also cut an extensive discussion on the dating of *The Duchess of Malfi* in relationship to the Howard–Carr marriage and the Overbury murder. The one chapter he envisioned but had not begun was on the 1640s. While that would have been relatively easy for him to write, it took me far from my areas of expertise. I have instead therefore indicated some of the directions that chapter might have gone in the 'Conclusion'. In focusing the argument, and clarifying points, some of his prose has been lost, and our writing styles are different. I have, when possible, kept his language, because his draft was full of his passionate and humane engagement with the people of early modern England.

Many of the ways I have expanded the manuscript follow the indications he gave in his notes. While he knew the pieces, some of them could fit in different places, and I have had to make those decisions. I have clarified and expanded the argument to place the discussion of inversion in the context of more recent theoretical concerns. As I have worked on the book, I have come to think that while this is a book I would never have started writing, it is a book that David would have never finished writing.

Throughout this process, I could not turn to David, but I have turned to friends for advice and assistance. In finishing David's book, I had to recapitulate some of his research, but I did not (and could not) redo all of it, so colleagues were very helpful in ensuring that what I had done made sense. Most of us when writing leave cryptic notes about directions we want to follow, or ideas we want to develop. I can usually reconstruct those notes that I have left myself, but David's were not always clear to me. I have had to lean on friends who are familiar with archival sources that have not been part of my scholarly life. For their help in unravelling these, I am especially grateful to Michael Young, Cynthia Herrup, Thomas Cogswell, Alastair Bellany and Maija Jansson. Frances Dolan and Dympna Callaghan allowed me to bend their ear on various issues related to Jacobean drama, and Katherine Steele Brokaw provided references, copies of books and reassurance when I felt I'd gone too far beyond my expertise. I am grateful to Rhea Riegel for discussions of *The Roaring Girl*, and to Ian Munro for sending me to *Volpone*. Laura Gowing generously helped me with transcriptions she had of cases. As I was finishing, Steve Hindle checked an obscure text at the Huntington Library and Amanda Herbert (as part of an epic Facebook thread) checked another at the Folger Shakespeare Library. Other friends have helped me when I had to cut some of David's examples, and have encouraged me when I struggled to make this my book as well as his.

As the manuscript developed, Fran Dolan read several chapters for me, and Cynthia Herrup generously read the entire manuscript. Grey Osterud read the manuscript and provided sage editorial advice. Brian Cowan and Beat Kümin, the series editors, and two anonymous readers provided invaluable comments. All of these readers alerted me to some egregious errors. Needless to say, the errors that remain are mine. It's been a pleasure to work with Rhodri Mogford at Bloomsbury on the production of this book.

I presented a version of Chapter 1 at the Merced Seminar in the Humanities; Matthew Kaiser's comments were provocative and helpful, but the whole discussion helped me sharpen the argument. I was also fortunate that Malcolm Smuts asked me to write two pieces that have shaped my thinking, 'Turning the World Upside Down: Gender and Inversion in the Work of David Underdown', which appeared in *History Compass*, and 'Cuckold's Haven', which appeared in *The Oxford Handbook of the Age of Shakespeare*. A version of Chapter 4 was originally published as '"But the Shows of their Street": The Wells May Games of 1607', by David Underdown in the *Journal of British Studies* (2011); it is published here with permission.

This work reflects research undertaken over more than thirty years in a variety of different archives. As I noted, David's attention to this project really began at the Huntington Library in 2002–3; I returned there on several occasions in

2014–15 to check references and explore new sources. I am grateful to the staff there for all their help. In the age of Early English Books Online (EEBO), it's still a treat to read original copies of books. In addition, I was able to bend the ears of some of the fellows there, especially Ann Little, Tim Harris, Chris Kyle, Dympna Callaghan and Susan Juster. The collections of the Yale University Library, and especially the Beinecke Library, were a critical resource for David's work, and again, I returned there to follow references; Kathryn James, the Curator of the Osborn collection there, was enormously helpful. I am also grateful to the staffs of the British Library and the National Archives, where I explored and further developed research that David had begun there. Significant work was also carried out at the Institute for Historical Research in London, the Norfolk Record Office and the Oxfordshire Archives; David had worked in the Wiltshire and Somerset Record Offices. Working as I do at a new university with a limited library, I could not have written this book without the support of Denice Swaratsky and now Dolly Lopez, our Interlibrary Loan Librarians (ILL): the efficiency of ILL in the University of California System is extraordinary, and I cannot express sufficient gratitude for it. The writing itself was made possible by a sabbatical leave from the University of California: I could not have finished this without the time it provided. My online writing group has provided support, encouragement and accountability over the past three years; I'm grateful to the participants, and the rotating leadership, for the ways I've been challenged and supported by them.

Finally, this is a book that has grown out of love and friendship. I was fortunate to have a marriage that was also a deep intellectual companionship. David and I were and are supported by friends who were colleagues. Now I see some of them on Facebook, but for many years it was the meetings in the archives and at conferences that mattered: they still do matter. My students are always surprised when I share information about, or from, scholars whose work they are reading, but of course the world of the academy is one where paths cross in multiple places over many years. I've mentioned some friends already, but there are many others. Tim Wales has been a friend and interlocutor since we met in the Norfolk Record Office in 1979; Kit French and I spent several recent summers sitting across from each other in the National Archives (which we both still call the PRO) while I read Star Chamber cases and she read wills. Allyson Poska, Judith Maltby, Rachel Weil and Margaret Hunt have all, in different ways, supported me and encouraged me. I want to especially acknowledge my fellow world historians at UC Merced, Ruth Mostern and Sholeh Quinn, and the Merced Seminar in the Humanities for the two years it focused on 'The World Upside Down'.

There are more personal acknowledgements as well. I relied on my New Haven friends, particularly the Pritchards, for housing and companionship when I worked again at the Yale Library. My extended family has been particularly important – Harold Underdown and Ann Rubin, Peter Underdown, and Philip Underdown and Nadine Lemmon; my granddaughter Simone is my New York theatre buddy, and my grandson Sam is just getting to know me. The wider Underdown clan has been a joy to get to know; it has been particularly fun to talk to my great-niece Beth Underdown about her forthcoming novel on Matthew Hopkins's sister. My natal family – my siblings, John and Gretchen, and my mother, Diane – has been a source of unending love and support. My father always liked to talk about my writing, and I am sorry he is not here to see the final result. My sister-in-law, Andréa Bailey, repeatedly welcomed me into her home however inconvenient it might be; and my niece and nephew, Sara and Christopher, have provided endless entertainment over the past two and a half years.

There are far too many people – not only David – who are no longer here to read this. I have been very aware, throughout writing this, of our connections to past scholarly conversations, but also to future ones. So this book is dedicated to the next generation: Simone and Sam, and Sara and Christopher. They, and their generation, will continue this conversation long after I am gone.

Susan Amussen

Abbreviations

BL	British Library
Chamberlain Letters	Norman E. McClure, ed. *The Letters of John Chamberlain.* 2 vols. Philadelphia, American Philosophical Society, 1939
CSPD	*Calendar of State Papers, Domestic Series*
Early Stuart Libels	*Early Stuart Libels: An Edition of Poetry from Manuscript Sources.* Edited by Alastair Bellany and Andrew McRae. Early Modern Literary Studies Text Series I (2005) http://purl.oclc.org/emls/texts/libels/
EBBA	English Broadside Ballad Archive http://ebba.english.ucsb.edu/
EEBO	Early English Books Online
HL	Huntington Library, San Marino, CA
HLQ	*Huntington Library Quarterly*
HMC	*Historical Manuscripts Commission*
JBS	*Journal of British Studies*
Middleton Works	*Thomas Middleton: Collected Works.* Edited by Gary Taylor and John Lavignano
ODNB	*Oxford Dictionary of National Biography.* Oxford, OUP, 2004
R.O.	Record Office
REED	*Records of Early English Drama, Somerset.* Edited by James Stokes
Statutes	*The Statutes of the Realm.* Vols 3 and 4, Pts 1 and 2. London, 1819. Available at Hathitrust.org
TNA	The National Archives, Kew

Citations to plays divided into acts and scenes are 1.2.3–4 (Act 1, Scene 2, lines 3–4). Citations to plays with only scene divisions are rendered as 1.2–4 (Scene 1, lines 2–4).

Spelling has been modernized throughout.

Introduction

Every degree of people ... hath appointed to them their duty and order; some are in high degree, some in low; some kings and princes, some inferiors and subjects; priests and laymen, masters and servants, fathers and children, husbands and wives, rich and poor; and everyone have need of other; so that in all things is to be lauded and praised the goodly order of God without which no house, no city, no common wealth can continue ... Take away kings, princes, rulers, magistrates, judges, and such states of Gods order, no man shall ride or go by the high way unrobbed, no man shall sleep in his own house or bed unkilled, no man shall keep his wife, children, & possessions in quietness: all things shall be common, and there must needs follow all mischief and utter destruction, both of souls, bodies, goods and common wealths.[1]

Comedians, and stage players, do often times envy and gnaw at the honor of another, and to please the vulgar people, set before them sundry lies, & teach much dissoluteness, and deceit, by this means turning upside down all discipline and good manners.[2]

'The Homily on Good Order and Obedience', often known as the Homily on Rebellion, was one of a set of homilies produced by the Elizabethan government to be read regularly in churches. Its assertion of a harmonious order where everyone knew their place was in tension with the fear that such order was threatened by multiple forms of inversion – in theatre, carnival and festive activities, but also in daily life and in politics. The tension between the hierarchical ideal and the world turned upside down was a central component of the mental world of early modern women and men. Its role in multiple settings is integral to understanding society, culture and politics in early modern England. The interconnected hierarchies of state, family, and household encouraged analogical thinking, which meant that inversion was frequently figured in terms of gender, with a focus on unruly women and failed patriarchs. While the obsession with order and the concomitant concern with the world upside down is widely acknowledged, its implications for our understanding of the early modern period have not been fully explored. In the chapters that follow, sustained attention to the way the upside down world depended on gender will demonstrate the significance of this dynamic for understanding the political scandals, social practices and literary culture of early modern England, while also demonstrating the centrality of gender to understanding the period.

Few ideas are more commonplace in discussions of early modern England than its obsession with order and hierarchy and the multiple linked hierarchies which could be invoked. There was the natural order, with God, humans and animals; there was the political order, with King ruling over his subjects, local notables governing their communities; there was a social order, with the nobility (itself ranked), gentry and common people; there was familial order, with a father/husband ruling over his wife, children and servants. All these orders intersected, yet they were not entirely parallel. Within national politics, it was generally assumed that the nobility had a better claim to rule than did those of lower social status, just as peers usually had more power locally than gentry. The gender order of the family was assumed to apply across all social orders, with the subordination of women to men taken for granted. The common use of analogies between the family and the state provided frameworks for discussion of politics.[3]

Early modern ideas of order presented two challenges to people of that time and to those of us who seek to understand them in the twenty-first century. First, people did not always agree on what constituted order or disorder: particularly in relation to festive culture, the boundaries of disorder were always contested. Second, even when people did agree, expectations of good order were constantly challenged by what happened in the world. For forty-five years, England was ruled by a queen rather than a king; subordinates – political, social and familial – constantly stepped out of their roles, or were more assertive than they were expected to be. Indeed, failure was almost built into the system, as one set of responsibilities was in tension with others. For instance, women were subordinate to their husbands in the family, yet their responsibilities in the household, whether work or directing servants of overseeing household production, required their active participation in the market; the skills and authority needed in these tasks were not always forgotten in women's dealings with their husbands. As a result of this paradox, early modern English commentators were as obsessed by the need for gender order as for social order. The popular author of pamphlets and jest books, Samuel Rowlands, certainly knew his audience when he wrote *The Bride*, a totally orthodox celebration of wifely meekness and obedience. The alternative to conventional marriage, he proclaimed, was a state of total inversion:

> When fish with fowl change elements together,
> The one forsaking air, the other water,
> And they that wore the fin, to wear the feather,
> Remaining changelings all the world's time after,
> The course of nature will be so beguiled,
> One maid shall get another maid with child.
>
> When every crow shall turn to be a parrot,
> And every star outshine the glorious sun,
> And the new water work run white and claret,
> That came to town by way of Islington,
> Women and men shall quite renounce each other,
> And maids shall be with child, like Merlin's mother.[4]

Rowland's link between natural disorder and gender disorder was typical. Forms of order supported each other, linked by the analogical thinking that was so pervasive in the period.

The world turned upside down, an inverted familial, social, or political order, provided a visual metaphor to represent disorder, and was integral to the mental world of early modern England. Sometimes the upside down world was a hopeful aspiration: let's turn the world upside down to obtain political or religious freedom, economic or social levelling, or gender equality, or simply to have fun by parodying official hierarchies and values. At other times it might have negative connotations: our world has been turned upside down by evil forces that are destroying the stable natural order ordained by God in family, church and state, and we must turn it rightside up by restoring the proper moral universe. The upside down world was licensed in festivals, but these rituals normally ended – or were supposed to end – with a return to the proper order. The world turned upside down was central to both elite and popular cultural systems during the sixteenth and seventeenth centuries. Inversion actually *requires* hierarchy and orthodoxy if it is to mean anything, even while it challenges them as illegitimate.[5]

While divine, natural, political, social and familial order could all be overturned, the language around the world upside down is frequently gendered. In part, because of the patterns of analogical thinking, gender could stand in for other issues; it thus provided a common framework for discussing an upside down world. Yet there were enough problems with the gender order itself to make it a central site for inversion. Two primary paradigms of gendered inversion were visible: unruly women and failed patriarchs. The women who were disorderly and the men who failed to govern their households provided the basis for these images. They were frequent targets of gossip and shaming, comedy or tragedy. They were central to political scandal and political debate; they posed a problem in families and local communities; and they provided a central dynamic of early modern theatre and popular literature. Tracing the gendered world turned upside down allows us to see how social, political and cultural history can fruitfully illuminate each other.

Our discussion ends before the civil war that engulfed Britain in the 1640s, partly to show that the idea of the world upside down, which was used so frequently during the war and its aftermath, had deep roots in English politics and culture. Our first serious encounter with this subject was Christopher Hill's wonderful book, *The World Turned Upside Down*, published in 1972, towards the end of that exciting period when the existence of a radical counterculture did not seem the outlandish idea of a handful of naive left-wing idealists.[6] Hill chronicled the radicals who emerged during the 1640s and 1650s when Diggers, Ranters, Quakers and other assorted visionaries were enthusiastically bent on inverting the old order in their pursuit (variously) of political, moral and sexual freedom. Hill's upside down world, a hopeful one that reorders the social as well as gender hierarchy, is not the whole story, however. When I (David Underdown) began to look at the world turned upside down in my own research, I soon discovered a very different version. Many people in seventeenth-century England were hostile to, even terrified by, the notion of an upside down world. At the heart of their moral universe was the assumption that God had 'created and appointed all things ... in a most excellent and perfect order'. That order, they were taught, was also inscribed in human affairs, and undermining it in one sphere would lead inevitably to its collapse in all the others, and to that situation of 'carnal liberty, enormity, sin, and Babylonical confusion' in which 'all things shall be common'. In the revolution of the 1640s, Diggers and Ranters enthusiastically welcomed that prospect as a liberating one, but during the previous century most people were inclined to believe the Homily on Good Order's warning at the head of this chapter that the inversion of order would lead to 'all mischief and utter destruction, both of souls, bodies, goods, and commonwealths'. Meanwhile I (Susan Amussen) set out to understand gender in early modern England, yet gradually became convinced of the importance of debates about gender to politics. Through our conversations with each other, it became evident that these two themes were deeply intertwined.[7] Hill's radicals appropriated a familiar idea in new ways; our task here is to show the scope and significance of the world upside down that made their use of it so powerful.

Gender and inversion

A pervasive anxiety about unruly women and their male counterparts, failed or ineffective patriarchs, haunted early modern society. Partly, this was rooted in understandings of women's nature, which was thought to be – following the example of Eve – prone to sin and disorder. Women's actual behaviour was implicated in turning the world upside down in three primary ways. First, women were expected to be part of patriarchal households, but not all women were. While some of these – widows and heiresses, primarily – were allowed to be independent, even they were a source of anxiety. Far more problematic were women who escaped from the patriarchal family by bearing a child out of wedlock. Not only did mothers of illegitimate children create families without a patriarchal head, but what was perceived as a moral failing had economic consequences: outside a patriarchal household they struggled to support themselves and their children, and often required poor relief.[8] Other women refused to provide the deference and submission that was expected of them; whether by beating their husbands or quarrelling with their neighbours, they aroused fears of a world with women on top. Such women could be the focus of prosecution for scolding, punished by a trip to the cucking stool; women who abused their husbands – often along with their husbands – were the targets of charivari, or skimmingtons, directed at their household.[9] Third, women were imagined as turning the world upside down through witchcraft. In England, prosecutions for witchcraft peaked in the Elizabethan period and declined through most of the first half of the seventeenth century; well over 80 per cent of accusations were made against women. Anxieties about witches loomed large in public discourse, whether on the stage or in pamphlets. Witchcraft was particularly frightening because it involved women's use of satanic powers to turn the moral and gender order upside down. 'Witchcraft', it has been observed, 'is an act of pure inversion'. Witches were rebelling not only against God, but also against their properly submissive position by trying to control their own or their neighbours' lives, taking revenge for the deprivations and oppressions that were normally their lot.[10]

In the early seventeenth century, the anxiety about unruly women was articulated in a lively pamphlet debate on the nature of women: Were they virtuous or sinful? Who was responsible for the failings of the gender order? This debate was an instalment of a centuries-old discussion, so the ideas about women's failure to conform to expectations were all familiar. Yet some of the defences of women moved into new territory, interpreting biblical texts as a basis for gender equality.[11] Because the debate had a perennial quality, what is significant is why it gained traction at a particular time. Its purchase between 1560 and 1640 is undoubtedly related to the anxieties about unwed mothers, scolds and witches.

These concerns were not random, but tied to specific challenges. One of the most important of these was gender at the royal court. The early modern period saw an unusual concentration of women rulers. Elizabeth I was not the only woman ruler in the late sixteenth century. From the perspective of many Protestant writers, the reigns of women in their own right or as regents, including Mary Stuart in Scotland, Mary Tudor in England, Catherine de Medici and later Marie de Medici in France, had led to predictable political (as well as personal) upheaval and bloodshed. John Knox's trumpet had blasted the monstrous regime of feminine government, while Philip Stubbes and other moral reformers proclaimed the danger to social order represented by women's appetite for luxury and ostentation in dress. National and anti–Roman Catholic prejudices did not overcome the admiration of historians from Holinshed to Camden for the masculine, disciplined and rational Romans as compared with the barbaric, gender-bending Britons, who allowed women to rule. An occasional writer, such as the pamphleteer Esther Sowerman, expressed admiration for 'the valiant Boadicea' for defending her country's liberty against the Romans. More often, Elizabeth was likened, paradoxically, to Augustus. Furthermore, Elizabeth's success was frequently explained as stemming from her reliance on her male advisors, a view expressed by the redoubtable Lucy Hutchinson later in the century as part of her criticism of Henrietta Maria's influence on Charles I. Preachers and political thinkers generally assumed that strong and independent women inevitably brought chaos and disorder upon those around them, and seventeenth-century drama contains countless moral tales that showed the disasters that such women, as Lady Macbeth and the Duchess of Malfi, brought in their wake. Elizabeth was the unexplained exception.[12]

The rule of women was not the only source of an upside down world at court. There was concern about the social upstarts who had achieved power above their natural station, whether through their abilities or their personalities: while there was a long history of skilled administrators moving into the upper ranks of the court, James VI and I had favourites who gained position more by force of looks and personality than of ability: Robert Carr, the Earl of Somerset, and

George Villiers, the Duke of Buckingham, were the most spectacular examples. But more often, and more strikingly, there were complaints of illegitimate feminine influence in government, politics being, after all, so obviously the masculine sphere. Buckingham's mother was a prime source of anxiety; perversely, Charles I's happy marriage raised concerns about the influence of his wife, Henrietta Maria, on his government.[13]

But unruly and unquiet women were by no means the only challenge: men regularly failed to govern their households appropriately. It was the responsibility of husbands, fathers and masters to ensure that their wives, children and servants behaved, so a man who fomented disorder, or who allowed his wife to step outside the usual bounds of behaviour, was particularly problematic. While the alehouse may have been a site of good fellowship, moralists worried that drunkenness turned the social, moral and gender orders upside down. Recent scholarship has reminded us that models of manhood, like those of womanhood, were socially constructed and contested. What has been called 'hegemonic masculinity' was challenged by alternatives, and not all men either wanted to, or were able to, fit into the expected patterns of behaviour.[14]

From the top of society to the bottom, then, the late sixteenth and early seventeenth centuries are full of instances that suggest a collapsing patriarchal order: in villagers' frequent resort to cucking-stools and skimmington rituals to enforce female subordination, as well as in solemn discussions of the theoretical and biblical foundations of the system by the elite. The political implications of disorder were clear at both levels. It is no accident that Sir Robert Filmer's famous *Patriarcha*, which argues for royal authority based on the natural role of fathers as heads of households, dates from the early 1630s. To suggest this connection between prescriptions of order and challenges to it does not imply that there were more unruly women in this period than at other times; the patriarchal order is by definition unstable. However, the sources of that instability, and the particular forms in which anxiety about it were expressed, constitute historical problems that need to be explained. There was a prevailing uneasiness about gender relations in early modern England.

Social order and social change

Naturally, we wonder whether there is any particular reason for the obsession with the world upside down. The idea is not unique to the early modern period; since it engages with a primary physical orientation, this image is found at many times in different cultures. But the early modern period seems to be a time when it had particular purchase. Inversion was intertwined with the religious controversy which followed the Protestant reformation, as each side saw the other as turning the world upside down. Medieval practices of seasonal inversion were amplified by the invention of printing, which allowed play scripts and ballads which recounted them to be widely disseminated. Religious controversy was more clearly contained after 1660, while the inversions that accompanied festivals and festive rituals became less culturally central as the distance between elite culture and popular culture widened in the later seventeenth and eighteenth centuries.[15]

Between 1642 and 1660, the civil war and revolution literally turned the world upside down; the parliamentary government placed the king on trial for treason against his people, and executed him. The challenges to the social and political order meant that an upside down world was not a metaphor, but a reality to be experienced. A 1642 pamphlet by John Taylor, *Mad Fashions, Od Fashions, All out fashions*, has a woodcut of the world turned upside down, which is also used in a later pamphlet with that title; 'All things are turned the Cleane Contrary Way', the author complains.[16] Several ballads from the period refer directly to the 'world turn'd upside down' by the Long Parliament's banning of the Book of Common Prayer, and the later banishment of Christmas celebrations. Another ballad, 'Hey then up go we', had both parliamentary and Royalist versions, but both emphasized the ways the revolution changed the social order. Gender was still a critical category of inversion, with gendered insults directed towards both sides, as well as refiguring of gender by some of the radical sects.[17] Following the restoration of Charles II, the fear of the world upside down does not disappear, but it was less common and appears to have held less power.

For both historians and literary scholars, the practices of festive inversion are the most familiar and explicit ways the world was turned upside down. In medieval Europe, and in much of Catholic Europe through the early modern period, these practices were semi-institutionalized in times of carnival, which were tied to the church calendar. While some customs disappeared in England after the Reformation, many festive practices lived on. There was a period of license in carnival right before Lent began; and May Day, Whitsun and Midsummer – all tied to church rituals – also provided opportunities for festive license. These events included varying degrees of formal performance. They often involved the portrayal of rulers by those who, like the medieval boy bishops who ruled the day after Christmas, came from subordinated groups, or featured pageants which mocked authority. These could be occasions for plays about Robin Hood, who was a central figure in English festive culture. Often the plays not only turned the social order upside down, as Robin Hood did, but also allowed women to perform roles that they did not normally hold. Such festivities presented an alternate order, and while the proper order was generally restored at the end, they provided an opportunity for subordinated groups to articulate parts of what is usually the 'hidden transcript' of their society. The London celebrations of the return of Prince Charles from Spain without a Spanish bride featured behaviour that both 'dissolved and re-established the social order'. At times, such festivities became the occasion for a wider political event, as in the French city of Romans in 1580; there the leader of a popular party was assassinated by the crowd in the middle of Mardi Gras. In London, Shrove Tuesday was a common time for apprentices to riot.[18] These practices were regarded with suspicion by groups that held opposing views on most other questions. Protestants frowned on many of these practices because festivity so often led to sinful behaviour. But the riotous disorder that such festivities might encourage meant that they were regarded with increasing disapproval by those in authority regardless of their religious views. Over time, the festive calendar in Catholic as well as Protestant Europe was more strictly regulated, and less likely to lead to disorder. Many of the practices that had been part of general culture became more centred in youth culture, as we shall see in Chapter 4. Yet even when the formal festivities disappeared, people continued to observe them in one way or another. For example, the disorderly escapades of one of the reprobates in the puritan town of Dorchester occurred at times of traditional festivity.[19] One reason for the gradual diminution of the significance of the world upside down is the narrowed range of festive events.

In addition to calendrical festivities, other rituals in early modern Europe turned the world upside down. The most familiar of these is the charivari and its English form, the skimmington. The charivari was a shaming ritual; usually directed at families which in some way violated community norms, it could also be directed at corrupt officials. In England in the sixteenth and seventeenth centuries, it was directed primarily at households where women stepped out of line and either beat their husbands or were unfaithful to them. Such rituals were paralleled by formal punishments, particularly for offenses which were seen as trying to turn the world upside down; the ritual re-enactment was thought to restore proper order.[20]

The concern with festive culture in all its forms was rooted in wider concerns about order anchored in social, religious, demographic and economic developments. The period from the Reformation to the civil war in England (1540–1640) was one of significant social and economic changes, which fed anxieties about disorder. On the broadest scale, this period was marked by significant demographic expansion, as the population of England and Wales almost doubled between about 1540 and 1640, from about 2.8 million to 5.1 million. The increase in population was accompanied by price inflation, a result of growing demand for food and other goods. These trends in turn contributed to the greater centrality of 'the structures and culture characteristic of a "market society"' within an economy that was increasingly national and capitalist. Engagement in the market also promoted agricultural specialization. The characteristics of such an economy were, in retrospect, predictable: for some, it offered the opportunity to accumulate ever greater wealth; but it also meant that a growing proportion of the population was dependent on wage labour. The increase in poverty and vagrancy was an ongoing challenge.[21] Furthermore, although women's work was eventually marginalized in the skilled trades and the labour market, at this point, dairying, malting and textiles were central to family economies, so some women gained additional power.[22] While these changes are not explicitly part of the story we examine here, they provide the backdrop against which our story took place and shaped English men's and women's experience of, and reactions to, these dramas.

These economic developments were facilitated by the disendowment of the church following the Reformation. The church had held as much as one-quarter or even one-third of the land in England, and about three-quarters of that was seized by the crown, and generally sold, between 1537 and 1547. Gentry and noble families expanded or consolidated their estates, successful merchants purchased landed estates and entered the gentry, prosperous yeomen bought land they had rented and many slowly accumulated larger holdings. In each of these cases, the availability of land reshaped local social hierarchies and enabled social as well as geographical mobility. That mobility, especially where some members of the community suddenly gained wealth and position over their neighbours, was often a source of conflict.[23] The increase in population and its greater mobility, accompanied by the growing ranks of the underemployed poor and unemployed vagrants, were a source of underlying tension and anxiety.

The economic polarization of English communities was mirrored by social and cultural polarization. That polarization came not because people had different values – everyone believed in order and hierarchy – but because people interpreted these in different ways. What constituted disorder and what constituted permissible play? Some kinds of behaviour were always frowned on: riots were bad, as was out-of-wedlock pregnancy. There was a shared belief in the value of good neighbourhood and the 'common peace': those who disrupted the community were bound over to keep the peace. And those who disrupted the peace of a community – scolds, disorderly poor people, vagrants and beggars – were very real people. But not all judgments about what disrupted the social order were shared: frequenting the alehouse or dancing on Sundays, for instance, were seen as problems by some people, but not by all. Those with more rigid and narrow views of acceptable behaviour saw themselves (and generally referred to themselves) as the godly, though they are now more commonly known as puritans; many of them had connections to continental Protestants, and eventually to colonists in New England. The boundaries between the godly and the rest were often fuzzy, but the religious policies of Charles I in particular emphasized the differences rather than the commonalities.[24]

Throughout, these cultural differences underlined and were underlined by religious differences. The Reformation, and England's erratic path to becoming a Protestant country, provides another important context for the conflicts and tensions we will trace. Between 1533 and 1559, there were repeated shifts in the contours of England's official religion; while the doctrinal and liturgical shape of the Church of England was established in 1559, it was never able to suppress alternative views. Some of those alternatives were more Protestant; while the Presbyterian movement under Elizabeth sought structural change in the church, the better known puritans were doctrinally orthodox, but wanted a more Protestant approach. From the late sixteenth century onwards, patriotism was tied to anti-Spanish and anti-Catholic sentiments. In addition, there was a small but important Catholic community which grew with the Catholic missions. This led to both 'cultural and religious indeterminacy and instability'. What is most significant for our purposes is not the substance of religious disagreements, but their existence; each group at different times levelled charges at the other that their practices or beliefs turned the world upside down.[25]

These demographic, economic, religious and social changes underlay, and were accompanied by, political challenges. The long reign of Queen Elizabeth provided stability, but it never resolved the fundamental fiscal problem of the English state: its revenues were inadequate to cover its unavoidable expenses. The English state's reliance on unpaid local officials for much of the work of local government was partly a result of this financial predicament. At the national level, while royal revenue supported the state adequately in times of peace, it could never cover the cost of war. The necessary funds could only come from parliament, which was understandably reluctant to vote for taxes; the members of the House of Commons were, after all, the same men who governed their localities. Thus, governing required collaboration as much as command. The succession of James exacerbated the state's difficulties. Elizabeth had been notoriously stingy and had no family to support; James had to provide for a family, and while complaints that English wealth was flowing to his Scottish subjects were overblown, he was far more generous than was his predecessor.[26]

Avoiding war was one solution to the financial problems faced by the English monarchy. Elizabeth did her best to avoid warfare on the continent, though she eventually did go to war with Spain. After making peace with the Spanish, James I was notoriously reluctant to get involved in the Thirty Years War, even to protect his own son-in-law. After the disastrous wars of the 1620s, Charles too stayed out of war – until he brought the Civil War upon himself. James's pacific nature was frequently contrasted with Elizabeth's martial valour. These qualities were gendered, so the comparison mapped on to ideas about the world turned upside down. James was seen (at least by some) as a failure for being too feminine. But the contrast between Elizabeth's 'masculine' (and hence successful) government and James I's 'feminine' (hence contested) government is overdrawn. Effective authority required a combination of feminine compassion and masculine vigour, and contemporary writers sometimes accepted this view.[27] Yet most people thought of masculine authority as natural and its feminine counterpart as illegitimate; the arrival of a king in the form of James was expected to make everything right, and instead it turned the world upside down in new ways.

These issues gained wider significance in the early seventeenth century than they would have earlier because of the vast expansion of both print and manuscript news. The Reformation coincided with the growing accessibility of printing technology, and the Protestant emphasis on Bible reading encouraged the dramatic expansion of printing in England. Although statistical precision is impossible, it is clear that by the early seventeenth century at least a third of adult men and a tenth of adult women could read. Devotional books played a central role in printing, but presses also turned out household manuals, jest books and ballads, along with poetry and plays. Government proclamations and official treatises articulated normative ideas about politics; while explicit opposition to royal policy was rare (and dangerous) in print, underlying issues or principles were frequently explored and debated. London had a lively culture of gossip, and a growing group of news writers kept the gentry outside the capital informed.[28] Print culture was particularly important in cities and large towns, where residents were able to easily buy ballads and books.

Watching and listening remained vital to literary culture. This was the great age of theatre: while Shakespeare is the most familiar of Renaissance dramatists today, writers like Christopher Marlowe, Ben Jonson, Thomas Middleton and John Webster each wrote at least some plays that rank with Shakespeare's. They were joined in writing for the stage – often itself a collaborative enterprise – by many who are today far less familiar: Thomas Heywood, Richard Brome and Nathaniel Field, along with many others who wrote the approximately 3,000 plays produced during the period. While Londoners had the greatest access to productions with theatres that were easily accessible to a wide audience, there had long been a thriving dramatic culture in provincial England; London companies toured, noble families often provided patronage and local groups performed. Putting on plays was a common educational practice at both grammar schools around the country and at the universities and Inns of Court. This theatrical life outside London was often connected to the festive calendar, to May Games, Whitsun processions, and bear and bull baitings. Although London companies appear to have spent less time touring as the seventeenth century progressed, ideas of performance and theatricality were widely familiar.[29] Throughout the period, plays were not confined to theatres: while professional theatres came into being, inn yards and halls were also used. The theatre, like the printed word, rarely engaged explicitly with political issues, but its concerns were often topical.

Early modern England did not conform to the ideal image of a stable and orderly society. Demographic, economic and social changes rendered the established social order precarious. A queen regnant and kings who were weak political leaders did not conform to the monarchical ideal, providing disturbing evidence that things were awry. All these issues, as well as ideas about what the world should be and how it had gone wrong, were discussed in books, pamphlets and the theatre. All these signs suggested that the world was indeed askew, perhaps even upside down.

Inversion, or the upside down world

Metaphors are primary tools of human thought. They are ways that we use concrete and familiar ideas to help understand abstract or complex ones. Conceptual metaphors embody key concepts that shape our experience of the world. Physical and spatial metaphors, based on the notion that 'UP IS GOOD/ DOWN IS BAD', are particularly common, as they are grounded in our shared experience.[30] Thus we speak of being 'down in the dumps', or 'high as a kite'; heaven is imagined as above and hell is down. High-flyers are successful people; when we root for the underdog, we know they may lose. While such metaphors are not universal, they are not 'radically relative or subjective'.[31] The world upside down places this spatial metaphor in time: the world was, and should be, right side up, but something has happened which makes it upside down. It is usually a negative metaphor, using our expectation of being upright as normal and good to define a situation as abnormal and in need of fixing, though what is upside down for one person might be right side up for another.

In Western Europe, the idea of the world upside down can be traced to the Greeks; its classical roots made it accessible to both theologians and secular thinkers. A sample from works published between 1600 and 1605 shows the range of its uses. In a set of sermons, the future archbishop, George Abbot, referred to the way an infidel reminds a Jew of his obligations, saying 'here the world is turned upside down'.[32] The infidel was better than the Jew: an unexpected outcome. In an argument against Catholicism, Abbot described how Christ 'turned all their [the Jews'] constitutions upside-down, and gave new interpretations of the Law'.[33] These meanings were essentially positive, in the first case because what was unexpected was virtuous, and in the second because salvation changed the world for the better. But religious language about the upside down world could function in more negative ways: Catholics and other heretics turned the world upside down with bad theology, as William Perkins charged that a particular view turned the 'causes of salvation and damnation' upside down.[34] The image could be used more generically to highlight that immorality inverts the natural and social order:

> While Vices mask in Virtues weed,
> And Reason made a Bawd to each abuse;
> While Beasts are fatted, good men suffer need,
> And all things altered from their proper use;
> So long the righteous gods will surely frown,
> And we shall find the world turn'd upside down.[35]

While the phrase was sometimes used literally, it was more often metaphorical: thus Richard Knolles describes 'tents and pavilions turned upside down' during a battle, but also talks about the state turned upside down by repeated shifts in government.[36]

Comic uses of the upside down world retain the metaphorical sense of something wrong, but often double it. In Thomas Dekker's and Thomas Middleton's *The Patient Man and the Honest Whore*, the patient man of the title, whose wife has given his robes of office to a servant, refuses to allow the servant to doff his hat to him because of the servant's clothes; if the noble clothes honour his poor dress, 'Then the world's upside down.' Of course, what was actually upside down was the servant wearing the master's clothes.[37]

But the world upside down was more than a literary trope. It described a way of acting. Traditional practices of carnival institutionalized inversion, with formal parades and pageants as well as the general expectation that people would step outside their normal roles. Carnival provided a license to joke, tell stories and mock those in authority. Such festive gatherings might allow the poor to challenge the rich, or the youth to take leadership. Such events were tied to particular festivals; it was a day of license, not some longer period which offered freedom, when, 'All things are Arsie-Varsie; upside-down'.[38] Charivari were directed not just at offenders against the gender order, but against those who undermined economic rights: the use of processions to shame offenders of various types had a long history. While these rituals were often carried out by ordinary people, they could also be official: carting was used as a punishment, particularly for sexual offenses. To have someone carried facing backwards emphasized that their actions had been backwards, and the punishment turned it around and set it right.[39] Some uses of the upside down world provided generic rethinkings of existing social arrangements. These practices took the structure of society and turned it upside down: for fun, to mock it, or to punish those who strayed outside its limits.

The multiple ways an upside down world functions is visible in Richard Brome's 1638 play, *The Antipodes*. The play combines comic uses of inversion with its enactment to restore order. Peregrine, a young gentleman, suffers from melancholy and is so obsessed with travel literature that he ignores his wife Martha, who is herself mad because she wants a child, and is still a virgin and ignorant of sex three years after their marriage. His father consults a London doctor, who stages an alternate reality. Peregrine is told that he will travel to the Antipodes, and after a drugged sleep, he wakes to a play within the play which enacts an upside down world, where everything is 'contrary': 'the people rule/ The magistrates', 'the women over-rule the men'.[40] When Peregrine arrives in the new country, in the city of Anti-London, he enters the actors' dressing room and attacks the props, and then declares himself King of the Antipodes by conquest, and proceeds to 'govern / With purpose to reduce the manners of / This country to his own'. In the upside down world of the Antipodes, adultery is licensed, servants order their masters and self-interest is confused with justice. A woman orders a male scold ducked, while the woman fencer's husband 'teacheth needlework/or some such arts which we call womanish'. Most striking to Peregrine is that women act as men do in England, and men as women: everything is 'contrary/In all that we hold proper to each sex'.[41] Peregrine marries his wife a second time in the Antipodes, and this time they go to bed. When he 'wakes up', his mind is restored, and his marriage righted. At the same time, his father, who has been a jealous husband to his younger second wife, is brought to see her virtue. In this play, the upside down world offers a satire on law and justice; it uses inversion to cure madness; it parallels disordered individuals and disordered society; and it uses a series of upside down marriages to set two marriages in the current world on the right track.[42]

The idea of inversion is central to literary modes of irony and paradox, where what is said is the opposite of what is meant; it is also a key element in humour. Anthropologists have found that ideas of inversion or reversal were seen as central to rites of passage; in events like carnival, it was seen as letting off steam. In some cases, an upside down world was the world before current order was established; in others, it was a way to explore what was not, to make visible alternatives. Those alternatives could be hopeful – the reign of God overturning the ways of the world – or despairing – the upside down world was devoid of virtue.[43] The upside down world carried symbolic weight. While it is predicated on everyone knowing what was right side up, it also reminded people that the world was not fixed.

These anthropological and literary approaches to symbolic inversion focused on a 'dimension of self-conscious, patterned behaviour'. They were structured and familiar. The festivities of carnival and other calendrical holidays fit into this category; so too did charivari. When these things took place, everyone knew the rules; they might not like them, but they knew what to expect. Similarly, the comic uses of inversion played with recognizable patterns. Reversal is a common form of comedy, especially with the switching of roles where 'prisoner reprimands judge, child rebukes parent, wife rules husband'. In *The Merry Wives of Windsor*, Falstaff, hoping to seduce two married women and thus cuckold their husbands, is asked to wear horns, the symbol of the cuckold, to an assignation with one of them.[44] Similarly, irony depends on a reader, or listener, knowing when someone means the opposite of what they say. All these forms depend on an existing structure, social or narrative, which can be challenged by inversion; indeed, you cannot turn a social structure upside down if there is no right side up. At the same time, the very instability of the social and gender order made the upside down world more threatening, as it was closer to reality.

The social significance of these practices has been the subject of much debate. Religious rituals of inversion such as baptism, when the child dies to sin in order to live in salvation, are rituals of belonging and incorporation. Festive rituals have been seen as a safety valve which allowed subordinate groups to play and criticize their betters but did not essentially challenge the structure. That interpretation certainly describes the general experience of these events. Others have seen a more liberatory possibility in such rituals, as they open up alternatives. In the early modern period they repeatedly extended outside their expected boundaries: the carnival in Romans was only the most dramatic example, but any occasion of festive license might cross its expected boundaries. Most historians working with this material have interpreted such practices as ambiguous: while it might serve as a safety valve, it also allowed people to imagine alternatives.[45]

Beyond these structured forms of symbolic inversion, some ways in which the world was turned upside down generated anxiety. People's behaviour in everyday life could challenge existing structures as powerfully as carnival performances, and the threat they posed was met by collective efforts to contain it. Examples include the scolds and cuckolds of early modern communities: women who quarrelled with their neighbours and husbands, and men whose wives were unfaithful. Men who allowed their households to be disorderly were a problem. So too were witches; although their behaviour was understood in terms of recognizable patterns, individual attacks were unpredictable. All these types of people were represented on the stage as well; so were other people whose actions overturned expectations. In all these cases we are dealing with behaviour that was familiar but reversed the usual order of society. The power of what are sometimes (to us) minor infractions or merely individual misconduct makes sense in terms of larger concerns about the social order.

To understand the significance of these forms of everyday inversion, we need to turn to more recent approaches to the study of early modern society. Over the past thirty years, we have become increasingly aware of the performative nature of early modern identity. This was visible in many ways, but perhaps most importantly through the importance of dress to identity, and the ways dress determined the ways people were treated. Dress was coded by class, and while continued proclamations tried to enforce a series of sumptuary laws that limited luxury fabrics to particular groups, their repetition, as well as the increasing complexity of the exceptions they offered, indicated their failure.[46] Assumptions about dress and identity also mapped on to gender: anyone wearing women's clothes was assumed to be a woman. That made the boys who played women on the English stage believable, and even allowed boys playing women to disguise themselves as men. Mapping gender by dress was mirrored in scientific views which suggested that gender boundaries were not rigid, and that in some circumstances gender identity could shift.[47] The importance of dress in identity caused anxiety because it suggested that people could claim a social position that was not really theirs; this was one of the major criticisms of the theatre. In a time of social change and social mobility, the potential to change one's identity was another source of instability.

Attention to the performative nature of gender and identity has also reminded us that the sources we have for the study of the period are stories, narratives told to make sense of, or to frame, particular events. The relationship between these accounts and "what happened" is always uncertain.[48] Yet the stories told are told to be credible, and thus reveal values and expectations.

It is also useful to think about the concept of 'patriarchal equilibrium', based on the observation that while women's work has changed over time, their social and economic position remained remarkably constant. Yet the mechanisms for maintaining this equilibrium are not at all clear. Here we show that the punishment of unruly women which was integral to containing the world upside down was one tool in this process. The expansion of market-oriented production enabled women who processed food, such as maltsters and brewers, to play a more visible and independent role in the economy both within the household and in the market. It is more difficult to track the role of women in dairying, particularly cheese making, but it is telling that many of the charivari directed against disorderly women took place in the cheese-making areas of the country. Accusing women whose work was becoming more significant in the economy of turning the world upside down, and shaming them with an inversion ritual, became a way to keep them in their place.[49]

Such ways of thinking remind us that the world upside down was not just patterned and symbolic: not only did people turn the world upside down through their ordinary behaviour, but responses to such behaviour had real consequences in the world. Many responses to the upside down world reflect a desire to maintain the appropriate order, which was under threat not just because of individuals' behaviour but because other aspects of society were changing. The power of the idea of the world upside down in early modern society was a response to the many changes taking place at the time, as well as the ways in which performative approaches to identity created additional instability. Patriarchal equilibrium was maintained by trying to police unruly women and failed patriarchs. The world turned upside down was a particular problem in a particular social world; responses to it sought to maintain order, as conventionally imagined, even as the growth of population, the expansion of cities and the increasing significance of the market changed relationships within society.

Looking forward

In the chapters that follow, we demonstrate the pervasive presence of gendered versions of the world upside down in the social and mental universe of early modern England, and show how it can be understood by exploring the connections between different aspects of society and culture. While the balance will vary among the chapters, every chapter will discuss politics, social practice and culture. The first two chapters examine the two faces of gender inversion. The unruly woman, whether a scold, or a witch, or just independent, was a constant reminder of the fragile nature of the gender order. The flip side of the unruly woman was the failed patriarch, the man who failed to govern her. Such men might be cuckolds, but they could also refuse to uphold normative masculinity. These two types provide the basis for the analysis of three case studies, which demonstrate how attending to unruly women and failed patriarchs illuminates a wide range of other social concerns. The third chapter focuses primarily on the ways the world upside down featured on the early modern stage; while tragedies suggested that illicit desire led only to death and destruction, comedies emphasized that inversion theatrical performances are tied both to politics and to social practices. The fourth examines the intersections of popular practice and politics in the city of Wells, Somerset, through a political charivari directed at members of the local elite. The last chapter takes witchcraft, which was from the start a form of inversion, and explores its appearance across society, culture and politics. Throughout, we trace the connections between social practice, politics and literary culture to show that inversion, and particularly the ideas of unruly women and failed patriarchs, provides an integrative framework for thinking; understanding the myriad meanings of the world upside down requires us to keep our lenses open wide.

1

Unruly Women

'Lust and uncleanness continually keeps them company, gluttony and sloth serveth them at the table, pride and vainglory appareleth them': these were just a few of the warnings given to husbands about what they could expect from their wives. The pamphlet in which they appeared, *The Araignment of Lewd, Idle, Froward and Unconstant Women*, proved to be one of the great bestsellers of the seventeenth century. It was, a critic noted, 'commonly bought up, which argueth a general applause'. The author announced himself as 'Thomas Tell-Troth', but subsequent editions (there were at least ten by 1637) revealed that he was an obscure fencing master named Joseph Swetnam.[1] Swetnam's work was largely a diatribe against vain, extravagant, assertive and immoral women – the vast majority, in his view. Men who chose wives for their beauty rather than their character would find that their only rewards would be the loss of all their money, and eventually sexual infidelity. And things might very well get worse. 'If thy personage please not her humour', Swetnam prophesied, '... her breast will be the harborer of an envious heart, and her heart the storehouse of poisoned hatred, her head will devise villainy, and her hands are ready to practice that which her heart desireth.'[2]

Swetnam was, in time, answered by three different pamphlets, all allegedly written by women. His name also quickly became a byword for ill-tempered misogyny, and in 1620 he was featured in a play, *Swetnam the Woman-Hater*. William Gouge's women parishioners were so upset by their minister's negative comments about wives when he first delivered his *Of Domesticall Duties* as sermons in 1616, that some denounced him as a 'hater of women', surely an echo of Swetnam's nickname.[3] Swetnam's sixty-four pages of wearisome abuse repeat most of the standard charges against women made by male authors in the age-old battle of the sexes. This unending controversy had one of its occasional flare-ups in the years before and after 1600, and behind it lay enduring fears of familial and social inversion, especially of the satanic usurpation of male authority by aggressive, disobedient women. In the conventional (male) discourse of the times, women were assumed to be by nature irrational, disorderly, dishonest, idle, excessively talkative ('their mouths cannot contain their tongues', the satirist and pamphleteer Samuel Rowlands observed) and directed by ungovernable sexual appetites; men, on the other hand, were by definition rational, virtuous, prudent, capable of control and self-mastery. But if men were not constantly on their guard, women were only too likely to turn the whole social and familial order upside down. These assumptions surfaced, sometimes in curious ways, in many familiar seventeenth-century disputes: between Protestants and Roman Catholics, between courtiers and country gentlemen, and between Civil War Roundheads and Cavaliers, for example.[4]

It may be that Swetnam was not entirely serious in his intentions; he ends his pamphlet by advising readers to 'take it merrily' and 'esteem of this book only as the toys of an idle head'. His subtitle, *Pleasant for married men, profitable to young men, and hurtful to none*, neglects to mention women, so they might well have disagreed with that claim. It is difficult from this distance to discern much 'merry' in Swetnam's diatribe: like all assertions that 'it's just a joke', his final comments are excuses.[5] The contrast between expectations and reality in the relations between men and women has, however, always been a great source for humour, sometimes of an uneasy kind, and the early seventeenth century was full of it. Incongruity – the disjuncture between the expected and what happens – has been understood as a source of laughter since ancient times; what is historically specific are the expectations that are upended.[6]

Plays also used humour as a way of talking about conflicts between men and women. Theatrical companies in the late Elizabethan and Jacobean periods all had plays whose subject was shrews; they went under various names, but after 1594, appear to be fairly widespread. The best-known example is Shakespeare's *The Taming of the Shrew*, a play in which laughter is shaped by incongruity throughout; the play can even be said to stage its own battle between 'the generic conventions of "happy comedy" and the demands of high seriousness'. From the early scenes when Kate is violent, through Petrucchio's torture tactics in 'taming' her, to the final scene where she exhorts other women to obey their husbands, we are constantly off balance. Shakespeare treats the subject jocularly, but Elizabethan audiences knew that Kate, like all the other strong women characters of the comedies, would have to conform to patriarchal expectations in the end. Her final speech, including her assertion that 'Thy husband is thy lord, thy life, thy keeper' and its reminder that 'Such duty as the subject owes the prince, / Even such a woman oweth to her husband' was obviously capable of ironic inflection and a knowing wink to the audience, especially as the audience knew the speech was delivered by a cross-dressed boy.[7] It also articulated commonplace political and marital ideals. Indeed, the final gesture in the speech, when Kate offers to put her hand under Petrucchio's foot, echoes the movement of the marriage ritual used until the Reformation; ironic readings of the end of the play undervalue its raw expression of patriarchal power. The play encodes debates about appropriate gender roles.[8]

The whole play is a comic commentary on inversion, though we are asked to laugh at violence and cruelty. It begins in a totally inversionary setting: the drunken tinker Sly is found by a noble band, dressed up as a lord, and a page dressed as his wife; the play we think of as *The Shrew* is the play that is acted to amuse him. We begin with a poor man dressed as a lord, then turn to another inversion, a shrewish woman who fails to play a properly deferential role. There are other upended hierarchies in the play: sons who do not obey their fathers, young men who fail to respect older men. The ubiquity of inversion both offers a critique of rigid hierarchy and suggests the precariousness of order. Kate's final speech reinscribes order, making the link between political and marital hierarchies explicit, but it cannot undo all the inversions that have come before. Petrucchio – and Kate in her final speech – articulate conventional ideas, but the play as a whole has emphasized how fragile the conventional hierarchy is. In *The Taming of a Shrew*, a 1594 play with a plot that parallels Shakespeare's, the play ends with Sly waking up, and telling the tapster that even if his wife abuses him when he goes home, 'I know now how to tame a shrew'. That ending turns the play into a lesson in controlling women.[9]

When John Fletcher wrote *The Woman's Prize: Or, the Tamer Tam'd* in 1610, he produced a play that was partly a sequel, but also embedded a critique of the shrew plays. In the play, the widowed Petruchio has carefully sought a biddable wife after the death of his first wife, who had remained violent and abusive throughout their marriage. Everyone fears for the virtuous Maria, for Petruchio 'will bury her / Ten pounds to twenty shillings, within this three weeks'. To everyone's surprise, the meek Maria, with her friend Bianca, takes charge, and with the help of other women, bars the doors to the house and keeps Petruchio out of it – and out of his marriage bed. By the end of the play, Petruchio and Maria are happy together; the resolution requires both that Petruchio respect Maria's independence and that Maria acknowledge her duty to him. But only, as she says, because 'I have tamed ye, / And now am vowed your servant'.[10] The Epilogue to the play is spoken by Maria, who argues,

The Tamer's tam'd, but so, as nor the men
Can find one just cause to complain of, when
They fitly do consider, in their lives,
They should not reign as tyrants o'er their wives;
Nor can the women from this precedent
Insult, or triumph: it being aptly meant,
To teach both Sexes due equality;
And, as they stand bound, to love mutually.[11]

Maria's final speech serves as a response to Katherine's in Shakespeare's play: men should not be tyrants, but should be collaborators. This version of 'due Equality' parallels the approach in domestic handbooks, as it sought to negotiate the balance between authority and cooperation. Yet this resolution required rebellion and turning the world upside down. The audience – and Fletcher's play was far more popular over the course of the seventeenth century than Shakespeare's – would have enjoyed the jokes about how men and women survived the sex strike, but they would have known that this balance was critical to the success of the household.[12]

The debate on women, whether in the form of Swetnam's diatribe or Shakespeare's play, can provide the basis for humour, however forced, because we read it against normative discourses of gender. Swetnam claims an inversion of the gender order while Shakespeare plays with the inversion of multiple orders. Both inversion and humour depend on knowing how things ought to be. You cannot turn a world upside down without knowing what it looks like right side up. Humour, especially, finds its purchase in the uneasy recognition of the gap between what we would like and what is. The gap between normative ideals and social practice was sufficiently large to provide ample material for laughter.

The debate on women

'Battle-of-the-sexes' controversies always have elements of an amusing intellectual game, with known rules and literary devices that were more or less observed by the contestants. Both Swetnam and Rachel Speght, who wrote the first response to him, were published by the printer Thomas Archer. Swetnam's style, however, suggests that his work was intended for a more popular audience than that engaged in the learned controversy. All three of the published responses to Swetnam displayed more erudition than he did. They all suggested that he was too ignorant and illiterate to observe these rules, that his arguments lacked the required scholarly underpinnings and that he was not part of the fashionable classes among whom such things were appropriately discussed. One of those critics recalled having first heard of *The Araignment* at a dinner party, attended by equal numbers of men and women. At such social gatherings, the author noted, 'nothing is more usual for table talk' than arguments about relationships between the sexes.[13]

The responses to Swetnam's pamphlet were therefore to some extent socially conditioned, with educated readers seeing it as a possibly unintentionally amusing contribution to a traditional literary game, while less educated ones (men, presumably) took it more seriously because it expressed conventional ideas. This might explain the tone of the play *Swetnam the Woman-Hater*, which was put on at the Red Bull theatre in 1618 or 1619. The play ridicules Swetnam as a comic figure, somehow injected into the familiar (to Jacobean playgoers) Italian world of amorous intrigue and court politics, and makes it hard to see how anyone could have taken his arguments seriously. The play features a debate between Misogynos (Swetnam) and Atlanta (who is actually a man disguised as an Amazon) which the judges decide in favour of Misogynos, though Atlanta's arguments were more coherent; a later scene replays the trial in front of a jury of women, with a correspondingly different outcome. The title, however incongruous in the light of its otherwise conventionally Italian plot, suggests that any mention of Swetnam was expected to arouse sufficient popular interest to be of use in promoting the production. At one point in the play Swetnam boasts,

How my Books took effect! how greedily
The credulous people swallowed down my hooks!
How rife debate sprang between man and wife![14]

The tone of Swetnam's *Araignment* is in fact so consistently ill-tempered and lacking in irony that it is hard to believe that he did not want to be taken seriously, and what little we know about the responses of his readers seems to support this. Many women clearly disliked his claims, and this reaction was given appropriate dramatic expression in a scene in the play when he is put on trial. But before we make too much of the tempting contrast between amused sophisticates and gullible common folk, it is worth noting that the only educated male reader whose reactions to *The Araignment* we know about directly was obviously sympathetic to its arguments. Rachel Speght, the young, unmarried daughter of a London clergyman, published a brief but vitriolic answer to Swetnam early in 1617, entitled *A Mouzell for Melastomus*. It was a learned attack on misogyny, grounded in biblical examples. While in part it responded to Swetnam, it also offered a rereading of biblical texts to critique current patterns of misogyny.[15]

One surviving copy of her pamphlet was copiously annotated by a contemporary reader; it is pretty clear that he was a man, possibly someone considering writing a response to her. While the annotations employed 'tactics which have proved to be quite durable methods for trying to keep subversive women in their place', he appears to have been educated.[16] The annotations were clearly made after reading the whole text, with comments at the beginning referring to the rest of the pamphlet. Their most immediately striking characteristic is the unrelentingly sneering, misogynist, tone. While the annotator did not necessarily like Swetnam, his abuse was reserved for Speght. He could not believe that she would have gone into print for any other reason than because she was herself pining for a husband. He first described her as a frustrated virgin (Speght offered a 'maidenhead for a husband' and the marginal 'Oh for a husband' is repeated several times), but then perhaps not a virgin at all ('You speak like a maid, not like a virgin … I am young, sir, and scorn affection, um, um, um'). He was indignant that a parson's daughter would do anything so unbecoming as to rush into print. He levelled similar abuse at the authors of the commendatory verses attached to Speght's pamphlet. Next to the verse that praises 'he that for his Country doth expose / himself unto the fury of his foe', the annotator asks, 'Doth she fight for her Cunt-rie?' When another declares that Speght 'bears the triumph quite away', he jeers 'Thy mistress bears prick and prize away'. We might be tempted to conclude that the annotator was a clever thirteen-year-old, but some of his comments were more substantive. He impugned Speght's biblical scholarship and countered her examples of virtuous women with observations about how few they were: Deborah and Hannah, for example, were simply 'two amongst ten thousand' and in any case were unlike those 'that now live in these our days'. Instances from 'the days of old' that contradict Swetnam's picture of female depravity, he points out, were not good enough; Swetnam simply argued that 'most part of those which now live, are so'. And he fell back on the traditional dichotomy of rational men and irrational women, contrasting men's superior 'policy and wisdom' with that of a 'weak and ignorant woman'. Many of the annotator's comments are simply abusive: Speght is 'a Devil incarnate', 'a desperate vanity', she has 'a wicked disposition'. In the end, Swetnam's characterizations of women, he asserts, were absolutely right: 'There is not one, that either is, or doth good, no not one'.[17] The reactions of a single reader prove nothing about the general reception of Swetnam's *Araignment*, but they suggest that his misogyny was not limited to the popular audience to whom he directed his work.

Swetnam must have known that there would be an enticing market for his little book among readers of this kind, and that there were a lot of them. Women took offence, though the two-year delay before Speght's response was published is longer than was common in pamphlet wars. Speght's *Mouzell* was quickly followed, also in 1617, by two other indignant rejoinders, both written under female pseudonyms: *Esther Hath Hanged Haman*, by 'Esther Sowernam', and *The Worming of a Mad Dogge*, by 'Constantia Munda'. Both followed Speght in impugning Swetnam's education, both paraded their own biblical and classical learning and both went well beyond Speght in answering invective with invective. Both cleverly turned the tables on Swetnam by pointing out that he was more guilty of scolding than the women who were typically convicted of this offence. Sowernam includes an episode in which Swetnam is put on trial, which may have inspired the trial scene in the play.[18]

Unruly women in local communities

Swetnam's *Araignment* and other pamphlets about disorderly women had a purchase in the imagination of early modern English men and women because they fed off the widespread concern about the 'woman on top' in contemporary society. There is extensive evidence, in multiple forms, of this concern. The ideal vision of society was one in which everyone lived in a household governed by a patriarch, with obedient women, servants and children; households would live in harmony, not only internally but also with each other. It did not happen that way, needless to say. Women undermined the ideal order in three primary ways. Scolding women were not always modest – in the sense of quiet and almost invisible – in public or private: *The Taming of the Shrew* played on recognizable characters. Nor were women always submissive to their husbands and fathers. And they did not always even live in patriarchal households. Those women who resisted the patriarchal order in any one of these ways were threatening, because in doing so they suggested that the expected order was not inevitable, and that there could be alternatives. The responses to disorderly women were one way to ensure that the social order did not change, and that patriarchal equilibrium was maintained.

Scolding women were the most familiar threats to patriarchal order. Scolds were usually married, but failed to be modest and submissive. At least in an earlier period, the women accused were generally from established families, which suggests a certain amount of economic power. Scolding was an offense that could be prosecuted in ecclesiastical courts, where it was a 'breach of Christian charity,' and in both manorial and royal courts, where it was a disturbance of the peace; it was primarily an offense of women, but men were prosecuted on occasion. Women's propensity for scolding was one more manifestation of their disordered nature. While the chronology and frequency of scolding prosecutions is unclear, prosecutions for scolding reflect 'a desire for order and justice, and conflicts about how to get [them]'. Prosecutions for scolding (or being a 'common barretor', who picked quarrels with neighbours) were sufficiently common that in 1580 the Wiltshire Sessions tried to limit their number. To scold was to disrupt the peace of the community through verbal abuse, but words could be a form of violence (as witchcraft cases also demonstrated). When prosecuted in the ecclesiastical courts, the penalty for scolding was penance; when presented in local courts, punishment could be a fine, but also often included being carted through the town and ducked in the cucking stool.[19]

Scolding prosecutions rarely provide more than the name of the offense and the guilty party. But even these brief mentions allow us a sense of how people thought about both the offense and the offenders. Often, punishments were imposed, but put on hold if behaviour improved; in Oxford, for instance, the 1615 Sessions ordered Katherine Forrest and Elizabeth Slye to be 'well ducked' for 'common strife and scolding', but because of their repentance, the punishment was only to be carried out if they offended again. The rare description of scolds' actions shows why their behaviour was threatening; they also show prosecution as a last, rather than a first, resort. In 1620, Oxford ordered Margaret, the wife of Edmund Slayman, be 'kept in safe custody' until she could safely be ducked, 'after many misdemeanors, daily disorders, abuse of officers and drunkenness'. The following year, they ordered Margaret Atwood 'to be put in the ducking stool at a time to be named for horrible scolding and base and scandalous words to Agnes Lee'.[20] Scolding was often joined to other offences: Mary, the wife of Lawrence Yate of Charlton, Worcestershire, was described in 1607 as 'a common scold and tale carrier'. As a local resident who would have received poor relief if necessary, she also stole produce from the fields, 'apples, crabs and corn, and has been seen to cut the barley'.[21] With such offenders, officials could punish offenses separately; when the inhabitants of Middleton Quernhow, Yorkshire, complained about Anne, the wife of John Sweting, 'a notorious scold, a common drunkard and a woman of very lewd and evil behaviour amongst her neighbours', it was ordered that whenever she was scolding, the constable was to duck her, but when she was found drunk, she was to pay her fine or be put in the stocks for six hours.[22] London local courts held special sessions in the late

Figure 1. A scold: illustration of John Taylor, *A Juniper Lecture*. RB 17686, The Huntington Library, San Marino, California.

sixteenth century to deal with 'harlots, bawds, and scolds'. In 1628, two 'scolding' 'fisherwomen' were taken up in London along with a third, 'pulling one another by the hair of the head': this was not a minor quarrel.[23] Women whose verbal abuse was more troublesome could also be suspected of witchcraft, with their words having malevolent power to punish their enemies.

Scolds disturbed the harmony of a community – good neighbourhood – through conflicts with neighbours, but local peace could also be disrupted by women who, like Kate in the *Taming of the Shrew*, defied the authority of their husbands. They might reject a husband's domestic authority, or commit adultery. While, as we shall see in the next chapter, henpecked and cuckolded husbands were targets of ridicule, they and their wives might also be the target of local shaming rituals. These have several names; across Europe they are called charivari, but in England they are usually known as 'skimmingtons', 'ridings', or 'rough music'. While we will discuss these in more detail in Chapter 4, they were one social response to unruly women. The riding directed at Nicholas Rosyer of Wetherden, Suffolk, and his wife, a neighbour reported, enacted 'an old country ceremony used in merriment ... whereby not only the woman which had offended might be shunned for her misdemeanor towards her husband, but other women also ... might be admonished'. Rosyer and his wife, needless to say, did not enjoy the 'merriment', and moved to the nearby village of Haughley, though his family had been established in Wetherden for two hundred years.[24]

While the refusal of daughters to obey their fathers was less often recorded than was conflict between husbands and wives, it too has left traces in the records, primarily around decisions related to marriage. The daughter of Sir Henry Ludlowe, a Wiltshire knight, was only one of many girls who married without her father's permission. A scurrilous libel circulated in Thaxted, Essex, about the way Richard Turner, a gentleman, had beaten his daughter: the libel's refrain was 'whip her arse Dick'. Turner, on the other hand, asserted that his daughter was a 'young wench' who had given him 'just cause of grief and offence', so he had given her 'such correction as in his discretion he conceived to be most fitting'. As with the 'correction' of wives, neighbours monitored men's behaviour to protect children.[25] Rebellious daughters counted as another sign that women were not willingly subordinate.

Finally, some women undermined the patriarchal order by living outside it. In theory, single adults continued to live in a patriarchal household, governed by their father or by a master. This was required not only by the Statute of Artificers of 1563 for all who did not have an estate worth 40s a year, or goods worth at least £10, but also by numerous civic regulations. Women who lived alone and 'out of service', with no household head responsible for them, were a particular problem. Demographic studies have demonstrated not only that the average age of marriage in early modern England was relatively late (twenty-six for women, twenty-eight for men), but also that a significant proportion of the population – as much as 20 per cent – never married.[26] Yet not everyone stayed in a household: vagrancy was common, though more men than women were vagrants. Single women might find a place as lodgers, a position in between living independently and being a servant, yet town authorities tended to assume that women living alone out of service were prostitutes. From 1579 to at least 1615, Southampton authorities repeatedly tried to crack down on 'charwomen', the 'divers young women and maidens which keep themselves out of service and work for themselves in divers men's houses contrary to the statute'. Southampton authorities were intermittent in their prosecution, but when they went after potential charmaids, they cast a wide net. In 1608, one of the women living in Thomas Foorde's house was his sister-in-law, who was recovering from ague. She was ordered to find service as soon as she was recovered, but some months later was still there, and now ordered to be gone in three weeks. With an eye on the potential costs of poor relief, in 1612, the beadles were chastised for neglecting to bring lists of migrants and charmaids, but in 1615, prosecutions had resumed.[27] Southampton may have the most detailed records of prosecution for living out of service, but authorities there were by no means unique. In Norwich, single women living alone were often imprisoned in the Bridewell, or house of correction. London authorities worried about women who lived out of service, which, they thought, inevitably led to crime or immorality. Independent women, not accountable to a head of household, were assumed to be sources of disorder. Most such prosecutions were in towns and cities; in rural areas, women charged under the statute were often living with their parents. As poor women faced more barriers to marriage than did wealthy women, the concern with unmarried women was tied to concern with the disorderly poor.[28] Such concern with women who lived outside patriarchal households emphasizes the household's importance to the social order.

The women who stepped outside of their expected roles, whether by living independently, or by arguing with neighbours, husbands and fathers, were not a new phenomenon. Nor, indeed, was elite concern with them, although the intensity of this concern does seem particularly strong between 1560 and 1640. New laws, for instance, policed infanticide and witchcraft, and simplified prosecution.[29] These concerns had greater purchase because they coincided with a series of court scandals that placed unruly women at the centre of politics. The court scandals played off of the pamphlet debate, and echoed local concerns.

Unruly women at court

Swetnam's *Araignment* was published two years after the widespread publicity generated by the first big Jacobean scandal, the annulment of Frances Howard's marriage to the Earl of Essex, and her marriage to the king's favourite, Robert

Carr, the Earl of Somerset. The scandal included sex and the alleged use of magic and ultimately witchcraft, all made more shocking (or at least titillating) by the involvement of members of the highest aristocracy and royal court. In 1613 the beautiful, and to some, malignant, Frances Howard, daughter of the Earl of Suffolk, succeeded in getting her marriage to the third Earl of Essex annulled so that she could marry Carr, James I's reigning favourite. Howard and Essex had been married in 1606 – Essex was fourteen, Howard a year younger – in one of those ghastly political unions so common among early seventeenth-century aristocratic families. This particular one was arranged, with James I's approval, to bring together two important court factions: the pro-Spanish, covertly pro-Catholic Howards, and the anti-Spanish, anti-Catholic friends of the young bridegroom's father, the second Earl of Essex, who had been executed in 1601. The marriage was a disaster waiting to happen. The couple did not live together until Essex returned from continental travels in 1609, but within a year Howard's dissatisfaction with Essex was the subject of fascinated gossip in court circles. A letter to the diplomat William Trumbull in July 1610 reported that 'plots have been laid' to poison Essex and that Frances was involved in them.[30]

The Church of England did not allow divorce, so the only way out of such a marriage would be an annulment; for this, there had to be proof that Essex was impotent.[31] Howard appears to have used all means possible, licit and illicit, to ensure that this was true. By 1611 Frances was in touch with the magician Simon Forman, getting prescriptions 'to inhibit the desires' of her husband, and at the same time to inflame Carr's love for her. Thus the first story, the unhappy marriage, was joined to a new one, her desire to choose her own sexual partner. This sinister story was revealed only later, but by the early months of 1613 the dire state of the Essex marriage again featured in the court news. Howard had apparently turned to a less famous healer, Mary Woods, of Stratton Strawless, near Norwich, known locally as 'Cunning Mary'. She was in the business of selling charms to women who wanted children, or who wished to obtain husbands – or get rid of the ones they already had; she also, like a witch, was reported to have a familiar who helped locate lost goods. Her cunning thus covers the range of activities such women undertook, and she worked with and for women. She responded to complaints with blackmail, threatening to accuse her clients of seeking to poison their husbands. Woods was examined between June and December 1612 for accusations of theft and threats of poisoning.[32] In February 1613 she was linked to Howard, and was questioned concerning a diamond ring and gold chain which Frances Howard had left with Woods (at that time working as a laundress in London), ostensibly to look after while the Countess was at a court masque, and which she subsequently tried to recover. Woods testified that the ring and chain were to be given to her, along with £1,000 in cash, in return for her poisoning Essex, though she also claimed that after some delay she had refused to do it: she was examined in Suffolk, having left London with the ring and the gold. By June she would admit only that she had sold a powder to the Countess so that she could have a child. When asked about the contradictions, Wood responded, 'what was true she best knew in her own conscience'.[33] Howard's known associations with Forman and Woods suggested that magic was the companion of female desire.

Whatever Woods's exact relationship with the Countess, by early February 1613 knowledge of Frances Howard's hatred of her husband was again circulating at court, and thus quickly becoming public knowledge. John Chamberlain, the news writer, picked up the story about Woods by 29 April, saying that the Countess had 'many conferences with a wise woman,' who alleged that she 'dealt with her to make away her Lord'; he noted that this had forced the Howards to think 'it not fit to proceed in the divorce'. If so, the delay was a brief one, as the case got under way in May, when James I appointed a commission to hear it, under the direction of Archbishop Abbot. Abbot and several other bishops on the commission strongly opposed the annulment. The sanctity of marriage, the archbishop declared, was 'instituted by God himself' and could never be abrogated. But the king's view that it was 'only a question of order and policy' eventually and perhaps inevitably prevailed, so Frances got her annulment; in November Carr became Earl of Somerset, and Howard and Carr were married at Christmas 1613. The annulment and remarriage were a subject of consuming interest both among insiders at court and, at second hand, among the large numbers of Englishmen and women from all social levels who had access to news of public affairs. At least some of those would have known that Frances Howard's mother, the Countess of Suffolk, was believed to be an 'enchantress', and that she was a close friend of the Bishop of Bristol's wife, Mrs Thornborough, who had similar interests. The whole affair is shot through with rumours of sorcery and witchcraft, which seemed to confirm the common assumption that masculine impotence was always the result of malign supernatural powers trying to invert the natural order.[34]

The annulment and the subsequent marriage were played out with much publicity, and interest in them extended well beyond the court. In 1613 and 1614 a number of derogatory libels about the couple and their marriage were being circulated in manuscript. One described Howard as 'A maid, a wife, a Countess and a whore'; another noted that in her escape from Essex 'lechery did consult with witchery'. The libellers were fond of using maritime metaphors based on aristocratic titles: Howard's ship sails from Essex to Rochester (Carr's title at the start of their courtship) and eventually lands in Somerset (Carr's later title), by which time she is 'fit for any sport'. The libels do not tell a love story, but one of inappropriate desire. They reflect popular interest in, and horrified – or just titil-lated – fascination with the events at court.[35]

The annulment and Howard's rapid remarriage were scandalous enough, with their overtones of female desire and magic. In the late summer and autumn of 1615, some six months after the publication of Swetnam's *Araignment*, they was overshadowed by the addition of poison to the mix, with revelations about the death of Somerset's former advisor and secretary, Sir Thomas Overbury. Overbury had died in the Tower in September 1613, after a four-month impris-onment, having, it transpired, been poisoned. He was ill when he entered the Tower, and was apparently slowly poisoned by pies and jellies sent by the Countess, and died as a result of a poisoned enema. He had made the mistake of opposing his patron's intended marriage, and as a result, Frances had become his implacable enemy; she allegedly orchestrated the poisoning, which was car-ried out by her agents. There had already been speculation about the actual cause of Overbury's death, occasioned partly by the Tower authorities' refusal to allow Sir Thomas's brother-in-law to view the corpse, and its suspiciously hasty burial. Rumours circulated before the full extent of the crime was evi-dent. One of the early libels against the Carr-Howard match had warned, 'Nor dare we say why Overbury died'.[36] In June 1615, the rumours finally seem to have spurred Secretary Winwood to investigate, which he did in a conversation with Sir Gervase Elwes, the Lieutenant of the Tower.[37] Eventually, the fact that Overbury had been murdered came out. After a series of sensational trials in the autumn of 1615, the underlings – Richard Weston, Overbury's keeper in the Tower; Sir Gervase Elwes, the former Lieutenant of the Tower; James Franklin, the apothecary; and the Countess's friend, Mistress Anne Turner – were found guilty and executed. Frances and her husband were also found guilty of murder; while they received royal pardons, they were disgraced and lived the rest of their lives in genteel seclusion.[38]

We might well wonder how much Swetnam knew about all this when he wrote *The Araignment*. He could not have known about the murder, but his work does contain some passages that hint at one phase or other of the affair, which had scarcely been secret; the scandal reflected precisely those aspects of court culture that he most deplored. If he had heard rumours about the murder, he was obviously aware that his work might get him into trouble if he was not careful, as he warned his readers at the outset, 'before I go any further, let me whisper one word in your ears, and it is this: whatever you think privately, I wish you to conceal it with silence'. Later, having deplored at length the foolishness of men who had ruined both their fortunes and their reputations 'for the love of wantons', he metaphorically throws up his hands: 'But what should I say? Some will not give their babble for the Tower of London'.[39] Apart from this mention of the Tower (which could in any case be a confused reference to Overbury's time there), the rest of the language could easily date from any time after the middle of 1613, when Frances Howard's intention to get her marriage to Essex annulled became public knowledge. But the scandalous gossip surrounding Howard and Robert Carr undoubtedly contributed to Swetnam's moral universe, as well as that of his readers.

The issues arising from the scandal – of women's agency, especially their sexual and marital agency – were explored in many contexts. The story itself, with magic, adultery and poison, reads like the plot of a Jacobean tragedy: the disastrous consequences that ensue when women pursue their own inclinations and claim initiatives that properly belong to men. The most familiar example is Shakespeare's Lady Macbeth, but there were plenty of others: John Webster's *White Devil* and *Duchess of Malfi* certainly fit. John Marston's lesser-known *The Insatiate Countess* had an apposite title, but was written long before Frances Howard became the most infamous personification of the female sexual appetite that is depicted in the play. Yet it was first printed in 1613, just as the annulment proceedings took place, and there was another printing in 1616, when the Overbury trials had given Howard's alleged sexual license even more widespread publicity.[40]

While its similarities to Jacobean tragedy link it to representations of inversion, the scandal also involves one of inversion's most frightening manifestations, witchcraft and magic. The stories about Frances Howard's dealings with Simon Forman and Cunning Mary confirmed public apprehensions about the satanic forces that were likely to be involved when women pursued their own sexual interests. The poisoning itself conveniently fitted into expectations about how independent women behaved, but it was linked to a wider set of political fears. As the details came out during the late summer of 1615, the whole affair began to take on the outline of a vast scheme to overturn morality and government. Just as Secretary Winwood was investigating the murder, Thomas Scot published a pamphlet, *Certaine Pieces of this age paraboliz'd*, dedicated to Essex. Scot contrasted England's providential rescues from the Spanish Armada in 1588 and the Gunpowder Plot of 1605 with the death of the anti-Spanish, anti-Catholic Prince Henry in 1612: if the 5th of November was a day of deliverance, the 6th, the date of Henry's death, was 'worst of all days to our Island past'. Henry's death was God's punishment for the kingdom's sins, which included that 'some wives may have two husbands'. He referred directly to the annulment of Frances Howard's marriage. God saw

> How holy Hymen's sacred bands are broken, . . .
> How goatish lusts needs all those waves to slake
> His scorching flames, hot as th'infernal lake.[41]

The connection to broader political threats was not entirely paranoid. The discovery of the Overbury murder coincided with other sources of concern about the future of the kingdom in the highest reaches of government. While Winwood was investigating the murder, he was told by William Trumbull, the English agent/ambassador at Brussels, of the existence of a dangerous plot which, Trumbull said, 'doth not only concern the life of his Majesty but the whole estate of his kingdom'. Trumbull quickly made arrangements to send his principal informant, Octavio Bonajuti, to London, to make a full report to Winwood, all in the deepest secrecy because other members of the king's government might be incriminated. He never arrived. The coincidence of the discovery of the Overbury murder and the purported threat to the kingdom is suggestive.[42] At the trial of the Overbury killers, Chief Justice Coke linked the murder to earlier Catholic threats to England, including the Spanish Armada and the Gunpowder Plot. It is entirely possible that Bonajuti and his intermediary, an Irish officer named Captain Walter de la Hoye, were among the sources for the great 'popish powder poison plot' against the king and kingdom which Coke so chillingly described.[43]

Challenging patriarchal power

Frances Howard and Robert Carr, already guilty of turning the moral world upside down by contracting an illicit marriage, were thus connected in many people's minds to a vast and sinister scheme to destroy the whole system of authority that God had ordained. The Overbury scandal pushed to the centre issues of female agency: about Howard's determination to control her marital destiny; about the likelihood that women would resort to seduction, witchcraft, even murder, if they were sufficiently determined in their rebellion against male authority. Seen in this light, Swetnam and the various *Shrew* plays were not so funny. Women were frequently blamed for scandals in which contemporaries discerned signs of satanic inversion; such scandals often had serious political consequences for the men involved. These scandals were not simply about sex, any more than the Frances Howard scandal was: they involved sex, power, or money or a combination of all three. Furthermore, in all of these scandals, women sought to control their own destiny. In 1619 – years after her daughter's disgrace – Frances Howard's own mother, the Countess of Suffolk, was accused of leading her husband, the Lord Treasurer, astray by her rapacious appetite for money, and thus being responsible for his conviction on charges of bribery and embezzlement.[44]

The association of women's sexual agency and political danger was familiar, and it did not need to involve women at the highest level. In 1599, Chamberlain wrote that Richard Fowler had been committed to the Tower 'for no less matter then suspicion of practice against her Majesty's person', though he suspected that Fowler was only 'foolish', not 'devilish'; the real problem was not Fowler but his wife, who, like Helen of Troy, was 'the cause of all the evil, carrying the right picture of a courtesan in her countenance'. This turned out to be true: a forged letter, with the goal of getting rid of Fowler and allowing Marie Fowler to escape her marriage, had led to the accusation. As a result, Mrs Fowler was to be carted to Bridewell and whipped. Her 'mignon' (so Chamberlain described him) Captain Heines (or Eynes) was sentenced to the pillory and imprisoned; he was later hanged for killing a fellow prisoner. Her brother, Henry Boughton, was heavily fined; in 1612, he and his sister were again in trouble, this time for coining. The heaviest penalty fell on Gascoin, a soldier, who was 'the principal actor, and the best proof came against him'. He was sentenced to life imprisonment, first being paraded in inversionary fashion, riding backwards, branded, and put in the pillory. The references to Mrs Fowler as a courtesan and the punishment – carting was the official form of a charivari – suggest that whatever was suspected was connected to gender.[45]

Unruly women were not involved only in sexual scandal. Lady Anne Clifford's determination to control her own destiny focused entirely on property. The Clifford lands were entailed, in an unusual arrangement, on the oldest *child*. As the oldest child of her father, the Earl of Cumberland, Clifford should have inherited his lands after his death in 1608, but instead he left the lands to his brother, who was heir to the title, and gave his daughter only £15,000 – a sizable sum, but far less than she would have inherited otherwise. Lady Anne's mother, the Dowager Countess of Cumberland, began a lawsuit on behalf of her daughter, which she could do as a widow. King James sought to mediate, and while

Clifford's husband, the Earl of Dorset, would have accepted the proposed settlement, Lady Anne refused. After her refusal to obey both the king and her husband in the matter of her property, she spent several years in isolation, unable to go to court. In 1617, the king again tried to enforce a settlement, which would have involved her giving up her property, but she – with the implicit support of the queen – refused. Ultimately the men agreed without her that the lands went to her uncle, and her husband received a handsome sum in return. Clifford was not a scold, but given her understanding of her rights and the family honour, she refused to obey either her husband or her king; her unwillingness to part with her rightful inheritance was one source of tension in her marriage, and her commitment to regaining her inheritance (in which she was ultimately successful by outliving her uncle and cousin) was the driving purpose of the remainder of her long life.[46]

Clifford's focus on her property was unusual but not unique. Most court scandals were the result of the well-known traffic in women, by which women were used as pawns to serve the financial or political needs of their fathers and brothers.[47] The problems of such arranged marriages were exacerbated by the influence of favourites at the court of James I: first the Howards, then Robert Carr, and finally George Villiers, who became Duke of Buckingham. While the Howards were an ancient noble family, James's other favourites were (relative) social upstarts, thus upending the social hierarchy. When such marriages fell apart, women implicitly rejected the authority of both their husbands and their fathers. One such case was the marriage of another Frances, the daughter of the redoubtable Sir Edward Coke, to Sir John Villiers (later created Viscount Purbeck) in 1617. Frances was fourteen when her father, recently dismissed from his post as Lord Chief Justice, tried to regain favour through an alliance with the rising star, the future Duke of Buckingham, who was Sir John Villiers's brother. Coke's wife, the formidable Lady Hatton, with whom he was on the worst possible terms, objected; as with Clifford the first issue was property, as Lady Hatton objected to his use of her first husband's property to benefit his children. Lady Hatton was put under house arrest, and Frances was bullied – by some accounts 'tied to the bedposts' and whipped – until she agreed to marry Villiers. The drama was undoubtedly fascinating – at one point, it was noted that many thought of Lady Hatton's performance 'that Burbage could not have acted better'.[48] Within a few years, Lord Purbeck was subject to fits of insanity, and perhaps not surprisingly, Lady Purbeck took a lover, and bore him a child; to Buckingham's dismay, however, she remained on good terms with her husband. As Chapter 5 shows, charges of sorcery figured prominently in discussions of

Purbeck's mental infirmity.[49] Not only was the marriage disastrous for the participants, but it did Coke no good either.

Then there was Lady Ros. Her father, Sir Thomas Lake, was a Howard client who became Secretary of State. In 1616, with the Howards under a cloud after the Overbury affair, he tried to strengthen his position by linking his family to the still influential Cecil clan, getting his daughter married to Lord Ros. Ros was the grandson of the elderly Earl of Exeter, who had recently remarried an attractive young wife. Within a matter of months there were disputes over the property settlement. The new Lady Ros ran away to her own family, her husband forcibly tried to get her back, and several of his men were injured in the resulting scuffle. Ros challenged his wife's brother to a duel, but had to flee to the continent to escape his massive debts. The Lakes then foolishly widened the quarrel by accusing the young Countess of Exeter of incest with Ros (her step-grandson), and of attempting to poison Lady Ros; the Exeters retaliated by spreading the story that Lady Ros had committed incest with her own brother. Eventually there was a Star Chamber suit – which reportedly ran to 17,000 pages of evidence – for slander which led to the disgrace of the entire Lake family.[50] Passing judgment for Exeter and his wife (presumably because of the lack of evidence for the charges) in the Star Chamber suit between the Exeters and their grandson's in-laws in 1619, James I compared the Lakes's slanders to the first fall of man, 'Sir Thomas Lake to Adam, his Lady to Eve, and the Lady Ros to the serpent'.[51] The comparison suggests the seriousness of the conflict and its potential implications.

The cases we have been talking about focus on women's inappropriate behaviour within the family, but women's behaviour also led to complaints about inappropriate feminine influence in government. While you could not complain of female authority while Elizabeth was alive, her rule did not dispel concerns about women rulers; later complaints may partly represent the release of anxieties that had been suppressed during Elizabeth's reign. A number of the sermons and tracts published after Elizabeth's death used the standard trope of 'The Queen is dead, Long live the King', but expressed special pleasure that there was now a *King*.[52] We are not primarily concerned with the truth or otherwise of any of the charges against women: what is significant is that they were levelled at women who were unusually independent and unwilling to cave in to patriarchal authority. Frances Howard had used her physical charms as well as magical charms to enslave Somerset; her mother was supposed to have dominated her husband and to have been responsible for his taking bribes; Lady Hatton, Lady Ros and Lady Purbeck were all seen as independent 'women on top'. After Lady

Ros refused to answer when being questioned by the Council, Chamberlain noted that she was thought to be 'a very pert lady' who domineered over her mother, Lady Lake, 'as much as her mother doth over some others'. Taken before the king's judges after she had given birth to an illegitimate child, Lady Purbeck wondered aloud 'what those poor old cuckolds had to say to her'. On trial for adultery before the High Commission, she challenged the bishops to swear that their own wives 'were free from all faults'. Convicted, she steadfastly refused to do penance for the adultery. She thus challenged the authority of church and state as well as of husband: heretical notions about gender relations in the family were apparently accompanied by similarly dangerous views challenging the authority of officers of state.[53]

In many ways these sordid disputes resemble those in earlier centuries; this is how the aristocracy had always conducted its affairs. They were the natural outcome of a system in which women were used to enhance the territorial power or political influence of their families. In all of them property was a central part of the dispute. Lady Anne Clifford wanted to gain control of property which was rightfully hers, while Lady Hatton owned large estates in the Isle of Wight which she wanted to keep away from Purbeck's family. The Exeter–Lake quarrel was touched off by a dispute over the manor of Walthamstow, a major component of the Ros's marriage settlement. These scandals meant that disputes about gender relations were a familiar component of public discourse. What is different, however, is the way these scandals echoed and mirrored other, seemingly unrelated, concerns with disorderly women.

The role of property disputes was critical in creating these scandals. If property was not at stake, it was possible for couples to have amicable (or semi-amicable) arrangements. Penelope Rich, sister of the Earl of Essex, had four surviving children with her husband when she began a widely acknowledged affair with Sir Charles Blount (later Earl of Devonshire); but with two surviving sons, the Rich inheritance was secure. The five surviving children she had with Blount were raised with her legitimate children, though provided for by their father. She continued to be a presence at court, and she continued to support her husband with her political connections while carrying on the affair; Rich supported her after she was imprisoned following her brother's rebellion in 1601. It was only fifteen years after the affair began that the marriage of the Riches was ended by the church courts.[54]

Paradoxically, a male ruler – at any rate the particular one on the throne after 1603 – may have exacerbated these anxieties. James I was sometimes feminized – covertly, of course, during his lifetime – because of his pacific foreign policies, so easily contrasted with the warlike, masculine representations of the great queen, his predecessor on the throne. As Thomas Scott of Kent wrote in the 1620s, 'There was in England, a King Elizabeth, there is now a Queen James'. Or, as Tom Tell-Troath wrote in 1630, 'for who would have thought we would have lost/but rather infinitely gained by changing the weaker sex/ for your more noble'. Just as celebrations at the accession of James I expressed coded anxieties about the rule of a queen, later praise of Elizabeth often served as coded criticism of James's failure to follow the 'manly' policy of robust military support for the Protestant cause in Europe.[55] As we shall see in the next chapter, James combined a deep commitment to patriarchal leadership with conspicuous failure at maintaining patriarchal order and discipline in both his immediate family and his court. But he continued to try to control unruly women; in 1619 he told his secretaries 'not to impart matters of state to their wives', as Lake had apparently been doing. He was, John Chamberlain reported, 'in a great vein of taking down high-handed women'.[56]

In the 1620s these controversies about uppity women took a new and in many ways more menacing turn. By the middle of that decade the Duke of Buckingham was undoubtedly the most hated man in England. The women involved in the earlier court scandals and their male allies or protectors were certainly unpopular. But the opprobrium attached to Buckingham was on a scale unmatched by any English minister since Cardinal Wolsey. He was already feared and disliked at court for his unbridled appetite for power, land, money, offices and titles for himself and for his kinsfolk; and the failure after 1625 of the war policies to which he had committed himself made him vulnerable to far worse charges. He was, many believed, either a secret Roman Catholic or a sympathizer, an agent of Spain and the Pope, and the author of the 'new counsels', the allegedly absolutist policies that Charles I began to adopt soon after he came to the throne.[57]

So there were plenty of reasons why Buckingham was disliked. But the ambitious women who surrounded and influenced him exacerbated the fear and hostility. This suspicion was easily connected to the alleged Catholic sympathies of the Villiers family: many people believed that women were fatally susceptible to popish advances. The duke's mother, Lady Compton, created Countess of Buckingham in 1618, was certainly a Catholic. A Jesuit named Fisher ruled the countess, it was said; and 'she the Duke, he the King'. The old countess 'never left working by her sweet instruments, the Jesuits', the memoirist Arthur Wilson recalled. Also Catholic, at different times, were Buckingham's wife and sister; so was his brother, Purbeck, who married Frances Coke. He dramatically proclaimed his allegiance at Wallingford House in 1622. After smashing a window from the inside, he waved his bloody fist at people passing in the street and shouted 'that he was a Catholic and would spend his blood in the cause'. This sensational public declaration was yet one more evidence of his mental instability; he was said to be even more under his mother's thumb than the duke himself.[58]

Furthermore, just as Lady Purbeck and her husband would hurl accusations of involvement in sorcery at each other, other members of the Villiers circle were also suspected of involvement in sorcery and witchcraft. No sooner had King James died in March 1625 than stories were circulating that he had been poisoned by Buckingham and his mother. According to a former royal physician, the king had been given a plaster and a treacle posset made by the countess from her own recipe, neither of them prescribed by the authorized physicians, though with the permission of a Catholic doctor who Buckingham employed. Once again we need not concern ourselves with the truth or falsity of these charges. The House of Commons took this accusation seriously enough to include it in the articles of impeachment against Buckingham in 1626.[59] Buckingham is relevant to a consideration of unruly women because he was widely believed to be at the centre of a circle which included a number of powerful women, who had access to the typically feminine black arts of poison and sorcery; that they were also Catholic made it all the more likely that they would employ nefarious means to achieve their goals. Ballads and subversive libels, whose circulation made a quantum leap as a result of the widespread interest in Buckingham, provided titillating details of the Villiers family's sexual habits – 'They get the devil and all, / That swive the kindred', one of them sneered. An undistinguished doggerel poem by a certain John Rhodes listed the family's crimes, brought about by '... poniards, poisons, swords, / With plaisters, potions, witchcrafts, coining Lords', and so on and so on.[60]

Similar masculine fears of dominant women can be found in continental European courts during this period, accompanied by the same assumptions that supernatural forces were at work. In France, after the assassination of Henri IV in 1610, his widow, Marie de Medici, governed the state for a few years, much as Catherine de Medici had done a generation earlier. Her Italian favourites, the Concini, whom she established in power, were hated both as foreigners and as upstarts, but also because they depended upon, and appeared to exercise, an illegitimate, feminine authority. A year after her husband had been assassinated in 1616 Léonora Concini was executed for witchcraft. Stories about the use of sorcery for political purposes also circulated in the Italian states at this time. The politically dangerous marriage of twenty-year-old Vincenzo Gonzaga, brother of the Duke of Mantua and Monferrat, to his elderly cousin Isabella in 1616, was alleged to have been brought about by supernatural means.[61]

Buckingham was assassinated in 1628, just a few weeks after his sorcerer, Dr Lambe, had been lynched by a London mob. The duke's spectacular career had occurred during a period unusually dominated by fears that assertive women, using illicit sexual and occult powers, were threatening to turn state and society upside down. Unruly or assertive women like Frances Howard or Lady Anne Clifford are not unique to this period, but the reaction to them suggests that their behaviour had a destabilizing effect greater than the practical consequences of their behaviour. From the top of society to the bottom, the evidence from the late sixteenth and early seventeenth centuries suggests a serious fear of a collapsing patriarchal order. It is no accident that Sir Robert Filmer's *Patriarcha* dates from the early 1630s. Filmer makes explicit not just the importance of an ordered state, but also the links between order in the state and the household.[62] Unruly women were a threat to the political order because they were just as much a threat to household order.

Reforming women

The widespread interest in Frances Howard and later sexual scandals was an invitation to moral reformers to set out their wares. Overbury himself was, posthumously, the first of these. As part of his campaign to turn Carr against Howard, he wrote a long and sententious poem, *A Wife*, which set out the conventional attributes of a good and virtuous partner in a way that suggested a striking contrast with the reputation of Frances Howard, married as she was to another man. It must have been written before the annulment proceedings began in May 1613, because Overbury was already in the Tower by then, and it is just possible that a version of it dates from 1612. But it was entered in the Stationers' Register on 13 December 1613, three months after Overbury died and a fortnight before Carr and Frances Howard were married. The poem was frequently reprinted, and Overbury's death was used as a selling-point long before it was known that he had been murdered: the first edition is entitled *A Wife, now a Widowe*. After the sensational news of the murder broke, later editions became even more marketable.[63]

A Wife is a meditation on the ills that follow when lust becomes the foundation of a marriage, and it is full of advice that was obviously relevant to Carr's situation. The prudent husband will choose his wife not for 'carnal beauty',

Overbury declared, but for her virtue: an observer might note that Frances certainly possessed the first attribute, but that she was perhaps deficient in the second. Furthermore, Overbury argues that Carr, the upstart Scot, should not imagine that he will be advancing his fame by marrying the daughter of an English Earl, and a member of the Howard family at that. 'Birth, less than beauty, shall my reason blind', Overbury proclaims, adding that the probable size of a bride's marriage portion does not increase her true worth. Instead, the wife should be distinguished by the conventional qualities always attributed to respectable women, not for unusual talents or behaviours. Virtue should be joined to understanding, gained not through book-learning, which belongs only in the masculine sphere, but through feminine intuition. Above all, the wife should be constantly concerned to keep her reputation secure: her behaviour served as a proxy for her chastity. Overbury would have regarded the advice as appropriate for all women, but particularly so for one with as dubious a past as Frances Howard:

> To keep their name, when 'tis in others' hands,
> *Discretion* asks; their *credit* is by far
> More *frail* than *they*: on likelihoods it stands,
> And hard to be disprov'd, *lust's slanders* are.
> Their *carriage*, not their *chastity* alone,
> Must keep their *name* chaste from *suspicion*.

The list of desirable feminine qualities in *A Wife* contains nothing original, and we do not need to suppose that Swetnam copied from it when he described desirable wifely qualities in his *Araignment*. But it may still be significant that, even in the midst of his consideration of these virtues, Overbury focused obsessively on the disastrous effects of sexual desire.[64]

Overbury's poem tapped into the public disapproval of the Howard-Carr marriage, for both moral and economic reasons. Francis Delaval wrote to his brother, Sir Ralph, that the king was paying for a masque, to be performed by 'Divers Earls and Lords', all being 'a means to make the Chequer [Exchequer] poor, but at last the poor subject shall pay for all'.[65] Dislike of the marriage was sufficiently well known that the poets who contributed their talents to the Somersets' extravagant marriage celebrations could not ignore it. In Thomas Campion's masque, performed in the Banqueting Hall at Whitehall on 26 December, the knights' journey to the affair is hampered by Error and Rumour, who are eventually put to flight when singers command them to 'dim not Hymen's golden light / with false illusion'.[66] There are similar mentions of a hostile public in George Chapman's poem on the marriage, *Andromeda Liberata*. Chapman's dedication urges Frances to ignore the 'factious brood / Whose forked tongues would fain your honour sting', and accuses her critics of themselves having hearts 'guilty, of faults fained in yours'. It contains repeated denunciations of what Chapman calls, with what is in retrospect unintended irony, 'the poisoned murmurs of the multitude'.[67] These murmurs, moreover, focused more on Howard than her former or new husband: it is the woman who is the source of disorder.

Other pamphleteers also took advantage of current events. Thomas Tuke, the curate at St Giles-in-the-Fields, published his *Discourse Against Painting and Tincturing of Women* in 1616. Tuke had apparently already written (but not yet published) a more general attack on the use of facial cosmetics by women, to which he now added an appendix, part of which was headed 'Of Poisoning and Murder'. The prefatory verses attached to the first part, and therefore presumably written before the Overbury scandal erupted, included a contribution by a certain Arthur Dowton, who reminded women that

> The chastest of your sex contemne these arts,
> And many that use them, have rid in carts.

These women had thus been punished as prostitutes with the judicial form of charivari; the use of cosmetics implied a violation of norms of sexual morality. Tuke added a lengthy passage written by a sixteenth-century Spanish physician, who declared that cosmetics were 'brought in by the devil, ... to transform human creatures of fair, making them ugly, enormious [sic] and abominable'. Tuke himself drove the point home, asking, 'Is not this an inversion of nature, to dissemble and hide the natural visage with an artificial?'[68]

The contemporary implications are much more explicit in the appendix, which refers specifically to Overbury's fate and to the role of Frances Howard's friend and confidante, Anne Turner. Turner was seen not only as Frances's accomplice in the approaches to obtain charms and potions from Simon Forman, and subsequently in the murder itself, but also as the epitome of feminine pride and luxury, corrupting other women by her daring espousal of new fashions of dress and cosmetic beauty – in which, of course, Frances Howard set an even more conspicuous example. Summing up at Turner's trial, Chief Justice Coke depicted her as an exemplar of most of the seven deadly sins: strumpet, bawd, sorcerer, Papist, 'a daughter of Forman' (Simon Forman the magician) and employer of witches. Whether she was also a murderer, Coke left to the jury, obviously confident that they would find she was.[69]

Tuke's first target was Mrs Turner's most famous sartorial statement, her provocative adoption of yellow ruffs and bands instead of the chaste white ones which modest women were supposed to wear. Such ruffs were signs of vanity and 'vain desires', for both symbolic and political reasons. Artists portrayed Judas wearing yellow, and it was also the colour of lust. Yellow dye came from saffron, which comes from stamens collected from saffron crocuses (thus its connection to lust), and it has always been expensive. Saffron usually came from Ireland, and thus was both Catholic and foreign. The ruff, like the yellow linen of which it was made, was also foreign, in this case a Dutch fashion. The starch which shaped it was made from wheat bran, so it was particularly fraught when there were poor harvests: a royal proclamation in 1596 outlawed making starch from English grain, and in 1607 the starch industry was blamed for creating the current dearth. The yellow ruff was a satanic colour, foreign and Catholic, and a cause of famine. At her execution, Turner tearfully repented not only of having committed the crimes of murder and witchcraft, but also of having been an exemplar of the sins of lust and vanity through the displaying of yellow ruffs. Her penitent performance on the scaffold – as was true of such performances in general – was an attempt to turn right side up the moral world which she and Frances Howard had so scandalously inverted.[70]

Mrs Turner also allegedly plastered on more than the normal amount of facial make-up, Tuke's second target. Painting of faces, he asserted, was 'a provocation and incitement to lust', and led women inexorably to 'practice love-potions by charms and sorcery', as Frances Howard had done, and in the end to murder by 'Italian devices' such as poison. Tuke had no difficulty in connecting cosmetics and fashions of dress, commending the repentant Mrs Turner's call to women to 'leave off their yellow bands, and of garish fashions, the very invention of the devil'. In a final addition to his pamphlet, 'The Pictor of a Pictor, Or the Character of a Painted Woman', Tuke suggested that the corrupt moral climate of the capital was largely to blame for these evils. To the painted woman, London was 'her Paradise, her Heaven, her All in all', and within London that scene of excess and conspicuous consumption, the New Exchange, was 'the Temple of her Idol'. But Tuke also drew an anti-popish conclusion: 'The Church of Rome, who as she is the Mother of spiritual fornications, magic, sorcery and witchcraft, so hath God given her over to defile herself with corporal pollutions and fornications'. Adultery, feminine excess, foreign fashions, diabolical interventions, Italianate poisoning and Popery, all came together in the Overbury affair to turn the ordered moral world upside down.[71]

Tuke was not alone in his obsession with cosmetics. One of the longest marginal entries made by the anonymous annotator of Rachel Speght's *Mouzell for
Melastomus* was on this subject. Speght had declared that the original creation of
women 'can not choose to be good, yea very good, which is wrought by so excellent a workman as the Lord'. Aha, pounced the annotator, but women's work 'can
not choose but be bad':

> For since He framed them, she hath put new colours of white and red upon her
> face, set in new teeth; either wear not her natural hair; or if it be, it is so pow-
> dered and perfumed, as she thinks she hath much mended her creator's work.
> Had they thrived as they were at first created, they had been excellent, but many
> are so changed in face, that you shall scarce know them from a pa[inting].[72]

Like Tuke, Speght's anonymous reader saw a close connection between cosmetics and dishonesty; others linked it to sin and witchcraft.

Dress was, if possible, more fraught than make-up. In a society where dress
encoded identity, what people wore identified class as well as gender. Sumptuary
laws, which sought to restrict the wearing of particular fabrics by class, dated
back to the middle ages. They were reissued under Philip and Mary, but by
that time the number of exceptions to the rules made it difficult to know who
could and could not wear particular fabrics. In the early 1560s, returns to the
Exchequer detailed women who wore particular fabrics in relation to their husband's military responsibilities. Complaints about 'the excess of apparel in merchant's wives and their daughters, gentlemen's wives and their daughters, and in
all degrees' continued through the century. In 1597, a proclamation was issued
regarding the enforcement of the sumptuary laws, but it was immediately followed by another 'Dispensing Certain Persons from the Statutes of Apparel'. In
1600, justices were urged to reform 'the vanity and excess of women's apparel'.[73]
Introducing a 'bill against apparel' in the House of Commons in April 1614,
Christopher Brooke condemned the cost of women's clothing, noting that they
'carry manors and thousands of oak trees about their necks'; his bill was particularly aimed at the wearing of gold and silver lace, which had been so conspicuous
at the recent marriage of Frances Howard to Robert Carr.[74]

Moralists and satirists joined the judges. Thomas Scot's catalogue of England's
sins included 'Fashions from Spain, France, Germany and Rome, / and Turkey
too, with their Religions come'.[75] Samuel Rowlands satirized the common female
assumption that following fashion was a hallmark of independence:

> We may delight in fashion, wear the same
> And choose the stuff of last devised sale;

Take tailor's counsel in it free from blame,
And cut it off, as soon as it grows stale.[76]

In addition, elite fashion often relied on foreign fabrics – silks and velvets – blamed for economic crises and associated with a decline in the moral fabric of the nation.[77]

Concerns during Elizabeth's reign focused on confusions of class, but James I was concerned with the confusion of gender that dress allowed. In January 1620 Chamberlain reported that James I had ordered the clergy to preach 'against the insolency of our women, and their wearing of broad-brimmed hats, pointed doublets, their hair cut short or shorn, and some of them [wearing] stilletoes or poinards and such other trinkets of like moment'. These were masculine fashions, and women should not wear them. A fortnight later Chamberlain noted that the clergy had obeyed: 'Our pulpits ring continually of the insolence and impudency of women'. Stage-players (an allusion to *Swetnam the Woman-Hater*, perhaps?) and ballad-singers had also joined in the campaign. The world was 'very far out of order', Chamberlain reflected, 'but whether this will mend it God knows'. And in spite of the king's strict views on women, when the Dean of Westminster refused to admit women wearing yellow ruffs to the pews in the Abbey, James told protesting aristocratic ladies that 'his meaning was not for yellow ruffs but for other man-like and unseemly apparel'. Mrs Turner's passionate speech on the scaffold does not seem to have had lasting effects.[78]

Perhaps taking advantage of the king's attack on women's unseemly apparel, two pamphlets published in February 1620 denounced the scandalous fashions which in recent years had been threatening to blur the divinely established distinctions between male and female: *Hic Mulier, Or, The Man-Woman* and *Haec Vir, Or the Womanish-Man*. The ungrammatical mixture of genders in their titles at once proclaimed their subject. 'Since the daies of Adam women were never so Masculine', *Hic Mulier* complained. The pamphlet drew explicitly on the Overbury scandal for its examples. Turner had adopted 'the false armory of yellow starch', which according to the rules of colour in heraldry depicted 'baseness, bastardy, and indignity', but were now being used in true inversionary manner as a statement of fashion. The Countess of Somerset had set an example of a monstrous 'deformity in apparel' by wearing styles that were shamelessly copied from those of men's clothing, and which were French into the bargain. To drive the point home, the author quoted lines on women's modesty and chastity from *A Wife*.[79]

In the second pamphlet the mannishly dressed woman of *Hic Mulier* encounters *Haec Vir*, the correspondingly femininely dressed man, and the pamphlet begins with a comic dialogue in which each professes to misread the other's gender from his/her clothing. Having established the true situation, Vir accuses Mulier of having unnaturally rejected 'the Creation of God and Customs of the Kingdom, to be pieced and patched up by a French Tailor, an Italian Baby-maker, and a Dutch Soldier', in other words, to be a puppet of foreign fashions. It is hard to know which is seen as more offensive, the rejection of divine order or the adoption of foreign styles instead of honest English ones. The second pamphlet, however, does provide a robust defence of women's independence, allowing Mulier to assert, 'We are as free-born as Men' and therefore have the right to choose what we want to wear. But eventually both participants repent of their folly. Mulier calls on men to be 'men in shape, men in shew, men in words, men in actions, men in counsel, men in example', and Vir agrees: 'Henceforth we will live nobly like ourselves'. The world of gender relations had been turned upside down by the what-to-wear crowd; now divine harmony has been restored, just as Joseph Swetnam (and Archbishop Abbot) would have wanted.[80]

* * *

Women were unruly and disorderly in many different ways. When they scolded with their neighbours, they disturbed the local peace. When they disobeyed their husbands and fathers, they challenged the patriarchal order, as they did when they acted on their own sexual desires. When women lived independently, their behaviour suggested that women could live outside patriarchal households. Such challenges to the expected order were fairly simple. The disorderly women we have seen here came from all levels of society, and from all ages. Their presence at the court – and in relation to some of the most powerful men at court – meant that they were a political problem, not just a social one. Unruly women are visible not just in historical sources, but in the literary and dramatic world of early modern England.

The publication of *Hic Mulier* and *Haec Vir* in 1620 was undoubtedly a bit of clever marketing by their publisher. They were part of a new stage in the debate on women, this one concerned with the maintenance of gender and moral boundaries through dress and fashion. The existence of this debate – in pamphlets and political tracts, sermons and royal proclamations – does not mean the horror of cross-dressing fashion was universal. In fact, one could argue the opposite: the regular laments about transvestite fashion existed because most people did not worry about them. The critique of cross-dressing was central to attacks on the theatre, which were certainly not successful. When we can gauge the reactions of people, they were remarkably calm about it. When Margaret Willshere, along with her 'dame' and her sister, dressed in men's clothing and headed to a neighbour's house, her master recognized her with 'some words of mirth'. Moll Cutpurse, the cross-dressing heroine of *A Roaring Girl*, is a trickster who rights wrongs, not a source of disorder.[81] Yet the polemics themselves crossed expected boundaries, with sources ranging from King James, distressed by popular fashion, to the Puritan polemicist William Prynne, distressed by court fashion. William Prynne's *Unloveliness of Lovelocks* argued that even the most sober man, if he did not watch out, would find that 'His Amourous, Frizzled, Womanish, and Effeminate Hair, and Lock, will draw him on to Idleness, Pride, Effeminacy, Wantonness, Sensuality, and Voluptuousness, by degrees; and from thence to Incontinency, Whoredom, Deboistness, and all Profaness, to the eternal wreck and ruin of his Soul'. Like the yellow ruff, the new styles were seen by their critics as a sign of the spread of cultural influences from popish countries. 'French men brought in this fashion that they must have their locks like to women', the minister Stephen Denison declared. The energy of this debate suggests that perhaps the gender boundaries were not as clear as everyone hoped: not only could Petruchio be tamed in Fletcher's sequel to *The Taming of the Shrew*, but identity was so much a social construction that mere changes of clothing could alter it.[82]

The manuals that described the proper government of the household insisted that the duty of government belonged to men. Both men and women had important roles to play in maintaining gender boundaries. Disorderly women were enabled in their offenses by men, whether fathers, masters, or husbands, who failed to maintain patriarchal power. A good patriarch would have ensured his wife's good behaviour and his daughter's obedience. The porous boundaries of gender in practice meant that these failed patriarchs were possibly more dangerous than were their unruly wives and daughters.

2

Failed Patriarchs

If the only challenge to order in early modern England had been unruly women, it might have been manageable. But even more dangerous than unruly women were the fathers and husbands who failed to govern their households effectively. Every story of an unruly woman can be turned around to focus on the patriarch – husband, father or master – who, deliberately or inadvertently, did not properly or effectively discipline his subordinates. Indeed, the central argument made by the author of *Haec Vir* is that women took on men's roles because men did not. While modern framings of power tend to focus on how elites subordinate others, early modern conceptions of power were decidedly reciprocal: superiors could expect obedience, but obedience was in response to their good government. The obligations of government were as significant and onerous as the obligations of subordination. One way to control disorderly women was for men to play their proper role. In the dedicatory epistle to *A Godly forme of Householde Government*, Dod and Cleaver argued that if householders wanted wives, children and servants to 'practice such duties as appertain and belong to them', they must 'be diligent & careful to reform themselves'. Patriarchy disciplined men, and made their proper performance of their roles as important as women's deference to their authority.[1]

To this end, advice manuals and sermons paid far more attention to governing than to obeying. It was, Dod and Cleaver noted, 'not a thing that men can stumble on by chance'. Furthermore, they argued, 'He that knoweth not to govern deserveth not to reign'. The entire treatise is directed to 'household governors' – primarily men, though their wives are 'joined' to them, 'as an helper' – and instructed them in how to manage their various inferiors: while husbands were responsible for the household, husbands and wives both had roles in governing children and servants. Householders were to tell their inferiors what to do, but also to call on them to do it, admonish them if they were resistant and finally correct them through rebukes or chastisements. The behaviour of inferiors was the responsibility of their governors. Dod and Cleaver built this notion into the structure of their tract: in every case, the discussion of the duties of the superior – husband, parent, or master – comes before and is longer than that for the inferior. After all, the role of the inferiors was to show respect for their superior, primarily by taking any guidance they were given and following it.[2] William Gouge emphasized a husband, father and master's responsibilities in his famous *Of Domesticall Duties* by balancing positive injunctions with examples of how people failed to fulfil their obligations. In relation to servants, masters made their authority 'despised' when they 'carry themselves basely and abjectly before their servants, being light in their behavior, foolish in their carriage, given to drunkenness, uncleanness, lewd company, and other vices.'[3] Men – in a line reminiscent of Fletcher's *The Tamer Tamed*, were to 'exercise authority tempered by love.'[4]

Marriage – which meant becoming the head of a household – marked the transition to full political adulthood; before marriage, most men lived in the households of their fathers or masters. Marriage was necessary for householders precisely because the economy was primarily based on a household model of production. Thus, the first and most important task of household government was embodied in a husband's relation to his wife. Most manuals detailed the duties involved quite carefully, devoting far more space to relations between husbands and wives than to the management of children or servants. The role of husband was more complicated and more important than that of a wife. Husbands had to balance a wife's subordination to them with her joint responsibility for the conduct of the household.[5] William Gouge, who details mutual duties of husbands and wives as well as specific duties of wives and husbands, begins his discussion of a husband's duties by noting that 'as the wife is to know her duty, so the husband much more *his*, because he is to be a guide and good example to his wife.'[6] Those duties include loving his wife and wisely maintaining his authority. Authority can be lost both through excessive strictness and by lewd, profane, or unthrifty behaviour. Furthermore, 'tender respect' for a wife needs to be joined to 'provident care' of her – in other words, financial responsibility. All his instructions follow from these general principles. His discussions of men's appropriate behaviour were always balanced by a description of what men do that is bad; like Dod and Cleaver, Gouge assumed that manhood and governance were acquired skills. For Gouge and the other authors of household manuals, the well-ordered household was critical to both a godly and well-ordered society: 'Necessary it is that good order be first set in families: ... good members of a family are like to make good members of Church and common-wealth.'[7]

Patriarchal authority was enshrined by both canon and statute law: heads of households were responsible for the attendance of the members of their households at church and, for children and servants, at catechism. The enforcement of these laws, particularly related to Catholic wives, revealed the contradictions of patriarchal government.[8] The mutuality of a marriage always existed in tension with patriarchal authority.

This model of household governance set men up for failure: husbands and fathers were responsible for the behaviour of people who they could never fully control. Wives, children and servants had responsibilities which took them outside the household, and thus gave them some degree of independence. Husbands and fathers could set the tone, and be more or less responsible for disorder, but they could never ensure that the behaviour of wives, children and servants would always support household and communal order.

James I and the failure of patriarchy

Given the analogies between family and state that were commonplace in advice literature and political thought, the royal court was expected to be a model of virtue and good government. While the household manuals were written for more ordinary households, they were equally applicable to the royal one. James I, in his *Basilikon Doron*, a book of advice written for his son Prince Henry, argued that kingship required not only 'establishing and executing' laws, but also 'by your behaviour in your own person, and your servants, to teach your people by your example'. This required the government of the court in 'all godliness and virtue'.[9] The king, as ruler of his kingdom and as father to his people, was supposed to set an example in the orderly government of his household. Elizabeth had largely done so, or at least so it was remembered. Sir Francis Osborne particularly noted that Elizabeth had no one in her household except those of 'stature, strength, and birth'; she was 'so exact a pattern' of behaviour for James. But, at least in the eyes of his critics, James failed to govern his inner circle properly. Two characteristics of James's court stood out in particular. First was the power given to his favourites, a series of young men (including Robert Carr) whose youth and relatively low birth made many think them unsuited to the highest positions in government. The second was the actual behaviour of courtiers. In spite of his advice to his son, James surrounded himself with a 'beggarly rabble' who were not 'of a good fame and without blemish' or from the highest levels of the aristocracy. James contributed to his son's fiscal difficulties 'through a profuse prodigality'. There were nationalist concerns as well: James's excessive favour to the Scots who dominated his court was seen as exacerbating English fiscal problems. Criticism of the Scots appeared in satires and public houses.[10] The power James gave to his favourites demonstrated that he did not observe the divinely ordained order that he espoused in theory; with his favourites, subordinates apparently ruled the master rather than the other way around.[11] Francis Osborne saw the inversion of hierarchy characteristic of James's relationships with his favourites echoed in Robert Carr's relationship with Sir Thomas Overbury. Osborne's idiosyncratic reading of the Overbury case, which focused on Carr rather than Frances Howard, was framed by the tendency of 'those in power to be guided by servants'. Somerset, he argued, 'was so enchanted with an opinion of Sir Thomas Overbury's parts that he preferred him from a Servant to such an intimate friendship', so that Overbury saw all his correspondence and knew all his secrets. It was Overbury's consequent 'arrogance' that 'kindled the ruin of them both'.[12] James's failure to govern his court involved moral, gender and social inversion; it is impossible to separate them.

Even more serious than the promotion of favourites whose chief apparent advantage was their good looks was the remarkable greed and excess of James's court. The drunkenness that sometimes characterized it quickly became legendary, and is brilliantly captured in Sir John Harington's account of the festivities that were put on for the king's brother-in-law, Christian IV of Denmark, when he came on a state visit in 1606. The royal parties were entertained by the Earl of Salisbury at his great house at Theobalds, where, Harington reported, there were women and wine 'of such plenty as would have astonished each sober beholder'. The English noblemen 'follow the fashion and wallow in beastly delights', and the women were not far behind. A masque based on the biblical story of Solomon and the Queen of Sheba at once got out of hand, with courtiers of both sexes vomiting and falling down drunk in the royal presence. Of the ladies playing the parts of Faith, Hope and Charity, only Charity was sober enough to complete her performance; Hope and Faith 'were both sick and spewing in the lower hall'. The disgusted Harington could not help contrasting all this with his memories of the Elizabethan court, where he 'never did see such lack of good order, discretion, and sobriety'.[13]

Keeping up with the Danes, who were notoriously hard drinkers, might partially excuse the disgraceful scenes at Theobalds. But James did not need his brother-in-law's example to encourage a lack of decorum and sobriety. Sexual laxity and extravagant gambling joined drunkenness as the fashionable vices. Preachers were constantly reminding heads of less exalted families of the disastrous consequences of this kind of behaviour. Recorded criticism of the Jacobean court is most often retrospective because it was too dangerous to make at the time, and it was closely connected to political criticism. Yet the particular criticisms levelled at James's court are consistent and different from those levelled at his son. The disenchanted courtier Sir Anthony Weldon blamed the Overbury affair not on Francis Howard, but on her new husband; Somerset, he suggested, having 'long wallowed in his Master's Bounty, and the Treasures of this Kingdom, he fell the foulest that ever Man did, upon the Rocks of Dishonour, Adultery, and Murder'.[14] Weldon also thought that things went from bad to worse after the promotion of Buckingham as the reigning favourite. At least in earlier days, women and children had been kept in their place, but with the Villiers family installed in the royal apartments, 'now you would have judged, that none but women frequented them', and little children were running around everywhere.[15] This was particularly odd, Weldon felt, because James 'naturally ... hated women' and preferred the society of handsome young men like Robert Carr and George Villiers. The French ambassador, too, observed that the king 'piques himself on great contempt for women'.[16]

The disorder of the court was exacerbated by the erotic charge of James's relationships with his favourites; while discussions at the time were coded, there were certainly rumours that they went as far as sodomy. These rumours and suspicions should be put in context, however. In early modern England and Europe more generally, sodomy was the sin 'amongst Christians not to be named'.[17] As with cross-dressing, it is easy to confuse legal and theological views with popular ones. The early modern concern was with practice and behaviour, rather than essential identity, and there was some flexibility about same-sex intimacy, which was not necessarily identified as homosexual practice, nor connected to homosexual identity. In general, sodomy was associated with foreigners, and with those who might be defined as 'other', and the insult of being 'sodomitical' might be totally detached from any allegations regarding sexual behaviour. Thomas Coryate reported that the Swiss Protestant Henry Bullinger (nephew of the reformer) showed him a book by the (Catholic) Bishop of Beneventum in Italy in praise of 'that unnatural sin of sodomy'. Benjamin Carrier, a Catholic priest, reported in 1632 that there was a group of some forty 'Sodomitical Persons' in London, all puritans. And in the account of Sir Anthony Sherley's travels in Persia, a friar who made his living procuring women for men (and who provided Sherley with a 'Persian courtesan to lie with him') turned out to have a taste for the two Christian boys that Sherley purchased in the market.[18] In all these cases, sodomy is associated with a hated religious other, Catholic or puritan.

The challenge for men was that proper manhood was threatened both by too close a relation to the effeminizing bodies of women and by the dangerous figure of the sodomite.[19] Although the normative order of early modern England depended on the conjugal patriarchal household (the church was probably the only profession where being single was not a bar to advancement), the homosocial worlds of education, politics and business provided multiple possibilities for intimate relationships.[20] But intimacy was not necessarily sodomy. Intimacy between servants who shared a bed, or between students at university, who were more or less equals, was expected. The importance of household order meant that such relationships attracted attention and became a problem when they undermined the formation and management of heterosexual households: if a master had an intimate relationship with a servant, it fostered disorder. Sodomy was not only a serious sin, it represented 'appetite ruling the mind rather than being ruled by it'. It was the dominance of appetite that threatened an ordered society; the control of appetites was a central component of patriarchal masculinity.[21] Men's control of their appetites allowed them to control the women of their household, whose appetites were naturally out of control.

Homosocial and homoerotic relationships were not uncommon, and even same-sex practice was sometimes tacitly (though not publicly) accepted. But fears that the king might have been guilty of the sin of sodomy raised disturbing possibilities of divine retribution on the whole kingdom for this fundamental inversion of sexual order. No one could *publicly* accuse James of sodomy, which he had vigorously condemned in his *Basilikon Doron*, but suspicions were embedded in the language often used by critics of court immorality, and were expressed more explicitly in private. In 1622 the puritan Simonds D'Ewes and a friend discussed things 'that were secret as of the sin of sodomy, how frequent it was in this wicked city ... we could not but expect some horrible punishment for it ... as we had probably cause to fear, a sin in the prince'. Some of the anonymous verse libels that proliferated at the time employed mythological analogies that would have been clear to all. One, beginning with the line 'Arm, arm, in London there is a faction', told the story of Jove and Ganymede, making the explicit parallel with James and Buckingham, and condemning Jove's sin 'for loving so 'gainst nature'. Another, *The Five Senses*, prays to save 'my Sovereign from a Ganymede'. Some historians deny that the erotic language in the correspondence between James and his favourites, particularly Buckingham, was anything more than the conventional exchange of friendly masculine compliments. But their letters suggest that something more than the common practice of sharing a bed was at issue, even if it did not meet the technical definition of sodomy.[22]

In light of these references, letters from the imprisoned Sir Thomas Overbury to Robert Carr contain some intriguing hints that Overbury may have thought that Carr could use intimacy, or its witholding, as a way of pressuring James to agree to his client's release. The letters are ambiguous, and their interpretation turns on the meaning of the one word, 'To', which is usually capitalized. 'To' was certainly a code word for some dimension of Somerset's intimacy with the king. It was possibly related to Somerset's sleeping in James's bedchamber, or refusing to do so, which was a later cause of complaint; in 1615, James complained of his 'withdrawing yourself from lying in my chamber, notwithstanding my many hundred times earnestly soliciting you to the contrary'. In one letter, Overbury asked his employer 'whether you will not use To for a fortnight rather than leave me thus [in the Tower]'; in another, he urged Carr first to tell James that he (Carr) is dangerously ill, and then 'take that To again, and not recover till I am out'. During his increasingly desperate appeals (he was ill from the effects of his poisoned diet), Overbury tells his master that if the king is still adamant, he should 'go to bed and take To, and not stir though he remove, till I be out'. If all else failed, there was only one remedy: 'To for a week'.[23] Whatever was involved in 'To', it was something more than the presence of courtiers in the semi-public royal bedchamber.

The details of the relations of James I with Carr, Villiers and possibly other favourites are less important than the widespread belief that homosexual behaviour was common at his court. Despite the exaggerated metaphors in the later fulminations of puritans like Lucy Hutchinson about the king 'wallowing like a swine in the mire of his lust', her picture of the disastrous moral example set by the court was accurate. She lists the courtly sins that were publicly known and not unmentionable: 'murder, incest, adultery, drunkenness, swearing, fornication, and all sort of ribaldry'.[24] We have already encountered instances of several of these, and more will follow in due course. Disenchanted courtiers like Sir Anthony Weldon remarked with disgust that known homosexuals were tolerated and even provided with cover in the form of well-connected wives. Sir Anthony Ashley, for example, 'who never loved any but boys', was snatched up by a Villiers kinswoman. An anonymous libeller remarked how well Ashley had done 'since he left sodomy'. Sir Francis Osborn, another gentleman with experience of the court, later recalled that young Lord Ros, who was enmeshed in disputes with the Lakes, became so totally besotted with all things Italian that he came to detest 'the meat, drink, and apparel of England'. Among other things, Osborn asserted, Ros adopted Italian fashions in sex, 'feeding his affections upon the barren and loathsome apples of Sodom'. A more famous example from James's court was the great Francis Bacon, Lord Verulam, Lord Chancellor and philosopher. He was impeached for corruption, but Simonds D'Ewes reflected that sodomy was 'his most horrible & secret sin' and that even after his fall he still kept 'one Godrick a very effeminate-faced youth to be his catamite & bedfellow'. His partners were servants, a libeller sneered: the combination of sodomy with servants doubly challenged the social hierarchy.[25] Here again, as with James, it is impossible to separate the inversions of the gender order caused by same-sex desire from inversions of the social order.

And it was not just James's favourites. James's own marriage stood in stark contrast to expectations of good conduct. He failed to govern his wife, or she refused to be governed by him and got away with it. In *Basilikon Doron*, James had argued for an authoritarian, though loving, relationship between husband and wife: a husband was directed to 'cherish her [his wife] as your helper … please her in all things reasonable'; yet his superiority was unquestioned – he was reminded to 'rule her as your pupil' and that it 'is your office to command, and hers to obey'. All this should happen 'with such sweet harmony as she should be as ready to obey, as you to command'. Yet James's marriage demonstrates the difficulties men faced in being good patriarchs. When he became King of England, his relationship with his wife, Anne of Denmark, was amicable if not close. Yet Anne had never provided the unquestioning obedience that James expected. In the late 1590s, she had converted to Catholicism, so she was not a member of the national church that James headed. After about 1607, Anne and James lived primarily apart. Anne had her own household, and was a noted patron of the theatre and arts. Her political inclinations were the reverse of his: more warlike, more active. She raised her eldest son, Henry (whose education she oversaw from 1603), to repudiate his father's pacific values. The masques Anne sponsored at court were often subtly subversive, emphasizing the way the queen's power complemented that of the king. The queen's support for Lady Anne Clifford, too, underlined a view of women's position that was seriously at odds with the subordination that James and others insisted on. Thus, though James believed that wives should be obedient to their husbands, he failed to ensure that his own wife would be so. In the words of one historian, the relationship of James and Anne was 'a surprising inversion of gender roles'.[26] James' failures as a patriarch emphasize the ways in which the gender order and the social hierarchy were linked; it was impossible to separate his failure to govern his wife from his intimacy with 'low-born' favourites.

Elite men as failed patriarchs

King James failed to set an example to the kingdom of a well-ordered patriarchal household, and his court followed suit. The court scandals discussed in the
previous chapter all represent failures of patriarchal authority. Neither the Earl
of Essex nor Lord Purbeck was man enough to control his wife. As with Essex
and Purbeck, the failures of patriarchy at court were mostly related to marital
breakdown, which was not surprising in a circle shaped by arranged marriages.
But the consequences of spousal strife at the highest rank of society were striking. The marriage of the Earl and Countess of Sussex fell apart in a spectacular fashion. In 1594, Sussex, then a young man, had travelled to Edinburgh as
Elizabeth's Ambassador Extraordinary for the christening of James VI's son,
Prince Henry. The relationship he established with James promised a bright
future after Elizabeth's death, but nothing came of it. As Sussex tells the story,
his marriage was a dismal failure, as his wife from the start 'neglect[ed] the duty
of a wife to her husband and so oppose [his] government and direction'. While
the earl complained of his wife's failings – though she was sufficiently dutiful to
bear him four children – the collapse of his marriage reflected on his ability to
govern both his wife and his own lust. From 1602 onwards, the earl and countess
lived apart, with an income charged on the earl's estate to support the countess
and their children. That year he was living with his mistress, a former attendant
of his wife, and outraged one observer by using a friend to tell his wife of the
expensive clothes he was buying her: 'not content to abuse her by keeping a
common wench, he strives to invent means of more grief to his lady'. In 1610, he
had a daughter with a second mistress, Mrs Shute, who remained his companion
until the countess died in 1623; he married her in unseemly haste the following
day. Chamberlain's contempt for Sussex is evident in his description of his scandalously rapid remarriage: 'He could make her none of the greatest nor richest,
yet she is become an indifferent common countess'. By then Sussex had wasted
much of his estate, and in 1622 he had sold his primary seat to Buckingham
for £21,000. As we shall see in Chapter 5, this was about the time Sussex and
his countess were engaged in duelling suits against each other, both including
accusations of sorcery.[27]

While the Countess of Sussex may not have been a saint, there is no evidence
other than Sussex's assertion that she had ever been other than an obedient wife;
the accusation of sorcery was lodged almost twenty years after the marriage had
collapsed. The early seventeenth-century reading of the situation, as is evident
in contemporary sources, would have placed the responsibility for her behaviour

on her husband. He was supposed to ensure her obedience. He was also expected to be a good husband: that did not include openly keeping a mistress, or indeed hiring his own sorcerer to harm her. His waste of his patrimony meant that both his wives suffered. Reciprocity was at the centre of early modern conceptions of order, and the behaviour of superiors was thought to determine the character of the household. Recourse to the courts, and recourse to sorcery, represented a failure of governance.

While Sussex's marriage may have failed because of his own behaviour, some examples of marital breakdown involved more mundane differences of opinion and personality. Lord Chancellor Ellesmere, James's chief legal advisor from 1603 onwards, had married his third wife, Alice Spencer Stanley, Dowager Countess of Derby, in 1600. As Ellesmere was the illegitimate son of a knight, his marriage to an aristocratic and wealthy widow must have seemed like a confirmation of his success. Instead, the marriage was a dismal failure. In 1610, he wrote that his wife's 'cursed railing and bitter tongue' had acquainted him with 'such tempests and storms'. In 1611, he composed a document entitled 'An unpleasant declaration of things passed between Countess of Derby & me since our marriage, and some directions for my son', outlining the causes of his conflict with his wife and planning for his son's management of his estate. The situation was especially difficult because Ellesmere's son (by his first wife), who was his heir and executor, was happily married to one of his third wife's daughters. The source of tension between Ellesmere and his wife was money: one biographer calls him 'covetous' and describes her as 'haughty, profligate, greedy and ill-tempered'. He alleged that after their marriage, his household costs ballooned, because of 'the train which the countess brought with her', including her three daughters, servants, attendants, and followers, whom he labelled 'a wasteful company'. He was particularly offended that she had only contributed a small amount from her extensive estate to the costs of the household when her daughters were still living with her, and none since they had married. In addition to the 'great loss and decay of my goods and personal estate', he had suffered from 'her proud and disdainful carriage, and her unquiet and turbulent spirit'. Since he had provided her with a jointure – property designated to support a widow – larger than he could afford, he wanted to ensure that nothing that was not specified should go to her. His instructions were undoubtedly helpful in defeating Alice's challenge to his will.[28]

Ellesmere would undoubtedly have said that the failure of his marriage was his only failure as a patriarch and that it was a result of his wife's behaviour, not his. But he was clearly interested in such failures, and in 1612 he took extensive notes on a Star Chamber suit brought by Sir Pexall Brocas of Beaurepaire, Hampshire, against another Hampshire gentleman, William Norton. The ostensible cause was an attack by Norton and his followers on Brocas, though six years earlier they had been involved in a dispute over leasehold land.[29] Ellesmere's attention probably reflected Sir Pexall's reputation. Pexall Brocas had inherited the family estate from his grandfather, Sir Richard Pexall, when he reached his majority in 1584; however, a deathbed revision of Sir Richard's will in 1571 gave his second wife a life interest in much of the property, and led to extensive litigation between Sir Richard's four daughters and his widow's second husband. It was not until 1618, when Sir Richard's widow died, that Sir Pexall took possession of the full estate, and even then he was involved in property disputes with his step-grandmother's surviving husband and step-children.[30]

Young Pexall Brocas appears to have aligned himself with a crowd of rowdy young men. At the time of his marriage in 1585, he was already in debt, and the situation did not improve. In the 1590s, his relationship with one of his associates soured, with disputes over land and debts, and he was charged with forging a release of a debt. Before 1603 he had been convicted of crimes including riot and forgery; he was also involved in the Essex rebellion. Notwithstanding being described in 1602 as 'a man of very lewd behavior and disordered course of life', he was among a large group of gentlemen knighted by James I on his arrival in London in 1603; in early 1604 he was pardoned for all 'riots and unlawful assemblies', for forging a deed, for forfeitures due to the forgery, or from any suits in any royal court.[31]

Although his early life was marked by debt, he was later better known for his sexual exploits: he was reputed to have fathered over seventy illegitimate children, some of them in London, others at his estates in Hampshire and Buckinghamshire. In 1605 a Hampshire farmer alleged that Brocas had 'forsaken the company of his own wife' and had for several years 'lived lewdly with other women'. He had bastards by at least two of the maidservants, and he also 'kept three or four other lewd women in his house', marrying two of them off to other servants (in one case, bigamously). One of the maidservants deposed that she had often seen another maid in bed with Sir Pexall. Several of the menservants were also reputed to be 'of very bad life'. Brocas's scandalous conduct was well known outside his household. In February 1612, just a few months before the Star Chamber hearing that Ellesmere took notes on, John Chamberlain reported that Brocas's 'young mignon' had recently had to do penance at St Paul's Cross; Brocas had 'entertained and abused [her] since she was twelve years old'. Always one for a good laugh (he employed his own jester), when Brocas himself had to do penance in 1614 after repeatedly defying the Court of High Commission's conviction of him for 'notorious adulteries with divers women', he eventually turned up with thirty men in scarlet livery, who accompanied him afterwards when he went to demand what he claimed as the customary free dinner from the Lord Mayor in recompense for the injury to his reputation.[32] From a conventional perspective Brocas was a failed patriarch, but he celebrated his rejection of the standards by which he was judged.

Brocas was on bad terms with his own son, whom he accused of trying to poison him with mercury powder in order to gain possession of his estates. He also appears to have been a bad neighbour, angering his tenants by putting huge flocks of sheep on the common at Little Brickhill in Buckinghamshire, where he also owned property, quarrelling with Hampshire neighbours over tithes and allegedly trying to intimidate 'honest men' with vexatious lawsuits. He was also accused of murdering his bailiff and ensuring a packed coroner's jury so that it was ruled a suicide rather than a murder.[33] On one level, then, Brocas's conflict with Norton, which attracted Ellesmere's attention in 1612, was not surprising. But when Ellesmere looked at Sir Pexall's Star Chamber suit against Norton (a case whose official records are missing), Norton's behaviour stood out more than Brocas's. During the summer of 1611 Norton had allegedly taken the lead in a succession of drunken orgies, many of them occurring on Sundays, during service time. 'Pails of drink' were consumed; healths were drunk to the devil (kneeling), to the pope and Romish priests; there were mock knightings of some of Norton's companions to reward them for their drinking prowess. Open contempt was expressed toward both church and government. If the Lord Chief Justice came, Norton declared, he would kill him. On at least one of these occasions, Norton was reportedly 'stark naked'. It is not surprising that the Lord Chancellor took copious notes on the depositions, which seemed to confirm the worst fears that he and many other people had about the inversion of order. From his perspective, these were no comic Sir Tobys or Sir Andrews from *Twelfth Night*: they were rebellious wastrels, led by gentlemen, flagrantly trying to turn their world upside down. William Gouge identified a central mistake of masters: to 'suffer their servants to be their companions, playing, drinking, reveling with them'. By this standard, both Brocas and Norton were failed patriarchs, in spite of their position, refusing to conform to hegemonic masculinity.[34]

As a knight, which was a personal rather than inherited honour, Brocas should have been expected to play a constructive role in society. Yet his career was marked not only by sexual peccadilloes that make for a good story, but large volumes of litigation, even by early modern standards. Brocas was involved as plaintiff or defendant in *at least* eighteen Star Chamber cases under Elizabeth and James, and six chancery cases. He was also cited in four cases in the Court of Exchequer.[35] The torrent of litigation in which he was involved indicates that his behaviour was not only extreme, but extremely disruptive. His failure extended from the household to the community.

The Earl of Castlehaven: sexual disorder and household disorder

These spectacular scandals may have had a greater impact, because over the course of the period from 1560 to 1640 there generally appears to have been a move towards greater moral strictness, at least among the country gentry.[36] When Charles I succeeded his father in 1625, apart from the survival of the Buckingham clan, the court was quickly cleaned up, as even Charles's enemies admitted. The most infamous of all failed patriarchs of the period came to light during Charles I's reign (though not in his court): the second Earl of Castlehaven of Fonthill Gifford in Wiltshire was tried by his peers and executed for sodomy and rape in 1631. The situation in that aristocratic family became public knowledge towards the end of 1630, when Castlehaven's son, Lord Audley, wrote to Charles I, appealing to the king as the father of his country to remedy the abuses of his biological father.[37] To understand its relevance to the subject of failed patriarchs, a brief summary is needed.

The second Earl of Castlehaven, Mervin Touchet, was born around 1593, and succeeded his father in 1617, less than a year after the title was created. From 1600 onwards, his father had lived chiefly in Ireland, but the second earl lived primarily in England. He had been given the family's English estates in 1608, and in 1611 he inherited additional English estates from his grandfather. In 1620, he bought his grandfather's principal estate, Fonthill Gifford, from his cousin. His second marriage had allied him with a prominent family: his new wife was Anne Stanley, daughter of the fifth Earl of Derby and his wife Alice, who was Ellesmere's troublesome third wife; Anne's first husband, Grey Brydges, Lord Chandos of Sudely, had died in 1621. She was apparently somewhat older than Castlehaven. In one of those intricate marriage alliances so typical of the aristocracy of that period (and following the same pattern Ellesmere had followed with his third marriage), the Earl married his son James, Lord Audley, to his new wife's daughter, Elizabeth Brydges – in other words, to his own stepsister, who was no more that fifteen years old when the events that led to the Earl's execution came to light.[38]

Castlehaven had long been on bad terms with some of his neighbours. In 1622 a man named John White, at Stourton Caundle, just over the Dorset border from Fonthill Gifford, was charged with 'scandalizing the Earl of Castlehaven'. It is tempting to speculate that he might have been spreading rumours about Castlehaven's private life, perhaps heard at the disorderly alehouse that White kept.[39] His words might also have had some connection with the dispute over who appointed the rector to the living of nearby Stalbridge, which ranged the earl against a group of substantial parishioners, both clerical and lay. That conflict had begun during the lifetime of Castlehaven's father, and continued after 1617, when the second earl inherited. In the course of the dispute, the earl's opponents allegedly invented 'many foul, odious, false and scandalous accusations' against him, though the only one mentioned in the resulting Star Chamber case was that the first Earl had made unlawful appointments to the living so that he could corruptly enjoy the tithes while it was vacant. Castlehaven's opponents also allegedly took over the church and installed Caleb Morley, a fellow of Balliol College, Oxford, as minister, and rang the bells to assemble their supporters. Unfortunately for them, the bells also brought some of Castlehaven's friends rushing to the church; one of them, John Anketill, had been the earl's page and proudly acknowledged him in the Star Chamber case as 'his lord and master'. He subsequently became an important figure in the Fonthill household and married Castlehaven's daughter. There were suspicions, never completely substantiated, that he was involved in some of the sexual improprieties at Fonthill.[40]

Thus, even before the stories surfaced about Castlehaven's family affairs, the earl was no exemplar of good government or good neighbourliness. After his son's letter to the king, an investigation was undertaken, and in 1631 Castlehaven was put on trial for rape and sodomy. According to the prosecution at his trial before his peers in 1631, Fonthill was the scene of almost every imaginable kind of sexual license, apparently encouraged by the earl. The prosecution produced evidence that Castlehaven had encouraged servants to rape his own wife, on at least one occasion himself participating by holding her down. He had also encouraged his son's wife to sleep with servants, had had homosexual relations with some of them and had imported a local prostitute into the household. He quickly became an inversionary, demonic figure: a neighbour was reported to have heard him say that 'his whole delight was to damn souls by causing them to do such things as might surely effect it'. Castlehaven's defence was that his sexually voracious wife had intentionally cuckolded him, and had conspired with his son to make up these stories and bring him to ruin so that between them they could enjoy his estates. Yet in the eyes of many of his contemporaries

Castlehaven's worst crime was his abdication of patriarchal responsibility for the moral well-being of his family and dependents. The earl was found guilty of rape and buggery and executed on 14 May 1631.[41] Fonthill Gifford was a household in which the whole moral order had been turned upside down, and only Castlehaven's death could turn it right side up.

It did not help matters that although he was neither Irish nor Catholic, he was widely suspected of being both. He had lived in Ireland, where the Touchets had extensive estates, and he was named as a Catholic in parliamentary lists in both 1624 and 1626, though on both occasions he denied it and declared his conformity to the Church of England. Still, in 1625 Castlehaven was listed as one of the suspicious Catholic peers and gentry in Dorset, suggesting persistent anxieties about his loyalty.[42] At his trial the attorney general said that Castlehaven was 'constant to no religion, but in the morning he would be a Papist and go to mass, and in the afternoon a Protestant and go to a sermon'. Young Lady Audley recalled that she had been married in Ireland 'by a Romish priest in the morning, and at night by a [Protestant] prebend at Kilkenny'.[43] The suspicions confirmed Castlehaven's status as an outsider and as a potential danger to the Protestant establishment. At his trial, the prosecutor reached back through the centuries to remind the peers of sodomy's Italian origins. It was, he declared, 'not known in England in ancient times', but was brought in by 'certain Lombards' during the reign of Edward II. Bad history, but an expression of 'the long-imagined association among the Roman Church, Italy, and sodomy'. Castlehaven's alleged connections with both popery and sodomy provided a perfect explanation for his encouragement of disorder in his household.[44]

Whether you believed the attorney general or Castlehaven, Fonthill was the site of a totally dysfunctional household, a place where servants were out of control and women, either by coercion or desire, unfaithful to their husbands; the moral order was totally turned upside down. The only dispute beyond this central point was whether the household's natural head had promoted and encouraged the disorder, or was its innocent victim. Yet this was an argument Castlehaven, like the Earl of Sussex, could not win: it was *his* duty to govern his household, and whether intentionally or not, he had failed. But no one else won: Lord Audley succeeded his father as Earl of Castlehaven, but his marriage had failed, and the dowager countess and her daughter lived the rest of their lives in seclusion and disgrace.

Fonthill may have been more isolated from the surrounding neighbourhood than aristocratic houses usually were, but some of these stories must have filtered through the news networks of local people well before the case became public knowledge towards the end of 1630. The news writer Joseph Mead reported that Castlehaven was arrested for 'cuckolding his own son', among other matters.[45] When the sensational details spread across London they inevitably provoked intense public interest. Charles I heard that 'some great ladies' wanted to attend Castlehaven's trial, so he promptly issued a proclamation which excluded women from Westminster Hall, to shield them from the unsettling details of 'that obscene tragedy'. The trial was, not surprisingly, a packed one.[46] The events at Fonthill were even more widely publicized and sensational than the Overbury murder, and may have contributed to a resurgence of interest in sexual irregularities like incest. Mead, in the same letter in which he reported that Castlehaven had been sent to the Tower, noted the recent conviction of 'an old knight', Sir N. Halsey, for bigamy, and in another letter a month later, of a Welsh gentleman for incest. In 1631, Sir Giles Allington, a Cambridgeshire gentleman, was fined £12,000 for marrying his half-sister's daughter. At about the same time, several clergymen recorded ballads about incest in their commonplace books. And in 1633, John Ford's incest tragedy, *Tis Pity She's a Whore*, was also published.[47] There was all too much evidence of failed household government.

Failed marriages

The Castlehaven case represented a spectacular case of patriarchal failure, but however difficult the marriage was, the case resembled many incidents of marital breakdown where there was no legal separation. More prosaic cases, too, represented a failure of manly government of the household. Without judging responsibility from this distance of time, we know that the usual response of the community to marital breakdown was to try to effect a reconciliation between spouses, and thus reconstitute the patriarchal family unit. When the marriage had obviously broken down irretrievably, there were two options, separation or annulment. Annulment depended on proof that the marriage was not consummated, or was otherwise invalid, and was extremely rare, the Howard-Essex case notwithstanding. A separation 'a menso et thoro', from bed and board, recognized the end of the marriage but did not allow remarriage; women could sue for separation on the grounds of abuse, men on the grounds of their wife's adultery. The process was lengthy, and often seen as a last resort.[48] The best evidence of the importance of patriarchal authority comes not from marriages that collapsed, but from accusations of adultery in ongoing marriages. When one or both spouses had been insulted, cases made their way into various courts. Those cases highlight the importance of a man's reputation for good government of his family.

Cuckolds, men whose wives had been unfaithful, were a familiar part of the social and cultural landscape of early modern England. While the most striking examples were those who, like Castlehaven, not only accepted adultery (which was bad enough) but promoted it, any suspicion of adultery on the part of a wife was a problem. And yet, in the Catch-22 so common with patriarchy, adultery was almost expected. In jest, at least, the assumption was that all men were cuckolds, and therefore on some level not responsible for it; but in practice, men were held responsible for the behaviour of their wives. A London landmark in the period was Cuckold's Haven, or Cuckold's Point, a little east of the city on the Surrey shore. John Taylor, the Water Poet, wrote, 'Unto that Tree all are plaintiffs or defendants … some cuckolds, some cuckold makers'. Taylor plays for some time with the assumption that to be married is to be a cuckold, and wonders whether there is 'of Whores, or Cuckolds any want?'[49] The symbol of the cuckold was the horn, and horn jokes are omnipresent in comedies of the period. In *As You Like It*, for instance, the lords and foresters sing:

Take thou no scorn to wear the horn;
It was a crest ere thou wast born:
Thy father's father wore it,
And thy father bore it:
The horn, the horn, the lusty horn
Is not a thing to laugh to scorn.[50]

Being a cuckold was the inheritance of a married man. The horns appear to be based on the mythological Actaeon, who was turned into a stag after seeing the naked Diana. While Actaeon is punished for what he does see (a naked goddess), a cuckold is mocked for what he does not see.[51] Thus the anxiety in cuckold jokes: if the point of horns was that you couldn't see them, then any man could be a cuckold. Men's vulnerability to being a cuckold, in addition to the social consequences of being one, fuelled the laughter.

While cuckolds were a subject of jest and humour, there is extensive evidence to show that men did not in fact laugh when they thought they were cuckolded. Whether you thought the horns were funny, after all, depended whether you were making the joke or its target. Cuckold jokes emphasize the sharp edge of ritual humour. Just using a horn as decoration identified a putative cuckold. In 1591, when parishioners at Westwick, Norfolk, decorated the church at Midsummer, George Elmer used two branches, 'the one bowed one way, the

Figure 2. A cuckold, linking the cuckold with the beaten husband; illustration of 'Courageous Anthony'. By permission of the Pepys Library, Magdalene College Cambridge.

other another way', at the seat belonging to Joan Holmes and her husband, to create a set of horns. In Charminster, Dorset, in 1609, ram's horns were hung up outside the church during a wedding, while the following year in Somerset, horns were hung outside the window of a newlywed couple: both suggested that the bride had had lovers other than her husband. More aggressively, in the late 1580s, Richard Lamberd of Helion Bumpstead, Essex, placed horns in the chancel of the church, thus defaming the minister.[52]

The horns were not always left to speak for themselves: in Norwich in 1609, a man threw a pair of ox horns into a shop, saying, 'take that for the key to your bedchamber door'.[53] In the midst of a conflict over church seats and other issues in Sithney, Cornwall, the minister, William Robinson, brought 'a great and huge pair of goat horns' and threw them against Edward Fosse's window, and followed it by 'bragging what he had done'.[54] Indeed, actual horns were not necessary for such insults. When Alice Phesey of London told William Dynes that 'thy horns are so great that thou canst scarce get in at thine own doors, take heed thou dost not break a hole with thy horns through thy neighbours wall', the vivid image obviated the need for a concrete symbol.[55]

Insults could be extremely elaborate, often in the form of libels, which were usually sung. In many cases, including those directed at Frances Howard and the Duke of Buckingham, written copies circulated either locally or, in political cases, more broadly.[56] When John Gordon, Gent., was suspected of adultery with Elizabeth, the wife of Edward Frances, Gent., in Melbury Osmond, Dorset, the first verse of the libel read:

> Francis Nedd / with Acteon's head / doth square up and down / his head being high / he doth stye [stay] / to master all the town / and Bess the bear / doth swell and swear / she will master be/ of all the wives for high degree / and well she may I tell you true, / be mistress in London of the Stews. / For pomp and pride she bears the bell / She is as proud as the devil of hell /, But her husband I might be / I would make her leave her venery.

This was spread in 'divers places in the county of Dorset', through multiple copies which were sung and repeated.[57] The verse moved from the learned reference to Actaeon to bear baiting, a rough sport. But it emphasized her husband's failure to control her. A libel that circulated in Bremhill, Wiltshire, against Michael Robbins and his wife began, 'Woe be to the Michael Robens that ever thou wert born, for Blanche maketh thee cuckold, and thou must wear the horn'.[58] John Gobert of Bosworth, Leicestershire, brought cases in the Star Chamber in two successive years. In the first, he complained of a libel circulated in Leicestershire designed to look like a list of articles presented to a court, which alleged that a local curate had slept with a number of women, including Gobert's wife Luce, to whom he had been married twenty-one years. While the libel was not primarily directed at Gobert and his wife, but at Edward Astill, the vicar, Gobert thought it sufficiently important that he brought a suit. The following year, the authors of the first libel, presumably annoyed by the Star Chamber suit, circulated another libel near Gobert's London home in Blackfriars, which called him 'cuckoldly clown', accusing him of giving his wife to Astill. Verse libels about him were soon circulating in the locality ridiculing him as a 'cuckoldy clown', accusing him of being a 'promoter and common cuckold'; the libel included the verse, 'if I be a cuckold it is no matter / for that it is horned luck / because others my wife do fuck'.[59] The insults in all these libels brought attention not just to a wife's (alleged) infidelity, but to her husband's failure to control her.

The local reaction to failed patriarchs and the disorderly women they enabled was evident in the skimmington ride, the English version of the charivari. As we saw in the previous chapter, the ritual called out unruly wives; but they were equally addressed to the husband who had failed to govern his wife. In Quemerford, outside of Calne, Wiltshire, the procession directed at Thomas Mills and his wife Agnes planned to 'wash her in the cucking stool' at Calne, referring to the usual punishment for scolds. But the man riding the horse had 'two shoeing horns hanging by his ears', suggesting that Thomas was a cuckold.[60] In 1653, a crowd of people came to the house of John Day in Ditcheat, Somerset, 'hooping and hallowing'; one man was 'riding upon a cowl staff', while another carried 'a great pair of horns'. They called Day 'cuckold, and threatened to throw his wife into the Pool'; once again, the cuckolded husband is shamed, but his (allegedly) unfaithful wife is threatened with being ducked like a scold. Those who were part of this procession planned 'to make merry with Skimmington', and were promised a 'barrel of beer'. The pleasure the participants took in the event was not shared by John Day and his wife.[61] In these cases, the ritual suggested that the husband had allowed the order of the household to be turned upside down, and he was the target of shaming. Skimmingtons, combining festive license with social criticism, emphasized the importance of properly governed households.

While the cuckold was a problem because he failed to govern his wife, the unfaithful husband was a problem because he failed to govern his appetites. While such behaviour seems to us like simple misconduct, it was an inversion of the proper gender order: turning the world upside down was not their goal, but it was the consequence of their actions. Like the Earl of Sussex, Richard Littleton, Gent., had apparently installed his mistress in his house and ejected his wife Margaret; as a result of their sinful behaviour, both he and his mistress had been excommunicated by the local church court. When Margaret complained to the Justices of the Peace, she noted that he had also intimidated her neighbours so that they would not support her. Richard, in turn, complained that with the assistance of another neighbour she had taken six featherbeds, brass pots and pewter, and that *she* had refused his 'company [and] maintenance'. Richard's silence about his mistress is notable, and Margaret's petition was supported by a minister and six neighbours.[62] While Richard tried to play on his patriarchal authority, his neighbours viewed his breach of good governance as a significant problem.

While formal separations were rare, informal separations and desertion were common, and most often it was the husband who was absent. Whether absence was related to work, incompatibility, or even criminal behaviour, a couple who had ceased to live together did not conform to social expectations of marriage. Stuck in such situations, both women and men often created substitute families, sometimes living together, sometimes going through a marriage ceremony. Women, of course, paid the price for their offences, even when those offenses resulted from their husband's failures in governing the household. Sir Griffin

Markham was exiled in 1604 after a failed plot to kidnap James I to force him to convert to Catholicism. His wife remained behind, and managed the household herself. Having been abandoned by her husband, according to a story circulating in 1617, she had married one of her servants. She was fined £1,000 and had to do penance at St Paul's Cross; some thought the couple were lucky to escape execution under a recent statute.[63]

Or consider the case of John Dey of Loddon, Norfolk. In 1581 he was prosecuted in the Archdeacon's court for a bigamous marriage to his wife Audrey. He had, it was reported, been married to Katherine Myles, a widow, some twenty-seven years earlier (c. 1554), but had left her after six years (that is, c. 1560), during which time she had borne two children. Aside from one reunion, they had lived apart ever since; he was now reported to have married Audrey. According to Dey, the separation had occurred because Katherine was 'grieved' with marriage, and their life together was 'unquiet'. He claimed to have received a divorce from the bishop – presumably separation from bed and board, which did not allow remarriage – and had married Audrey in church in 1574, also (allegedly) with the permission of the bishop, after reading the banns. In 1617, some thirty-six years after Dey had appeared in court for bigamy and more than sixty years after his first marriage, this story was repeated in court as Audrey Dey sought to confirm her right to dower. One witness reported that while he lived, Audrey had lived together with John as husband and wife for close to forty years, though 'in much variance', and there were persistent rumours that Dey had another wife living when he and Audrey were married, but no one had ever seen her. John Dey's original story – that he left his wife because of their unquiet life and her discontent with marriage – is repeated in the account of his second marriage, which was apparently also marked by quarrels.[64] While Dey was not an ideal patriarch, the community's acceptance of a bigamous and contentious marriage suggests the importance of a patriarchal household. But people were watching, and they did not forget the back story.

Local concern with marital breakdown was exacerbated when the failure of patriarchy was combined with sexual relationships with servants. In these cases, as at James I's court, both class and gender orders were turned upside down, or at least challenged. In 1629 the people of Beeston, Norfolk, complained about Thomas Vyollett, Gent., who was violent and abusive, threatening his wife Susan and servants with a knife at various times; servants left his service to protect their lives. But even worse, in recent months Vyollett had introduced Elizabeth Hewes into his household as a servant. Hewes was described as 'a roaring, swearing, debauch and swaggering woman', but Vyollett took all the keys, including those for trunks and coffers containing his money, from his wife and gave them to Hewes, so that she could 'rule over his said wife and children and household'. Elizabeth had mistreated both Vyollett's wife and children, ordering them about 'more like dogs than Christians'. When one of his relatives remonstrated, and reminded him of his duty to love his wife, Vyollett responded that he cared no more for her 'then I do for a fart that falls from my breeches'. No wonder Susan Vyollett had left her husband's house.[65] An extreme case of the failed patriarch was Walter Calverley, a Yorkshire gentleman. He betrayed a young woman to whom he was betrothed by marrying another, and then wasted his fortune. When he realized the suffering his behaviour had cost, he killed two of his children and attempted to murder his wife; because the property of felons was forfeit to the crown, to protect their inheritance, he refused to plead and was pressed to death instead. The story was sufficiently sensational that several pamphlet accounts, a ballad and a play were based on the events.[66]

Thomas Vyollett turned the world upside down by putting a servant above his wife, but a husband's authority was especially challenged when his wife was unfaithful with a servant. Even suspicions of such relationships were a problem. Richard Bolter and Henry Seafowle were both gentlemen from South Creake, Norfolk. Bolter accused Seafowle of spreading stories that Bolter's wife and daughter had had sexual relations with a married shepherd, and of enlisting 'common fiddlers or musicians' to publicize libels composed by Seafowle. 'When shepherds become gentlemen / Sure their mistress doth them love', one of the doggerel verses ungrammatically declared.[67] The use of libels and allegations of sexual infidelity were familiar aspects of early modern society.

Husbands sometimes resorted to violence against servants suspected of illicit liaisons with their wives. Yet the need to resort to violence was itself a failure of patriarchal authority. In 1618, Roger Day, Gent., entered the service of Sir Francis Ashby of Harefield, Middlesex, and soon made apparently welcome advances to Lady Ashby. According to the enraged husband, Day 'would kiss and dally with her before … his fellow servants'. When he found out about it Ashby immediately dismissed Day, but soon discovered that the pair were meeting in nearby woods and exchanging letters, using another servant's wife as the go-between. In a plot reminiscent of the theatre, Ashby had one of his male servants disguise himself as Lady Ashby (wearing her clothes) and lure Day to a late-night rendezvous in the fields by sending a bogus invitation from 'her'. When Day arrived he was promptly beaten up by men hidden nearby, and then committed to Newgate Prison by Ashby's neighbour, Lord Chief Justice Sir Henry Montagu.[68]

One of the reasons the aggrieved husband had to act, Ashby said, was that other servants heard Day tell Lady Ashby that he knew of another case in which a servant had had an affair with his mistress; they then poisoned the husband and got married. Although Day had been in Ashby's service, he was close enough in status to Lady Ashby to make such a match conceivable. Fears of such petty treason – the killing of a husband, father, or master – were fanned by pamphlet accounts that slide from adultery between mistress and servant to the murder of a husband. The pamphlets all insist that they are telling a true story, and they are not the only sources for such events. John Chamberlain reported in March 1613, shortly before the Frances Howard affair became the talk of the town, that the town clerk of London had died of 'horn sickness' after being driven to 'melancholy and frenzy' by an affair between his wife and a servant. The relatives of unfaithful wives might also be among their victims: the diarist John Manningham noted the case of a woman consumed by 'lascivious love for her man' who plotted to have her own brother convicted of theft and consequently hanged because he opposed the relationship. 'So violent and unnatural a woman's malice', Manningham reflected, though happily she did not succeed in the desired fratricide.[69]

These concerns moved readily from life to the stage. Murders by adulterous wives were a staple of Jacobean revenge tragedy. Two plays from the 1590s, *Arden of Faversham* (1592), and *A Warning for Fair Women* (1599), concerned the murder of husbands by adulterous wives; they were joined by a wide range of texts on petty treason.[70] If men did not govern the women in their lives properly, women were dangerous.

Failed households

While the proper performance of patriarchy was most visible in the government of wives, the cases we have discussed remind us that the household included not just wives, but children and servants. It is more difficult to trace such misgovernment, because the legal framework made them less visible. We generally know of these accusations indirectly, when they are brought up to undermine a litigant's credibility or gain revenge by producing evidence of improper social or sexual behaviour, which was a common tactic in seventeenth-century courts. In these situations, we have no way of determining the truth or otherwise of the charges, but their frequency suggests that accounts of such misgovernment were plausible. A man who did not properly govern his household could not govern his community. In a typical case, George Froome, the high constable of the hundred of Bere Regis in Dorset, got some of the local neer-do-wells indicted for robbery. But his reputation for being of 'a very contentious disposition' encouraged them to repeat old allegations that led to his being bound over to Dorset Assizes on a charge of incest. We shall never know the truth about the incident (the grand jury brought in a verdict of *Ignoramus*), but the charges certainly played into anxieties about a world turned upside down.[71]

As in the case of Day and Lady Ashby, such cases were complicated by the ubiquity of service in early modern society. Masters like Thomas Vyollett who supported disordered servants could be used to disrupt local order. Equally, abusive masters undermined the authority of all masters. Maids who were pregnant by either their master or their master's son were familiar: while this is impossible to quantify, in at least one village, such cases account for as much as a quarter of cases of unmarried pregnancy.[72] The men accused of paternity seldom got off scot free. Robert Dey, the Rector of Cranwich, Norfolk, was accused of fathering a child on one servant, Elizabeth Purkey, and attempting to rape a second, Agnes Greene. In both cases, his behaviour was less visible because each was the only servant in the household with his elderly aunt, who was an 'old blind woman'. All three shared a room – a relatively common arrangement – but Dey had also come after Greene while she was washing dishes and making beds. Dey brought a defamation case against Greene when she spoke of his behaviour, as well as one against Elizabeth Purkey and those who alleged he was the father of her child.[73] When John Fuller of Great Rollright, Oxfordshire, confessed to impregnating one of his father's servants, he asked that he be allowed to give money to charity rather than to perform penance, as it would be a 'great disrepute to him' and a 'hindrance to his preferment in marriage'.[74]

The failure of patriarchal government is most visible when masters abused servants, but servants, like wives, could refuse to obey masters. One case joins a disorderly daughter with a disobedient servant. The servant of the Wiltshire knight Sir Henry Ludlowe, Joel Kinge, had 'very lewdly and wickedly betrayed his master' by eloping with Ludlowe's daughter. Kinge was, Ludlowe claimed, 'a very mean and base fellow', though his father was in fact a minister. Ludlow then repeatedly 'maliced' Kinge and 'attempted his overthrow': the language emphasizes the political nature of Kinge's offence. Some of Ludlowe's clients attacked Kinge on the road to Reading, where they hanged him from a tree with his horse's bridle, then cut him down and partly strangled him before pins were thrust down his throat. Miraculously, Kinge recovered, and the affair was too much even for the Star Chamber, which would normally have been disposed to uphold the authority of a father over his daughter and servants: the perpetrators were heavily fined.[75] Ludlowe failed doubly as a patriarch: he failed to control his daughter's behaviour, and in reacting to that failure, he overreached.

* * *

The challenge for men was that it was almost impossible to be a successful patriarch. This conundrum is most evident in humorous depictions of cuckolds, but it was impossible to ever fully control the behaviour of inferiors. *Tarlton's Newes from Purgatorie*, a book of jests 'fit for gentlemen to laugh at an hour,' by 'Robin Goodfellow', tells stories of various men's afterlives. 'A Tale of Three Cuckolds' offers an anatomy of cuckoldry which defines three types and describes their fate. The highest ranked in purgatory was the wittol, the man who knew and accepted that his wife was unfaithful, but loved her so much that he did nothing. His emblem was a ram, with two large horns. Next was the man who trusted his wife, and was unaware of her many betrayals. His emblem was a goat, as the horns were behind, and he couldn't see them. The final cuckold in *Tarlton's* catalogue was the man whose wife was beautiful and honest; because of her beauty, he did not trust her, and assumed she was unfaithful if she as much as looked at someone else. His emblem was an ass: he thought the long ears were horns, but they were just ears. In this scenario, a man had three choices: acceptance of a wife's infidelity, misplaced trust in her fidelity, or misplaced suspicion. The usual way to judge honesty was through 'credit' – a judgment that focused on a combination of economic worth and moral virtue – but this was not possible when a husband looked at his wife, as her virtue was in question, but her economic status was his. Tarlton makes each of these men a gentleman in purgatory, and none is punished for his faults, as their miserable lives are thought to be punishment enough. In this patriarchal fantasy, men's suffering at the hands of their wives in life is reversed after death: the upside down world is righted again. This message was emphasized by the last paragraph of the tale, where the rewards of husbands in purgatory are matched to the punishments of disorderly women, with scolds being hung by their tongues.[76] If in life women's misbehaviour was inevitable, after death it could be controlled.

Ben Jonson's *Volpone* (1606) is in part an extended meditation of failures of patriarchy; in this play, however, men fail because of their greed, not the behaviour of their subordinates. Yet two characters ultimately fail as patriarchs, the one as a husband, the other as a father. The drama revolves around three men who are scheming to inherit Volpone's fortune, and the schemes that Volpone and his servant Mosca use to extort gifts from them. While the play is about relations between men, there are two named women in the play, both married, and both defined in relation to their attractiveness and potential unfaithfulness. Lady Would-be, the wife of the English traveller Sir Politique Would-be, 'hath not yet the face to be dishonest', while Celia, wife to Corvino, one of the three men angling to be Volpone's heir, is beautiful and desirable. She is

> ... A beauty, ripe as harvest!!
> Whose skin is whiter than a swan, all over,
> Than silver, snow, or lilies! A soft lip,
> Would tempt you to eternity of kissing.[77]

Her jealous husband keeps her 'as warily as is your gold'. Inevitably, Lady Would-be is more than willing to be unfaithful to her husband, while Celia is virtuous. Greed trumps jealousy, however, as Mosca convinces Corvino that if he allows Volpone to sleep with Celia, he will indeed be Volpone's heir: for a fortune, the jealous husband was willing to be a wittol. When Celia refused Volpone's advances, he, Mosca and Corvino colluded in accusing her of adultery with Bonario, the son of Corbaccio, one of the other men seeking to inherit Volpone's fortune: Corvino argues it is better to be a cuckold than a wittol, for 'Now it is her fault'. Greed also allows Volpone and Mosca to set Corbaccio against his son, disrupting paternal as well as spousal authority. When the elaborate set of lies is revealed, and the plots unravelled, both men are punished. Corvino not only has to return his wife to her father (with triple her dowry) but – in a scene combining the emblems of *Tarlton's News from Purgatorie* with a charivari – he is to be rowed around Venice along the Grand Canal, 'wearing a cap with fair long ass's ears / Instead of horns'. Corbaccio is imprisoned, and his son is vested in all his property.[78] For their failures as patriarchs, Corvino and Corbaccio lose both their wealth and their reputations.

The concern with the proper performance of patriarchy in the period between 1560 and 1640 was not anything new. What is different is the way such concerns were connected to, even central to, politics and culture. The expansion of cheap print and the theatre both amplified isolated events to create an image of crisis. What might seem to us mere individual misbehaviour could appear far more dangerous to people at the time. We have reactions to failures of patriarchy from all levels of society. Such failures of patriarchy enabled inferiors – women, children, or servants – to take the position or role of their expected governors. Patriarchy was a defence against the dangers of inversion. These dangers were visible not just in court scandals and local disputes, but in the theatre, where they form a central theme. Murderous wives, weak husbands, incest, witchcraft and poisoning all appear on the stage. While the Italian setting of many early modern plays distances these issues from England, these are as alive in England as anywhere else.

3

Performing Inversion: Theatre, Politics and Society

The closing scene of *Volpone* reminds us that concern about unruly women and failed patriarchs was visible across society, and was a central theme in the theatrical world of the late sixteenth and early seventeenth centuries. Comedy uses inversion to provoke laughter. In early modern comedies both unruly women and failed patriarchs are the focus of attention. In the revenge tragedies of the period, it is often the ways in which women and men act on their own desires that cause disaster. Some plays, like *Swetnam the Woman-Hater*, were in direct dialogue with contemporary events. Even plays less directly tied to current events used the dramatic context to reflect directly or tangentially on contemporary concerns. Because of the dialogic nature of drama, plays do not have a direct message, but they often articulate debates and tensions of the society in which they live. Dramatic characters act in a world shaped by contemporary concerns.[1] After all, in addition to producing plays to gain a mass audience, leading playwrights were connected to the political world and its scandals. Elizabeth and James, as well as several leading aristocrats, sponsored theatrical companies. Shakespeare's company regularly performed for the public at the Globe, but also at the Inns of Court, where young gentlemen were studying law, and at the royal court. Ben Jonson wrote masques for the court, as well as plays for popular theatre; Thomas Middleton wrote a pamphlet on duelling published under James I's name, as well as a number of civic pageants for the City of London; and John Webster was effectively the literary executor for Sir Thomas Overbury. Plays could be used explicitly as political tools, as was, for instance, Middleton's *Game at Chess*. Yet in these contexts, the reception of the plays was always 'inherently dialogic, intensely glossable, indeed ultimately uncontrollable'.[2] Reading plays with a focus on inversion as we have already seen is illuminated by, and at the same time illuminates, the ways the theatre was connected to contemporary social and political concerns.

The early modern period is known for its flourishing theatrical culture. Particularly in London, the emergence of multiple companies producing plays for the public stage led to a remarkable number of plays being written and performed. Shakespeare is the most familiar of these writers, but it is estimated that about 3,000 plays were written and performed in England between 1560 and 1640, of which only about 500 survive. This was also a period of transformation in theatre: the Renaissance theatre brought together traditions of mystery and morality plays performed in civic contexts, festive performances (like Robin Hood plays), court masques and entertainments, and educational plays designed to help boys learn their Latin and Greek. The boy companies and traveling companies of the early Elizabethan period soon gave way to professional companies based in London. Genres proliferated, as comedies and tragedies generated sub-genres, including city comedies, which made London a character; tragicomedies, where a happy ending is pulled out at the end; revenge tragedies set in foreign courts; and domestic tragedies, which took ordinary people rather than rulers as their subject. The large public theatres and smaller private ones created niche markets: the Red Bull, where *Swetnam the Woman Hater* was performed, had a more plebeian audience than the Blackfriars Theatre, where the *Duchess of Malfi* was first presented.[3]

Drawing direct analogies from the plays to current events is tempting, as it was to theatregoers at the time. Ben Jonson ridiculed the popular game played by Jacobean audiences of reading literal or topical meanings in the plays they saw; and in the opening 'Induction' to *Bartholemew Fair*, he warned against trying to 'search who was meant by the Ginger-bread woman, who by the Hobby-horse-man, … what great lady by the pig-woman, what conceal'd statesman by the Seller of Mousetraps'.[4] Yet while direct analogies are not useful, plays were an ideal place to explore the dynamics of an upside down world because they made room both for the tensions which emerged from the internal contradictions of the gender system and for the ways in which individual behaviour could disrupt it. Each of these added layers of unpredictability to the supposedly ordered world, on stage and off. Theatre is both a product of its culture and helps create that culture. Thus, plays generally identify anxieties and challenges more than they provide specific messages; the explicit message at the end of the play is often undermined by what comes before. Each genre engages with the problems of unruly women and failed patriarchs in different ways, and to different ends. Theatre's multiple engagements with the world upside down make its production of inversion and gender central to our historical understanding of the period.

The Duchess of Malfi and court scandal

John Webster's play *The Duchess of Malfi* illustrates both the ways a play refracts current concerns, and how it might be shaped by the author's connections to contemporary events. The play reflects on the distinction between good and bad patriarchs and on unruly, or at least independent, women. The play begins with the Duchess's two brothers, Ferdinand and the Cardinal, warning the young widow not to remarry: 'They are most luxurious / Will wed twice ... Their livers are more spotted / Than Laban's sheep.'[5] Ferdinand does not rely solely on his warning, but places a spy at her court. The Duchess, however, asserts her own independence and secretly marries her steward, Antonio; in their courtship she takes the lead. She bears him three children – again, secretly – but secrets are few at court, and eventually rumours circulate that she is a 'strumpet'. Informed by Ferdinand's spy, her brothers come after her, and by the end of the play, the duchess, Antonio, and two of their children, as well as her two brothers and the cardinal's mistress, are all dead. The tragedy can be read as the result of the duchess's secret marriage to Antonio, in defiance of her brothers; it could be the result of a widow's uncontrolled sexuality; equally, it could be seen as the result of her brothers' attempts to govern her from a distance, using corrupt methods. The play begins and ends with reflections on good government; in the middle, female desire and male corruption both undermine good governance in the duchy.[6]

Webster wrote *The Duchess of Malfi* in 1612–13, and the first performance was apparently in late 1613 or early 1614, when London was full of gossip about Francis Howard's remarriage to Robert Carr. The play was based on an Italian case from the early sixteenth century, when the widowed Duchess of Amalfi married Antonio Bologna. Webster's play is connected in multiple ways to contemporary literary culture. The text contains borrowings from several works published in 1612, including passages that parallel *A Monumental Column*, his own elegy on the unexpected death of the king's eldest son, Prince Henry, published in December 1612. There are other contemporary references, including a number of borrowings from Sidney's *Arcadia*, published in a new edition in 1613. The masque performed at the marriage of Princess Elizabeth to the Elector Palatine in February 1613 may well have inspired the scene involving madmen in Act IV.[7] *The Duchess of Malfi* is a play deeply embedded in contemporary life.

In the very first scene, Antonio describes what he had observed during his recent visit to France. The French king, he reports, had expelled from his court all 'flattering sycophants' and all 'dissolute and infamous persons'. A monarch's court, he continues,

> Is like a common fountain, whence should flow
> Pure silver-drops in general: But if 't chance
> Some curs'd example poison 't near the head,
> Death and disease through the whole land spread.

The council should unhesitatingly pass on to the king whatever grievances come to their attention, for

> Though some o'th' Court hold it presumption
> To instruct Princes what they ought to do,
> It is a noble duty to inform them
> What they ought to foresee.[8]

These sentiments, while utterly conventional, could be read as a coded series of recommendations for King James. Antonio's description of good government hangs in the air; while it is not directly addressed by what follows, it shapes our vision. There is no 'king' in the play; its setting is primarily the duchess's court. She fails as a patriarch because she is a woman. Furthermore, she was a young widow, and therefore not a virgin. As a widow, the duchess, at least in English law, was able to make decisions for herself. And in the play, she chooses remarriage. Widows' independence led to a 'pervasive cultural ambivalence' about them. First, widows' sexual experience in marriage was thought to render them lustful, and therefore sexually uncontrolled. In addition, a widow often controlled property both from her natal family and from her husband, and remarriage endangered the inheritance rights of siblings and children. Furthermore, remarried widows had a reputation for trying to rule their new husbands. Widows might not be unruly, but they were outside patriarchal control.[9]

Ferdinand and the cardinal failed as patriarchs because they were *not* patriarchs in relation to the duchess. The 'fratriarchy', as one critic has called them, want to control her, but because of her independence, they cannot do so directly. Their warning against remarriage is a kind of moral blackmail; not satisfied with that, they insert a spy into her household. The play's repeated use of the word 'tyranny' suggests that, even outside their relation to their sister, neither Ferdinand nor the cardinal was a successful patriarch. Unlike the King of France as described by Antonio, Ferdinand wants to be surrounded by sycophants, telling his courtiers to 'laugh when I laugh, were the subject never so witty'. The cardinal is unable to marry, but has prevailed on Julia to be his mistress. Even those who are more or less honest interlocutors throughout the play show dubious judgment: Delio, an honest friend and confidant to Antonio, tries to bribe Julia into being his mistress; the Marquesse of Pescara, who serves as the honest ruler at the end of the play, is willing to give Antonio's lands, seized illegally, to Julia.[10]

The duchess, too, fails to live up to social expectations. A widow should run the household, but if she remarries, her husband has authority over her. By undertaking a secret marriage, the duchess evades the normal patriarchal order of marriage; her husband, who should rule her, is her steward. Her marriage is one that 'began with the woman on top'.[11] Furthermore, in spite of her political authority, the duchess is invisible as 'governor' in the first half of the play: instead, she is playful and sexual. Only when her brothers begin to threaten her is she seen exercising the responsibilities that were hers all along.

The Duchess of Malfi is deeply concerned with issues of gender and political order, so its first performance at about the time of the Howard-Carr marriage is significant. When we follow the story of the marriage and the closely linked murder of Overbury, we encounter at every turn reminders of inversionary thinking, of the world turned upside down. As they read of Frances Howard's misdeeds, people were fascinated by the corruption at court, as well as the dangers posed by dominant women with political influence and the spectre of a pro-Catholic foreign policy. But Webster's masterpiece may have had a closer connection with the scandal than the mere coincidence in time. The play opened shortly after Sir Thomas Overbury's death in the Tower, though long before the suspicious circumstances of his death became public knowledge. Webster, Overbury's friend who acted as his literary executor, may have known a good deal about Overbury's opposition to the Carr-Howard relationship. Webster, like other Jacobean playwrights, often created characters who were types, illustrating the preoccupations of their times and exploring the dramatic possibilities they suggested, and he had already explored the theme of the strong and independent woman struggling to escape from subordination to her menfolk in *The White Devil*, which was performed early in 1612.[12] So this was clearly a matter of concern for him. But it is difficult to imagine that Webster did not think of contemporary events, including the Howard-Carr marriage, when writing.

The connection between Overbury and Webster also illustrates the connections between the court and theatre. The two men were from very different social backgrounds: Webster was the son of a London coach maker who was a member of the influential Merchant Taylors Company, and Overbury came from Warwickshire gentry stock. But they were only two years apart in age (Webster was born between 1578 and 1580, Overbury in 1581), and they were law students at the Middle Temple at the same time. The Inn had a strong dramatic tradition, and the Revels put on there in the late 1590s were especially lively and uproarious. His friendship with Overbury might explain Webster's decision to dedicate *A Monumental Column* to Robert Carr in December 1612 – a time when, whatever Overbury's doubts about Frances Howard, the relationship between patron and client was still outwardly intact. After Overbury's untimely death, Webster repaid the favour, seeing successive editions of *A Wife* through the press, apparently at the same time as *The Duchess of Malfi* was performed, and composing many of the 'Characters', or brief sketches of types, which contributed so much to the work's later popularity. The poem was frequently reprinted, and Overbury's death was used as a selling point long before it was known that he had been murdered: the first edition is entitled *A Wife, now a Widowe*. After the sensational news of the murder broke, later editions became even more marketable.[13]

Given the rumours circulating in London, Webster would not have had to rely on Overbury for information about Frances Howard. Her desire to escape from her marriage to the Earl of Essex had been the subject of court gossip for years, and as an informed and literate Londoner, Webster would have known a good deal about it. The story of a beautiful aristocratic woman trying to control her own marital destiny had obvious parallels in the plot he was constructing for *The Duchess of Malfi*. And while *A Wife* was prompted by the Howard-Carr courtship, it was also relevant to the story of the Duchess of Malfi. In addition to the poem's implied strictures on the Carr-Howard relationship, Overbury harps obsessively on the disastrous effects of sexual desire.[14] The evil consequences of desire were thus central to the two projects Webster was working on at the end of 1613.

The duchess was, however, a far more sympathetic character than a friend of Overbury's might have been likely to create if he were thinking solely of Frances Howard; furthermore, there was nothing at the time of her marriage to Carr that might suggest any negative consequences of her actions. It is more useful to think of the duchess as reflecting a concern with unruly women in authority that was provoked by a number of independent-minded women who placed desire ahead of duty. The king's mother, Mary Queen of Scots, and his cousin, Arbella Stuart, both suffered because of their choices about marriage. They were far closer to the king, and the imprisonment of Arbella for her marriage in 1610, and the reburial of Mary in 1612, meant that they – and their attempts to shape their own marital and sexual lives – would have been as familiar to London audiences as was the behaviour of Frances Howard. Their stories were more complicated, but the price they paid for their agency was already evident.[15]

Mary Queen of Scots, a female ruler who twice married a subject and thus brought herself to (inevitable) ruin, 'was a precise charting of the consequences when a ruler places her private desires above reputation, political realities, and public responsibilities, and her will above the weal of her subjects'.[16] Twice widowed, she remarried men who were her social inferiors, against the advice of her 'protectors'. Mary was also implicated in the murder of her second husband, the king's father. She had been forced to abdicate in favour of James when he was barely a year old, and fled to England a year later; he never saw her again. Yet the king worked hard to rehabilitate his mother's memory, providing her with a splendid tomb in Westminster Abbey, larger and more imposing than that he built for his predecessor, Queen Elizabeth. The removal of her body from Peterborough Abbey, where it was buried after her execution, to Westminster, and the splendid ceremony for its interment, took place in 1612, just as Webster was writing *The Duchess*. The re-burial may have provided a reminder of the complex story of Mary's life, and the dangers of a woman ruler who allowed her lust to drive her policy.[17] Critical reference to the king's mother would carry its own dangers, but as with Frances Howard, the play is full of allusions rather than direct references.

Arbella Stuart was James I's cousin, who had married, without the king's consent, William Seymour, the grandson of Catherine Grey, the younger sister of Lady Jane Grey, thus uniting in a dangerous way two people with potential claims to the throne. The couple had been imprisoned shortly after the marriage in 1610, escaped, but were recaptured; Arbella was then put in the Tower, where she died in 1615 of 'suicide by starvation'. Webster was writing *The Duchess* during her imprisonment, when her condition was the subject of numerous rumours around London; some suggested that, like the duchess, she had secretly borne a child. There is no evidence Webster intended a direct parallel between Arbella and the duchess, any more than there is a direct parallel to Mary Queen of Scots or Frances Howard, but he was certainly taking advantage of contemporary interest in her plight. Webster's audience at Blackfriars would have been aware of 'the real tragedy which was creeping to its close in the Tower'. A play about the misfortunes of a woman who based her marriage on affection rather than duty thus had echoes across a number of contemporary cases.[18] Two of the most prominent cases had already ended badly. The combination of a woman, power and sexual agency was, apparently, quite dangerous.

Arbella Stuart and Frances Howard were both alive when Webster wrote *The Duchess of Malfi*, Mary recently reburied. At the time of its first performance, it was known that Howard had wanted to escape from her marriage to Essex and marry Carr, and that she had achieved this through the nullity suit; rumours of foul play were confined to her use of spells to render Essex impotent. Most people thought no worse of Howard than that her decision to put her personal happiness above her social duty was bound to have bad consequences, just as the duchess's decision to marry her steward, Antonio, leads inevitably to the dark ending of *The Duchess of Malfi*. The *Duchess* is not about any one of them, but their presence reminds us that female independence, particularly female sexual independence, was not an abstraction, but a matter of real concern that was performed, discussed and glossed in multiple ways in contemporary London.

Given this context, Antonio's initial remark that if there were 'Some curs'd example poison't near the head, / Death and disease through the whole land spread' leaps off the page. While Webster had no way of knowing that his friend had been poisoned, rumours were circulating that Prince Henry had been poisoned.[19] It is easy to see the passage's general relevance, as it was common form to denounce the extravagance and immorality of the court and the baleful influence of the Scots. In 1610, Sir John Holles complained in parliament that Scots 'monopolize his [the King's] princely person, standing like mountains betwixt the beams of his grace and us'. In the 'Addled Parliament' of 1614, John Hoskyns was more explicit, urging James I to send the Scots home, and complaining about the 'ill examples of all riot and dissoluteness' in the court; he also made a reference to the Sicilian Vespers, thus offering an implicit threat of rebellion against foreign courtiers.[20] During the first half of James's reign, a number of verse libels mocked the wealth the Scots had gained since James's accession. These ideas were also voiced outside the elite: in 1610 a Norfolk villager called another man a 'Scottish rogue', adding that 'all Scots are rogues and rascals'.[21] In Antonio's speech Webster expressed views that were embedded in the conventional anti-court discourse of the time.

Other speeches in *The Duchess of Malfi* echo the preoccupations of the early Jacobean period. Much ink has been spilt over the probable views of Webster and his audience about widows' second marriages. While their views on widows were not relevant to Frances Howard, whose marriage had been annulled, Ferdinand's condemnation of second marriages is striking, and a little further on Ferdinand says something that could easily have been said by anyone who knew that Frances had consulted the sorcerer Simon Forman:

They whose faces do belie their hearts,
Are Witches, ere they arrive at twenty years.[22]

Later, in Act III, a conversation between Antonio and the recently returned Delio may also contain echoes of 1613 London gossip. Antonio does not tell his friend that the duchess has been secretly married to him since they last met, but he does mention that she has had two children, who thus appear illegitimate. When Delio asks, 'What say the common people?' Antonio answers, 'The common-rabble do directly say / She is a Strumpet'. That particular characterization of Frances Howard was circulating in verse libels at the time of her marriage to Robert Carr. It is also implied in the revealing defences of the marriage in the masques and other poems, in which the adverse public opinion is openly confronted.[23] The 'common people' would not have found anything strange in an aristocratic lady being a strumpet.

The pamphlet war that was touched off by Swetnam's *Araignment* was closely connected with the court scandals, and thus with the political world on which plays like *The Duchess of Malfi* were commenting.[24] Like that debate, Webster's play illuminates important elements in the intellectual climate of the time. The events surrounding Frances Howard, Arbella Stuart and even the reburial of Mary Queen of Scots may in turn give us a deeper appreciation of the play. When women like Frances and her mother, the Countess of Suffolk, were achieving such dangerous prominence, old certainties about male authority were clearly being threatened. Frances in particular was a convenient symbol of inversion; so, in spite of being presented sympathetically, was Webster's duchess.

Revenge tragedy and the failures of patriarchy

The Duchess of Malfi is an example of revenge tragedy, a genre popular in England for about forty years from 1587, when Thomas Kyd presented *The Spanish Tragedy*. Like *The Duchess of Malfi*, revenge tragedies took courts as their subject and dramatized the ways sex and power corrupted government; almost always there is a terrible crime that has gone unpunished, and characters find private rather than public means of revenge. *Hamlet* is undoubtedly the most familiar example, with the action of the play driven by Claudius's murder of his brother; Hamlet seeks a private revenge, and then Laertes seeks revenge on Hamlet. As in the final scenes of *Hamlet* and *The Duchess of Malfi*, revenge tragedies usually end with many dead bodies on the stage, often with creative (and darkly humorous) forms of death.[25] The relatively short period in which these plays flourished underscores the tensions around politics and gender at the turn of the sixteenth century.

Two plays by Thomas Middleton illuminate the centrality of inversion and gender to revenge tragedy, as well as the ways sexual corruption and political corruption were linked. The first, written around 1606, is *The Revenger's Tragedy*. This court, it is apparent, is entirely corrupt. Nine years before the start of the play, the duke had poisoned the beautiful, chaste Gloriana, who was betrothed to Vindice, because she would not 'consent / Unto his palsy lust'.[26] Vindice has kept her skull, and nursed his resentment. At the start of the play, he and his brother Hippolito are both angry at the duke's treatment of their father, who has recently died, at least partly of grief from the duke's ill treatment. The duke is a failed patriarch on many levels, leading a court filled with lust and ambition, where personal gain trumps the good of the state; rather than trying to control these tendencies, the duke allows himself to be swayed by lust and affection. He first appears at a trial, where his step-son, Junior Brother, has been convicted of raping the wife of a courtier. The judges are about to sentence him to be executed when the duke accedes to his wife's pleas and postpones it. The duke, who had murdered Gloriana because she would not indulge his lust, is reluctant to execute the step-son who had lustfully forced himself on a woman. Lust is everywhere: the duke's son, Lussurioso, wants to seduce Vindice's and Hippolito's sister; he is 'past my depth in lust', but 'The dowry of her blood and of her fortunes / Are both too mean.'[27] The duchess is incestuously in love with her husband's bastard son, Spurio. The duchess's other sons, Ambitioso and Supervacuo, lust not for a woman but for position, aiming to inherit power from the duke.

In this court, men of power are not held accountable for their crimes. Uncontrolled desire feeds on itself. Since the ordinary course of justice is inadequate, Vindice has turned to private revenge. With the help of Hippolito, Vindice presents himself (in disguise) to Lussurioso as a pander who will help him get access to Castiza, their sister. He uses that role both to test his sister's and his mother's virtue, and to plot his revenge. Throughout, concern with female sexuality is central. Vindice is haunted by the fear that his sister might not be chaste, and horrified when his mother promises to try to convince her to give in to Lussurioso. He uncovers the duchess's infidelity, marvelling that the duke's horns 'are newly revived', and tells Lussurioso, who promptly seeks revenge.[28] When Vindice is finally able to exact revenge on the duke, he does so by poisoning the lips of Gloriana's skull, so that the duke is poisoned by kissing the earthly remains of the woman he had poisoned. Men's sexuality might be uncontrolled, but women are also dangerous, because their virtue is never to be trusted, and they are able to make choices. Castiza makes good choices, but not all women do.

Gendered imagery litters the text. For instance, Vindice tells his sister that 'The law's a woman', and he wishes that his sister's robust condemnation of rape would govern its actions. In the courtroom, Lussurioso suggests that 'offences / Gilt o'er with mercy show like fairest women'.[29] In these cases, the gendered language plays off assumptions about women's unreliability, which arose both from the ways they disguised their true selves, and from their changeability. The duchess complains that if she does not obtain mercy for her son, she would be 'fruitless' – 'a wonder in a woman'; she later remarks that 'Law / Is grown more subtle than a woman should be'.[30] While the judge asserts that rape is a 'Double adultery', Junior Brother insists that he could not resist the woman: 'Her beauty was ordained to be my scaffold'. The repeated slippage from real lust for actual women to gendered imagery emphasizes again and again the centrality of gender to political life. Actual women were dangerous because of the way they tempted men, but even feminine imagery provides excuses for patriarchal failure.

Middleton's *Women Beware Women: A Tragedy*, written some fifteen years later, follows two parallel plots, in each of which older men use younger women for their own interests. The multiple failures to live up to expectations for household and state governance drive the story. The main plot follows the fate of Bianca, a wealthy young woman from Venice who secretly married Leantio, a relatively humble merchant's factor from Florence. His first failure as a putative patriarch is that they did not marry with the consent of their parents. A secret marriage, as in *The Duchess of Malfi*, lacks the protections of social recognition. He brings her – again secretly – to his mother's house, but when Leantio has to return to work for his Florentine master, Bianca is seen by the Duke of Florence, and he arranges to meet her. This assignation is arranged by the widow Livia, who takes advantage of her widowhood to serve as a pander. She invites Leantio's mother to her house and encourages her to bring her 'guest'. Once Bianca is at Livia's house, the duke is able to rape her. He violates his role as patriarch and protector, putting his own lust above her marriage vows. The failure of patriarchal norms continues as Bianca, while consumed by a sense of her own sinfulness, falls in love with the duke. The duke has Leantio killed so that he can marry Bianca, and thus incurs the enmity of Livia, who has fallen in love with Leantio.[31]

The sub-plot also involves a young woman on the brink of marriage, in this case Isabella, whose father has happily arranged her marriage to a slow-witted and unattractive, but wealthy young man, Ward. She and her uncle, Hippolito, are very close – a relationship in which he recognizes desire but she sees friendship. She is about to refuse the marriage when her aunt, the same Livia who arranged the duke's encounter with Bianca, tells her (falsely, as it turns out) that her mother was unfaithful, so her uncle is not really related to her. Suddenly marriage to Ward becomes a cover for an adulterous and incestuous relationship with Hippolito.

The duke's wedding banquet sees the death of most of the remaining characters. Some of the deaths are integrated into the wedding masque, which undermines the celebration of marriage. Isabella poisons her aunt Livia with incense smoke; Livia kills Isabella by shooting her with arrows of flaming gold. Hippolito breaks character (he is a shepherd) to provide the moral commentary: 'Lust and forgetfulness has been amongst us ... Vengeance met vengeance'. He then impales himself on a soldier's halberd when he realizes Isabella is dead. Meanwhile, in the audience of the masque, the duke has drunk the poisoned wine Bianca had intended for his brother, so she too drinks poison. What was supposed to celebrate marriage instead revealed the corruption of 'fearful lust'.[32]

Throughout the play, men articulate their power as patriarchs over women, only to misuse it; older women fail to help govern the household, deliberatively or inadvertently acting in ways that make young women vulnerable. While men fail as patriarchs, older women are, if not unruly, entirely unreliable. While *The Revenger's Tragedy* clearly defines rape as a crime, both against the woman and her husband, in *Women Beware Women* the duke's failure as a patriarch is emphasized by the way he not only rapes a married woman, but has her husband killed, and makes rape the basis for marriage. Yet one of the consequences of the gendered divisions of society is that women were needed to enable the abuse of other women. As she is dying, Bianca laments, 'Oh, the deadly snares / That women set for women'.[33] Yet, in her case the women acted at the behest of men. Leantio decided to keep his marriage secret, and thus deprive Bianca of the protection the public acknowledgment of her marriage would provide. The duke asked Livia to set him up with Bianca.

Both Bianca and Isabella acted in response to the sort of arranged marriages that caused so much trouble at the court of James I. Like Frances Howard, Isabella was sold to the highest bidder, never mind compatibility. Bianca escaped such a marriage by eloping with her lover, but then finds herself imprisoned in secrecy. Once ensconced as the duke's mistress, unfaithful to her marriage, Bianca reflects

'Tis not good, in sadness
To keep a maid so strict in her young days.
Restraint breeds wand'ring thoughts, as many fasting days
A great desire to see flesh stirring again.
I'll ne'er use any girl of mine so strictly.[34]

Bianca's upbringing had not prepared her for the temptations presented by men who admire her; but rather than criticizing men, she sees this weakness as the fault of other women. In her final line she looks forward to being a mother and correcting the errors of her upbringing.

The play, written in 1620 or 1621, is in dialogue with the debate on women, as well as with contemporary scandals. The title echoes several other warnings about the women's behaviour. In *Swetnam the Woman Hater*, Misogynous seeks to demonstrate the 'follies' of women, so that 'henceforth men of women may beware'. Scholars have noticed the echoes in a ballad called 'Mistris Turner's Farewell to All Women': on the scaffold Frances Howard's companion rejects Lady Pride, and asks women to 'by me beware'. These echoes underline the sense of tension and conflict in relations between the sexes. In *Women Beware Women*, social order is overturned by men who disregard their roles as good governors, and by women who follow their own desires.[35]

Domestic tragedy and tragicomedy: gender and generic disruption

The characters in *The Duchess of Malfi*, *The Revenger's Tragedy* and *Women Beware Women* acted on a public stage, and the plays emphasized the link between politics and the household. Yet the problems of failed patriarchs and disorderly women are even more evident in tragedies focused on the household. These plays also emphasize the economic role of the household and the importance of women's work and market activity. The anonymous play, *Arden of Faversham*, dating from 1592, foregrounds the unruly and unfaithful woman who plots to kill her husband so she can marry her lover; the plot is possible because her husband has neglected his domestic responsibilities in pursuit of money. The play is based on a 1551 murder recounted in Holinshed's *Chronicles*. According to Holinshed, Arden was killed because he swindled a widow for property; the play instead foregrounds his failures as a 'domestic patriarch'.[36] The play is bound up with the economic changes wrought by the dissolution of the monasteries and the crown's seizure of church lands. It focuses on the plot hatched by Arden's wife, Alice, to kill her husband so that she can be with her lover, Mosby. Alice is an unruly wife; like Frances Howard, she is determined to choose her own husband. She has even taken a lover of lower social status; though she and her husband belong to the gentry, Mosby was a tailor who has managed to become steward to a local landowner. 'Love is a god, and marriage is but words', she announces early in the play, so Mosby 'shall be mine'.[37]

Yet before all the responsibility for the disaster that ensues falls on Alice, the play makes it clear that Arden was not a good husband. His avarice and his husbandly failings are linked; he neglects to govern the household because his attention to his property takes precedence over his attention to his wife. Arden was committed to accumulating property at all costs – even, it turns out, his life. The play opens with the announcement by Arden's friend Franklin that the Lord Protector has given Arden the lands of the Abbey of Faversham. Almost immediately, Greene, one of his tenants, complains that Arden's new patent has deprived Greene of lands that had previously been granted to him. 'Desire of wealth is endless in his mind', Greene complains, leading him to 'wring from me the little land I have'.[38] Greene promises a revenge that will make him wish that he had never received the Abbey lands. Toward the end of the play, another of Arden's victims, a sailor named Dick Reede, accuses Arden of wrongfully taking a plot of land from him, thus leaving his wife and children in poverty. When Arden refuses restitution and instead promises imprisonment, Reede, like Greene, vows vengeance.

Alice Arden is able to recruit Greene to aid her plot against her husband, though to do so she alleges not only that he beats her, but that he is unfaithful, frequenting other women 'in every corner' of Kent, and 'such filthy ones' in London.[39] The play suggests otherwise: while Arden knows that his wife is unfaithful and even confronts Mosby, he still leaves home and heads to London to see to business. While he takes on the role of provider, he does not take on the role of governor of the household. Arden's murder is possible only because of his failure to discipline his wife. He repeatedly forgives Alice for her relationship with Mosby, and foolishly trusts her to govern the household in his absence.

The play foregrounds the disastrous consequences of allowing desire to govern behaviour. Arden's attention is focused on building wealth, so he 'hoards up bags of gold'.[40] While he mistrusts Alice, he leaves for London instead of ensuring her obedience. Alice's desire for Mosby, like her husband's for wealth, drives her to neglect her duty as a wife. Such unbridled desire troubles Mosby, who recognizes that

> You have supplanted Arden for my sake,
> And will extirpen me to plant another.
> 'Tis fearful sleeping in a serpent's bed,
> And I will cleanly rid my hands of her.[41]

Alice herself has a moment of remorse, remembering how much her husband loved her and suggesting she had been 'bewitched' to love Mosby, who was

'A mean artificer, that lowborn name'. She fears that Mosby wants her for her wealth, not herself – a fear that is borne out by Mosby as he fantasizes about what will happen when he 'sit[s] in Arden's seat'. Both Mosby and Alice have moments of regret: Mosby reflects that 'My golden time was when I had no gold'; Alice wishes for her former 'happy life', though now she could only be 'honest Arden's wife – not Arden's honest wife'.[42] But desire has led them both to a point of no return.

The mixture of economic and sexual tension in *Arden of Faversham* draws attention to the social changes and conflicts of the period, rather than the political ones. Arden profited by the dissolution of the monasteries, but Greene and Dick Reede were impoverished by it. Those same changes, as well as elite patronage, enabled Mosby's progress from tailor to steward, though no one forgets his origins. Alice Arden, who takes advantage of Greene's resentment to get him to plot against Arden, is also able to draw her servant (Michael) and a painter with knowledge of poison into her plot by promising both of them marriage to Susan Mosby, her maid. Michael does his best to help the plotters murder his master, thus refusing the deference he owed him. Household order and economic order are both turned upside down in the play. The multiple thwarted desires, economic and sexual, lead to disaster. Both men and women have obligations, and when they are neglected or distorted, the result is tragedy that envelopes not just the guilty parties but many others.

The Yorkshire Tragedy, probably by Thomas Middleton, was published in 1608, but it was based on events in Yorkshire in 1605, when Walter Calverly murdered two of his children and wounded his wife after accusing her of adultery and the children of being bastards. In the play the characters have been reduced to their positions in the family, as their names indicate. While Arden focused too much on the accumulation of wealth, Husband in *Yorkshire Tragedy* is too profligate with it. The play is framed by the relationship between marriage and property. The opening scene shows a young woman who has (foolishly) waited for more than three years for her lover to return from London to marry her; a servant arrives and informs all that the errant lover has married an heiress in London and the couple has had three children. The woman waiting for him is lucky, however, because he beats his wife and has consumed all his wealth. The scene shifts to London, where Husband rages at Wife for not selling her dowry for him; when he realizes his brother has been imprisoned for his debts, he is seized with regret for the impact of his actions, so he murders the two children currently at home and severely wounds his wife, who was protected by the stays on her gown. Husband had abdicated his responsibility as a patriarch. According to one writer at the time, it was only in Spain that it was acceptable 'for the father to kill his innocent son, or the husband his chaste wife'. The acceptance of domestic failure, like other forms of inversion, was thus linked to religion.[43]

The play, which was apparently one of four performed at the same time, is short, a mere eight scenes and 700 lines. There is no time spent setting up the situation; it begins in the middle, as a man and a marriage are unravelling. The dynamic between Husband and Wife emphasizes her loyalty and submission, and his tyranny. As she declares, 'He says I am the cause – I never yet / Spoke less than words of duty and of love'. When, instead of selling her lands, she provides him with a post at court that will give him an income, he complains, 'Shall I, that dedicated myself to pleasure, be now confined in service to crouch and stand like an old man I'th'hams, my hat off, I that never could abide to uncover my head I'th'church? Base slut, this fruit bears thy complaints'.[44] In doing so he indicts himself for evading his role in the social hierarchy, which is not just to command, but also to serve. When the master of his brother's college comes to tell him of his brother's imprisonment for debt, Husband is possessed. The disaster that follows, as he later recognizes, is a result of his own abdication of responsibility. Unlike Bianca's warning to beware of other women, Husband gives his advice to other fathers: 'look into my deeds, / And then their heirs may prosper while mine bleeds'.[45] His neglect of his role as provider and protector of his family had led to the death of two of his children and, ultimately, to his own. While patriarchy rarely failed this disastrously, the play, like the repeated accounts of Calverly's crime, serves as an important reminder of the importance of the proper performance of manhood. In the domestic context, the breakdown of patriarchy that caused tragedy came from economic rather than political malfeasance.

The pamphlet debate on women that shaped these tragedies was the more immediate foil for a pointed tragicomedy, a genre that veers from potential tragedy to a happy ending. The anonymous play, *Swetnam the Woman Hater, Arraigned by Women*, explicitly refers to the debate on women, not just in its title, but in its text.[46] It takes on the same issues of royal governance and marriage that are central to *The Revenger's Tragedy* and *Women Beware Women*, but it overlays the tragedy with a play on comic disguise and a dramatization of the debate on women to pull out a happy ending. The play begins with the King of Sicily, Atticus, mourning the apparent death of his son Lorenzo in the battle of Lepanto. He also seeks to block the marriage of his only (known) surviving child, his daughter Leonida, to Lisandro, whose father the King of Naples is an old enemy of his; instead he wants her to marry his elderly advisor, Nicanor.

When she refuses, and then is found to have had a meeting with Lisandro, she and Lisandro are tried; but since the law forbids two people to be executed for the same offence, the judges need to determine whether the meeting was instigated by Leonida or Lisandro. Each tries to take responsibility, and the decision is made to recruit 'Two Advocates, to plead this difference / In public disputation, Man and Woman', to decide whether the man or the woman in love gives 'the first and principal occasion of sinning'.[47] When the time comes for the debate, the position of men is defended by one Misogynos, who is Swetnam in disguise; the position of women is defended by one Atlanta, who is the king's son Lorenzo disguised as an Amazon. Both participants are in disguise, but the impression of female sub-ordination is emphasized by the fact that the women's position is defended by a man pretending to be a woman; women do not speak for themselves. The debate is a draw, but the judges give the victory to Misogynos, declaring that 'Women are the first and worst temptations / to love and lustfull folly', so Leonida is sentenced to be executed, Lisandro to exile. Queen Aurelia pleads for mercy for her daughter, but the king refuses, saying, 'A King is like a Star, / By which each Subject, as a Mariner, / Must steer his course. Justice in us is ample, / From whom Inferiors will derive example'.[48] A clever stratagem designed by Atlanta / Lorenzo allows Leonida's execution, and Lisandro's suicide, to be faked.

Meanwhile, Misogynos has fallen in love with Atlanta, not realizing that she is Lorenzo. Atlanta consents to a meeting with him, where he is set upon by women, including the queen, and tried for slandering and defaming 'the whole Sex of women'. During this second trial, his servant tells his history, declares that he is not even the fencing master he claims to be, but rather a rogue and swindler who had been run out of the country when his book 'made a thousand men and wives fall out'. His sentence – harking back to the pamphlets – was to wear a muzzle, and to be whipped and led to the coast, all the while being 'bayted by all the honest women in the Parish' where he was exiled 'to live amongst the Infidels'. The muzzle echoes to the title of Rachel Speght's pamphlet, *A Mouzell for Melastomus*.[49] The punishment, a judicial shaming orchestrated by women, echoes that given to vagrants, who were whipped to the borders of the parish. The play ends with a series of masques which not only reveal Lorenzo's true identity, but also have Atticus perform the marriage of Leonida and Lisandro, both still in disguise. When all is revealed, Atticus admits his error, and good order and harmony are restored.

In *Swetnam the Woman-Hater*, concerns with political order and gender order are woven together. While the Misogynos plot has its comic dimensions, the outcome of the trial, the decision to execute Leonida for the faults attributed to her sex, is hardly amusing. Throughout, the nature of gender relations and political authority are put in question. In an upside down world, Atticus's wife and son have to intervene to protect his daughter, and Queen Aurelia has to speak up for her daughter and all women. Like the duke in *The Revenger's Tragedy*, Atticus struggles with a central questions of political life: What constitutes justice? What mercy? When Atticus decides that he cannot bend the law to protect his daughter and the execution of Leonida must go forward, there are political consequences: as William Gouge had noted, those in authority had to avoid being both too strict and too merciful.[50] Two guards who have witnessed the execution, unaware that it was a sham, decide to leave the country; even the courtiers despair. In the words of one gentleman, 'The time is full of danger every-where'; in the words of Nicanor, 'A melancholy King makes a sad Court'.[51] The king's decision to punish his daughter for her love, when both Leonida and Lisandro assert the virtue of their meeting, is seen as tyranny, not justice. The queen is enraged, and after she has berated Atticus, he complains about being scolded. In the end, good government of a wife and daughter turn out to be critical to good government of the kingdom. The order that was destroyed by the supposed execution of Leonida is restored by her life and reinforced by the return of Lorenzo in his proper person. The two trials in the play both foreground questions of women's virtue or vice. In the first, the judges use the old assumption that women, like Eve, are the origin of temptation, and use that to justify the execution of Leonida, which turns justice upside down. The second trial, from the perspective of the queen and her women, turns things right side up by reasserting female virtue. The debate on women is central to understanding the problems caused by the inversion of gender and political order, and to its restoration.[52]

The debate between men and women, and the presence of Swetnam on the stage, links this tragicomedy to contemporary debates. But the play actively intervenes in that debate and turns the world upside down by foregrounding the perspective and agency of women and protesting the injustices of patriarchal tyranny. *Swetnam the Woman Hater* was performed at the Red Bull by the Queen's Servants; it was published immediately after Queen Anne's death, with an impressive illustration on the title page, which placed the queen in the centre as the judge. As we have seen, Queen Anne had a complementary view of marriage, as opposed to her husband's hierarchical one; her position could be seen to be expressed by Queen Aurelia as she led the defence of women. The play acts as an additional response to Swetnam: the subtitle of the play is 'Arraigned by Women'. While the first judicial trial in the play consists of familiar attacks on

SWETNAM,

THE

· VVoman-hater,

ARRAIGNED BY

WOMEN.

A new Comedie,
Acted at the *Red Bull*, by the late
Queenes Seruants.

LONDON,
Printed for *Richard Meighen*, and are to be sold at his Shops
at Saint *Clements* Church, ouer-againſt *Essex* Houſe, and
at *Westminster* Hall. 1 6 2 0.

Figure 3. *Swetnam the Woman Hater*, title page. RB 69600, The Huntington Library, San Marino, California.

women along with equally familiar defences, the trial in front of the queen turns that around. By focusing on Swetnam as a 'woman-hater' who ultimately gets his comeuppance, the play dramatically expresses ideas in defence of women that were articulated outside of the theatre as well.[53] The gender order was never unquestioned.

Comic reversal and the upside down world

Comedies, like revenge tragedies and even tragicomedies, are interested in the challenges of living up to social expectations, but they turn the misunderstandings and mistakes to comic ends. The engagement with inversion is inevitable in the comic form, as the reversal of expectations is key to comedy.[54] To see how this functions in early modern comedy, we start with the stock figure of early modern humour, the cuckold. Running jokes about the inevitability of being cuckolded recur throughout the courtships in Shakespeare's *As You Like It* and *Much Ado About Nothing*: being a cuckold was the inheritance of a married man.[55] Yet Shakespeare turned the joke upside down in *The Merry Wives of Windsor*. In that play, Falstaff plans to seduce Mistress Ford and Mistress Page, and assumes that they will be unfaithful: Ford's wife 'gives the leer of invitation', while Page's wife 'gave me good eyes'. However, he makes the mistake of sending identical letters to the two friends, so while he boasts of how he will place cuckold's horns above the heads of Ford and Page, the two women plot to humiliate him. The series of tricks played on him persistently turn expectations upside down. Falstaff is ducked as a scold, as if he were a woman, and then, although he is unmarried, is the target of a charivari. In the final trick of the play, Falstaff is promised a meeting with Mistress Ford if he comes to an oak tree at night, dressed as Herne the hunter, with horns on his head. He finds instead both Mistress Ford and Mistress Page, and instead of making Page and Ford cuckolds, Page remarks, Falstaff is 'a knave, a cuckoldly knave'.[56] The would-be adulterer is the butt of the joke, while the wives show their virtue. While Falstaff seeks to turn marriages upside down through adultery, Mistresses Ford and Page collaborate to maintain proper order by shaming both Falstaff and Master Ford, who had mistrusted his wife. In doing so, they challenge the misogynist assumptions of much early modern humour. The laughter provoked by the play is most centrally based on incongruity: every expectation of the play and of its viewers is upended. Falstaff's assumption that women are available is proved wrong, and instead of placing horns on the heads of their husbands, Falstaff himself ends up wearing the horns. Jokes about women who are expected to fall for a lover but instead resist seduction allow virtuous women to feel superior to others. Like the queen and the women in *Swetnam the Woman-Hater*, Mistress Page and Mistress Ford unite agency and virtue in feminine form; in doing so they challenge the idea that female agency was an inevitable source of disorder.

Many of the comedies of the period were set in London, peopled with recognizable characters, and make London almost a character in the play. Thomas

Middleton's *A Chaste Maid in Cheapside* explores the way sex and money are intertwined in the lives of London's citizens through four intersecting plots. The failed patriarchs of the play enable multiple forms of disorder. The primary plot centres around the goldsmith, Yellowhammer, who with his wife is plotting the family's ascent into the gentry. They plan to marry their daughter Moll to a Welsh knight, Sir Walter Whorehound, and their son, Tim, a student at Cambridge, to Sir Walter's 'niece', who is in fact his mistress. Yellowhammer and his wife, like aristocratic parents at court, are intent on arranging advantageous marriages for their children in spite of their children's feelings; their ignorance of the world into which they wish to marry their children allows Sir Walter, whose surname denotes his character, to take advantage of them. Moll, who is not the loose woman suggested by her name, resists the planned marriage because she is both virtuous and in love with Touchwood Junior, a gentleman but a younger son. The eventual marriage between Moll and Touchwood Junior takes place after they have both feigned death and risen up from their coffins.[57]

The second plot is an extended meditation on cuckolds, wittols and cuckold-makers, which suggests that the central problem of the cuckold is his lack of control over his wife, not her infidelity. Master Allwit's wife is yet another mistress to Sir Walter Whorehound, and has borne him three children; initially, Allwit is the object of scorn as a wittol. Yet Allwit sees this not as a problem, but a benefit: he is 'clear ... from the charge' of a wife, because Sir Walter pays for all the expenses of the household; being a wittol is 'his living'. However, after a duel with Touchwood Junior, Sir Walter thinks he is dying; he then attacks the Allwits as wittol and whore. Allwit throws him out of the house, and the Allwits present a united front as virtuous husband and wife; he is now in control of his wife. They decide to move to the Strand and open a brothel: they are still making a living off sex, but now as a formal business. In the end, it is not Allwit the wittol, but Sir Walter, the scheming adulterer, who is ruined. The Allwit's new business reinforces the link between sex and money central to the play.[58]

The last two plots feature two married couples. Sir Oliver Kix and his wife are wealthy but childless; as a result, Sir Walter is his heir. Touchwood Senior (Touchwood Junior's older brother) is an impoverished gentleman who has decided to live apart from his wife because they already have more children than they can afford, and she becomes pregnant whenever they have sex. Indeed, he admits, his extraordinary virility means he always makes women pregnant. Touchwood Senior promises a medicine that will make Lady Kix pregnant – a drink, best delivered when she is lying down! – and of course he is successful. Sir Oliver pays him handsomely, as he now has a heir. Lady Kix's pregnancy ends

Sir Walter's hope of repairing his fortunes through inheritance, and it leads to his imprisonment for debt.

In these intersecting plots, the men are all conspicuous failures as patriarchs. Yellowhammer fails less as a husband than as a father who is willing to force his children into marriages solely for social advancement; he is successful only in marrying his son to a Welsh whore. Allwit fails because he is a wittol who profits from his wife's unfaithfulness. Sir Oliver Kix's and Touchstone Senior's failures are less notable: Sir Oliver has been unable to father children and seems unaware of the true nature of Touchstone Senior's 'drink' for his wife. Touchstone Senior is unable to control his sexual desires; he may be a loving husband, but he does not control his own behaviour. The wives in the play are 'good wives' in that they act in concert with their husbands. Yet the intermingling of sex and money repeatedly suggests that a good wife is not always modest and virtuous.

The frequency of disguise and cross-dressing in plays means that playing with gender identity and the performance of gender was a familiar trope across dramatic genres. In comedy, these became layered jokes because all the actors were male: women disguised as men meant that a boy dressed as a woman then dressed as a man; the whole audience was in on the joke. This institutionalized cross-dressing was one source of the puritan attack on the theatre: such disguises were a provocation to sin.[59] Yet while moralists objected, dramatists often used cross-dressing to raise questions about existing gender norms. The humorous potential of this critique, and the way comedy exploits both unruly wives and failed patriarchs, are evident in Thomas Middleton's and Thomas Dekker's *The Roaring Girl*. Moll Cutpurse, the Roaring Girl of the title, was based on a real woman in early modern London: Mary Frith apparently began her career as a petty thief, but became a prosperous business woman acting as a receiver and broker in stolen goods. She was notorious for dressing as a man, and her multiple engagements with courts included an appearance at the London Consistory Court for indecent dress. Although she married, the relationship appears to have been brief, and she and her husband lived apart.[60] She was, in sum, an unruly woman, not controlled by any man.

The whole play is aware of its theatrical setting: jokes related to the Fortune theatre, where the play was first performed, occur throughout, and there is evidence that Mary Firth sang at one performance of *Roaring Girl*.[61] Moll's stage version, which is just one of multiple representations of her in popular culture, starts with the characteristics which made her notorious in her lifetime. In the play, Moll is independent; she remarks that she will not marry because 'a wife, you know, ought to be obedient, but I fear me I am too headstrong to obey, therefore I'll ne'er go about it'.[62] Her acknowledgement of the proper patriarchal order positions her to be both a truth teller and a fixer who restores patriarchal government. It is, it turns out, the unruly woman who sets things right, sees through the tricks, and protects the vulnerable from plots against them. In particular, she helps to remind two fathers that their duty to their sons includes more than the accumulation of wealth. At the start of the play, Sir Alexander Wengrave has turned against the marriage he had originally planned for his son Sebastian to Mary Fitzallard, the daughter of Sir Guy, because the bride's dowry is not large enough. Sebastian and Mary love each other, however, and Sebastian informs Mary, who comes to him in disguise as a sempstress, that he is pretending to be in love with Moll Cutpurse so that his father will be so appalled that he will again approve his marriage to Mary. In defending his supposed courtship of Moll to his father, Sebastian argues, 'She is loose in nothing but in mirth'; while her dress and behaviour may be unconventional, she is virtuous. Indeed, when Laxton, a City gallant, offers her ten angels to meet him for what he thinks will be an assignation, she shows up in men's clothes, throws his money back at him, and bests him in a sword fight. 'Thou'rt one of those / That thinks each woman thy fond flexible whore / ... What durst move you, sir, / To think me whorish?'.[63]

Moll may be honest and virtuous, as well as willing to collude with Sebastian in tricking his father, but she plays with the fuzzy boundaries of virtue and law. She knows the ways of criminals and rogues, and makes judgments about right and wrong, not what is lawful and unlawful. She figures out that Trapdoor, who has offered to serve her, is trying to trick her into committing a crime so that she can be arrested; she repeatedly foils his attempts to put her in the wrong, and refuses to translate his thieves cant for more ignorant characters.[64] She also subverts the dishonest plot of the play's second troubled father, Sir Davy Dapper; Dapper is so worried by his son Jack Dapper's spendthrift ways that he arranges to have him arrested by a false claim and placed in London's debtor's prison. Moll figures this out, and alerts Jack so that he escapes arrest.

Moll's truth-telling is at odds with the world of deception in the play. While some deceptions, like Sebastian's, are for good ends, others are not. All of the deceptions, however, reflect the failure of households to meet the expected standards. This problem is evident in the main sub-plot of the play, centred around three shopkeepers and their wives. As often happens in a comedy, the wives rule their husbands; they can do so because they are vital to the success of their husband's businesses. Two of them are involved in flirtations with London gallants. Laxton, before he tries to seduce Moll, is stringing Mistress Gallipot along to get money from her; he is proud of his ability to convince her that it is only lack of opportunity that has blocked their sexual coupling. Goshawk, on the other hand, tries to convince Mistress Openwork that her husband is keeping a whore at an inn in Brentford, but she discovers he is lying. Even as the lies are discovered, the women, who manage their husbands' shops, boast of their ability to manage both the gallants and their husbands. But the play reminds us that deception, particularly related to sex, is never without cost, whether financial or reputational.

The Roaring Girl ends up resolving only one plot with a happy marriage: Sebastian and Mary are married, and Sir Alexander admits his error in opposing this marriage and misjudging Moll. Although one failed patriarch has admitted his fault, and the marriage of Sebastian and Mary promises to model the patriarchal ideal, elsewhere the proper gender order seems fragile or remains inverted. The other plots are less fully resolved; the gallants will, presumably, continue to court married women, failing to take up their own role as patriarchs. They will also presumably boast of their conquests, and often falsely name men as cuckolds. As Moll observes, 'Were all men cuckolds, whom gallants in their scorns / Call so, we should not walk for goring horns'.[65] It is the open rebel against the gender order who upholds it best; the other characters seem to lack an internal compass that guides them to the right. The concern with proper order expressed in this play informs Swetnam's *Araignment* and Rachel Speght's response, which were also published by Thomas Archer.[66]

While the central comedy of *The Roaring Girl* lies in the way Moll calls attention to men's abuse of women and the failures of patriarchal governance, Nathan Field's *Amends for Ladies* (1618) finds its comic energy in the disjunctures between how well people think they can negotiate patriarchal expectations and their actual inability to do so. The characters are types, not individuals. The play opens with a dialogue between a Maid (Lady Honour), a Wife (Lady Perfect) and a Widow (Lady Bright), with each explaining why her position is best. Yet almost immediately, the virtues each claims are challenged. Lady Perfect has boasted of her husband and her chastity, but her husband suspects her of being unfaithful. Lady Honour has praised her freedom as a virgin, but is in fact in love with one Ingen. Widow Bright has asserted her freedom to choose her next husband and her control over her property. In spite of her love for him, Maid refuses Ingen's offer of marriage, claiming she will never marry; in response, Ingen suggests they just enjoy each other without marrying, so she spurns him. To test his wife's virtue, Lady Perfect's husband encourages his friend Subtle to seduce her, asserting that 'there is no woman in the world / Can hold out in the end'. He sets her up by asking her to 'Make much of Master Subtle'. Lady Perfect refuses, insisting on her virtue and her duty to her husband.[67] Bould, who loves Widow Bright, disguises himself as a woman and gets hired as her servant: he takes advantage of the custom of servants sleeping with their mistress to get in bed with her. He assumes sex is the way to a widow's heart. After the widow discovers Bould's identity, she throws him out, promising not to report his attempt. And she notes, ''tis my pride / To assure you that there are amongst us good, / And with this continency.'[68] The courtship between Ingen and Lady Honour proceeds erratically, with the Maid disguising herself as a page to bring a message from herself to him, and Ingen disguising his brother as a woman and pretending to marry him/her, and he pretends to marry another woman, who is in fact Lord Feesimple disguised as a woman. If you're counting, that's four characters in disguise. Bould disguises himself as a woman to get close to his beloved Widow; Bould and Ingen pretend to marry men who are disguised as women in order to convince the women they love to admit that their love is reciprocated, and thus marry them; Lady Honour disguises herself first as a page and later as a servant, first to try to prevent Ingen's (fake) marriage and then to prevent a threatened duel between Ingen and her brother. By the end of the play, the husband has admitted his wife's faithfulness, Lady Honour has married Ingen, and Widow Bright has married Bould. So the proper patriarchal order has been upheld – but not by the men. It is only upheld by the actions of the three women, each of whom proves to be honest and chaste; every attempt to corrupt them fails. The maid has to defend her own interests both in marrying Ingen and in deflecting her brother's plan to marry her to an elderly widower. The widow is willing to resign Bould to a younger woman, but when she does marry him, it is evident that the marriage is from love, not lust. The wife has the last word, as she proclaims, 'Yet mine is now approv'd the happiest life, Since each of you hath chang'd to be a wife.'[69]

The comedy of *Amends for Ladies* comes from the fact that women have to work to ensure the proper patriarchal order. Lady Perfect complains that women are 'made the disgra'd subjects, in these plays' when it is men who are 'full of gross and base corruption'. When Bould has got into Lady Bright's bed by pretending to be a woman, the widow is outraged, regretting that 'fond opinion' that 'This is the way to have a widowhood / by getting her to bed'. The characters, as they play with disguise and challenges to the gender order, repeatedly remind viewers of theatrical practice. Their multiple disguises also remind viewers of the performative nature of identity. There is a cameo by Moll Cut-purse, who acts as an intermediary for a citizen's wife who cuckolds her husband. It repeatedly refers to the theatre: some of the men plan to go see a play about *Long Meg*, a play about a mannish woman, at the Fortune, the same theatre where *The Roaring Girl* was produced. In a later scene, 'roarers' in an alehouse worry that two gentlemen have arrived to take notes for playwriting; a mocking reference to Falstaff and honour is used against Lord Proudly, the maid's brother, when he is arrested.[70] *Amends for Ladies* foregrounds the ways women act to repair the damage caused by their husbands, brothers and suitors.

* * * * *

All the roles on the early modern English professional stage were played by men, so every play in some fashion turned the world upside down. Yet theatrical inversion goes well beyond boys dressed as women, or even boys dressed as women dressed as men. Across theatrical genres, failed patriarchs and unruly women shape the central conflicts of drama. In the upside down world, where men and women did not know their place, household government failed. The plays suggest the internal tensions within the patriarchal model, both its vulnerability to desire and the popular female critique of its norms. They also provided a way to explore contemporary debates without taking on overt political discussions. Tragedies portrayed the inevitable consequences when men failed in their roles as patriarchs, or women were unruly. The dead bodies that litter the stage at the end of tragedies testify to the evil consequences of their deviations from expectations. Comedies turned those expectations around: while they were equally concerned with failed patriarchs and unruly women, both their characters and their plots challenge expectations in a way that leads to laughter rather than death. These plays contributed to contemporary debates, because both the tensions they explored and the behaviours they presented were recognizable. The endings, whether marriage or death, reaffirmed the proper order. The self-conscious references to theatre in both *Roaring Girl* and *Amends for Ladies* remind us that early modern playgoers were aware that they were performing roles in their lives as well. The inversion so visible on stage could be played by friends and neighbours, not just by actors. The most common way to do this was through charivari. Here too, the world was turned upside down, and everyone was reminded both of the proper order and of its fragility.

4

Performing Inversion in Civic Pageantry and Charivari

In April 1608, the constable of Wells, Somerset, a clothier named John Hole, made a complaint to the Star Chamber.[1] The previous summer, he reported, a group of young people, aided and abetted by some of their elders, had carried on the traditional May festivities, and taken umbrage when he tried to limit them. Annoyed by Constable Hole's interruption of their innocent (or not so innocent) dancing and merriment, the young people, encouraged by some of their elders, continued the abuse of Hole and his friends in a series of pageants that were part of a church ale designed to raise money for the local church. Two pageants in particular were problematic. In one, Hole and his friends, John Yarde, Hugh Mead and Humphrey Palmer – all prosperous merchants and tradesmen – were caricatured as poor men in need of borrowing money from a usurer. Even the mayor thought that 'there was knavery in it'. For the final pageant in the series, on 25 June,

> The said riotous & disordered persons by the abetment aforesaid did … maliciously & slanderously procure a board of a yard long & half a yard broad to be painted by the said Walter Smith with a picture of a woman in the midst thereof having a hat in the one hand & a brush in the other & likewise the pictures of two men by her on the same board the one standing on the one side the other on the other side of her.

The bottom of the board had nine holes, 'the bigness of a ball', and there was another board a yard long attached perpendicular to the images. The length of the board referred to John Yarde, a hatter, and the woman pictured was his wife. The two men depicted were 'near to the likeness and resemblance' of John Hole and his friend Hugh Mead.

> The which board thus fastened together the one standing upright upon the other & painted with the said pictures & nine holes as aforesaid the said confederators in further accomplishment & execution of their said combination, plot, &

practice have unlawfully routeously & riotously assembled & gathered together Three thousand persons by sounding of drums, armed & weaponed ... & did then & there procure & cause to be openly carryed on horseback through the street of your said City by William Gamage with two other persons riding on two other horses on both sides of him namely one Jasper [blank], servant to John Guilbert riding on the right side of the said Gamage having a desk before him with a paper book & pen and ink upon it representing a scrivener or notary to set down in writing whatsoever the said Gamage should appoint him; the other riding on the other side of the said Gamage with a pair of Gards & a Noddy board between both which persons the said Gamage riding in the midst with his said board having a little ball or boule in his hand did cast & trundle the said Boule or ball upon the said under board towards the said nine holes saying with a loud voice so as many people might hear him, 'He Holes it for a Crown', & then presently it was answered aloud by some other of that confederacy standing by and then and there appointed for that purpose, 'He Holes it not within a Yarde for a Crown', thereby meaning & naming your said subject John Hole by alluding to his name & the said John Yarde who dwelleth at the sign of the Crown ... Some other of the said confederacy did then & there in like sort with a loud voice often say unto the said Gamage these words, 'Holing is against the king's proclamation & not sufferable in the streets & therefore if you will needs Hole it go Hole it in the Mead', whereupon the said Gamage speaking to the said pretended scribe or Notary said with a loud voice, 'Set it down, Notary, Holing is against the king's proclamation', thereby not only deriding your Majesty's said proclamation but also slanderously traducing the said Hugh Mead & your subject John Hole & that in the view & presence of three thousand people at the least. By all which devises pictures & words the said lewd & ill disposed persons laboured falsely & unworthily to defame the honest reputations of your subject & of the said John Yarde, Hugh Mead & the wife of the said John Yarde & thereby to cast an imputation & scandal of incontinency upon them.

The suggestion in this final pageant that John Yarde's wife was having an affair with Constable Hole provides some explanation for Hole's agitation. Because 'yard' was a common slang term for penis, the sexual word play of hole and yard was obviously tempting. But while the sexual insult explains Hole's attitude, it does not explain why the case ended up as one of the longer Star Chamber cases, with 265 sheets, nor does it explain why members of the Privy Council paid serious attention to it. The events in Wells in 1607 illuminate the ways in which inversion was performed not just on stage, but in the streets and fields of early modern England, and how that intersected with local structures of power.

The pageant that Hole described on 25 June echoed a charivari. Such processions, usually called ridings or skimmingtons, were shaming rituals that simultaneously performed and symbolically corrected inversion. While we are most familiar with charivari as popular rituals, similar processions were used by courts to punish misconduct, as in *Volpone*. Charivari were also part of the vocabulary of political and economic protest. In the western forest riots of the 1620s and 1630s, the targets were courtiers, and several leaders took the name of Skimmington, or Lady Skimmington; the allegations were that the moral order had been overturned, and a skimmington was necessary to right things again.[2] One of the most famous images of a charivari from the period is a satire, published, coincidentally, in 1607. In this image, a beggar leads an ass toward a judge. On the ass is a well-dressed young man, described in a text bubble as a clown, riding backwards charivari-like while a courtesan tries to pull him off. On one side of the ass a young gallant is trying to climb on, as is an old man, and the ass is followed by another gallant and a fool. Each of the characters offers a couplet, but the ass asks, 'Will all get up upon me? All together? / At once? Clown, Gull, Punk, Pandar, Fool and Feather?' The ass worries whether his back will break with all the weight, and suggests all might be happier if he took them one by one. Yet the image of a crowd seeking to ride the ass suggests widespread moral corruption.[3]

The complaint by Constable Hole describes both a charivari and an accompanying verse libel targeted at him in 1607; the libel, a doggerel by William Gamage, who had played the leading role in the charivari, was circulated after the procession. In that year, to help raise money for the repair of the tower of St Cuthbert's Church in Wells, the authorities allowed the churchwardens to sponsor a church ale, with a series of guild processions and pageants, after the traditional May Games. The Star Chamber case concluded with Gamage and another young man punished with a judicial charivari. The lawsuit involved at least three gendered inversions: alleged sexual misconduct, a charivari, and after lengthy legal proceedings, a charivari punishment. It brought up issues of public order and local politics, as well as gender and sexuality. The events were part of a debate on how local communities should be governed; because Wells was a cathedral town, there were competing authorities, and in different versions of events, both ecclesiastical and civic authorities could be seen at various points as failed patriarchs. The Wells events also link the festivity of the skimmington with the festive year. While the Reformation had done away with many of the occasions for public festivity, a few remained, either translated for Protestant sensibilities or enduring in spite of Protestant attempts at reform.

It is worth examining the common features of skimmingtons before we turn to events in Wells in 1607. Ridings were raucous processions, which involved the re-enactment of the offending event, usually by neighbours. Participants made great noise on their way to the house of an offending couple, with one person (representing the husband) riding backwards; the actor – often the next neighbour to the offending household – rode a horse or donkey, or was carried on a pole. Sometimes a second rider dressed in women's clothing acted the role of a wife, and often the man revealed his shame by holding a distaff or other symbol of femininity. The next neighbour was used, Thomas Platter wrote in 1598, because he had not 'come to his neighbour's assistance when his wife was beating him'. Skimmingtons often included the use of horns, suggesting that men whose wives ruled them were also, inevitably, cuckolds: a woman in Cawston, Norfolk, told another that 'if you beat poor cuckold your husband about the horns again we will have a better riding than we had before'. In cases with a juridical component, the offenders themselves were carried on horseback. The ritual was sufficiently familiar in Somerset that the Phelips family placed a plasterwork representation of a skimmington – a woman beating her husband, and the neighbours parading the next neighbour on a pole – in the great hall of Montacute House when it was built in the early seventeenth century.[4] Many elements of the processions were based on judicial shaming punishments; by mirroring formal legal practices, popular disapproval was made clear.

While there is much that could be (and has been) said about charivari, for our purposes what is important is the way charivari play with the world upside down. The original offense, whether a wife beating her husband or being unfaithful to him, turned the world upside down, so the ritual re-enacted that inversion in order to restore order. The riding directed at Nicholas Rosyer of Wetherden, Suffolk, and his wife, mentioned in Chapter 1, responded to her beating him when he came home drunk. In the riding, Thomas Quarry, who lived 'at the next house', was carried around the town on a cowlstaff dressed in women's clothing, telling 'all wives to take heed how they did beat their husbands'.[5] Of course, people were not always so high-minded: in 1653, the crowd that came to the house of John Day in Ditcheat, Somerset, 'hooping and hallowing', planned 'to make merry with Skimmington', and had been promised a 'barrel of beer'.[6] The festive dimension was never far away.

The charivari in Wells was also connected to more traditionally festive events. The May celebrations included music, dancing and courting among local unmarried people; such festivities, with their potential for unsupervised romance, were often a sources of anxiety, especially by more Protestant local authorities. It is

Figure 4. A political skimmington: Renold Elstrack, 'While maskinge in their folleis all doe passe, though all say nay yet all doe ride the asse.' British Museum PPA93995 – 1855, 0114.189 © The Trustees of the British Museum.

Figure 5. A skimmington: The 'Stang Ride' or 'Skimmington Ride', plasterwork panel in the Great Hall at Montacute House, Somerset. This depicts both the wife beating the husband, and the village ritual. © National Trust Images / Nadia Mackenzie.

easy to miss, however, the ways festivity could be used by young people to mock their elders: young people may not have had a formal role in civic life, but they had opinions about local notables. In contrast, civic processions were by their nature political: in towns and cities they often recognized the election of new members of the local council or, as in London, a new mayor.

Festivity and subversion

The events in Wells in 1607 took place in a festive context. The festive year was marked by the distinction between carnival and Lent, which divided the ritual year into times of festivity and austerity. During carnival inversionary behaviour of almost every possible kind was tolerated, as normal barriers to excess in matters of food, drink and sex, as well as customary gender and social distinctions, were temporarily removed, and it was not only permitted, but expected that authority would be lampooned and ridiculed in ways that turned the social and political worlds upside down.[7] The wild scenes that were still repeated at Venice and other Italian cities were no longer permitted in Protestant England, but attempts to perpetuate annual civic festivities of less lurid kinds nevertheless occurred in many late sixteenth-century English towns.[8]

The ritual and festive year in early modern England had two high points, November and May–June. In November, festivities were connected with Gunpowder Treason (Guy Fawkes) Day on 5 November, and with another originally anti-Catholic festival, the anniversary of Elizabeth I's accession on the seventeenth. The Gunpowder Treason celebrations had been brought in as a safely patriotic substitute for an older tradition that the authorities wanted to get rid of. That older one was Halloween, which seventeenth-century Protestants regarded as an evil survival of paganism, or worse yet, of popery.[9] Most reforming Protestants liked the festive merrymakings that occupied the late spring and early summer even less than Halloween. May Day, Whitsuntide, and Midsummer were all occasions for communal feasting and playing, for drinking and sexual license. Maypoles symbolized the old festive culture that zealous Protestants were trying to stamp out, and there were countless local struggles over whether they should be abolished.

The prominence of May as a time of festivity was visible across English culture. Among the elite, it was a frequent subject of pastoral poetry. Robert Herrick's 'The Argument of his Book,' the table of contents for his *Hesperides*, emphasizes the sexual nature of May:

> I sing of May-poles, hock-carts, wassails, wakes,
> Of bridegrooms, brides, and of their bridal-cakes.
> I write of youth, of love, and have access
> By these to sing of cleanly wantonness.

On a more popular level, the first song in Thomas Dekker's *Shoemaker's Holiday*, focused on a Shrove Tuesday celebration, begins,

> Oh, the month of May, the merry month of May,
> So frolic, so gay, and so green, so green, so green!
> Oh, and then did I unto my true love say:
> 'Sweet Peg, though shalt be my summer's queen.'[10]

Ballads, too, took for granted that May was a time of license, of dancing, courtship and sexual activity. While there were interruptions for work, the festive season continued into June, with Whitsun and Midsummer both identified as times of misrule and sexual license linked to agricultural fertility: the woods in *A Midsummer Night's Dream*, with lovers wandering about unsupervised, were a recognizable part of early modern culture.[11]

The sexual dimensions of May celebrations made them an obvious target for reformers. But puritans also took aim at other traditional customs: morris dancing, play-acting, as well as church ales. Church ales were parish festivals, organized to raise money for keeping the church fabric in repair, a sort of alcoholic version of the modern church bazaar. The profits came from the sale of beer, so it is not surprising that they became known for drunkenness and disorder. Yet, their defenders insisted, they had a useful function even beyond the fund-raising, for by bringing people together for merrymaking, they reinforced the good fellowship that linked them as a community.[12]

Other communal celebrations could also easily get out of hand. Many English towns had traditionally held processions at midsummer, typically organized by the local craft guilds, through which the identity of the community was annually reinforced and expressed. Some of them – late medieval York and Chester are famous examples – were accompanied by elaborate theatrical productions on familiar, usually biblical themes. By the late sixteenth century, these dramatic performances were less common, but other civic performances emerged. In many towns, a procession, including pageants of varying levels of elaboration, accompanied the installation of the mayor or town council. In general the messages presented in such staged pageants were predictable representations of civic and moral virtue. Yet the very dramatic context of such performances – as in the plays we examined in the last chapter – allowed for oppositional voices to emerge. In London, where the Lord Mayor's pageants became increasingly elaborate, Thomas Middleton, Thomas Dekker and John Webster all wrote pageant scripts. In a ceremony designed around the mayor taking an oath to the king, they often included a defence of the city's privileges against the Crown; in some of the pageants from the 1620s, London displaces the king, or becomes a realm in its own right. And while they are outwardly conformist, in their dialogue with current drama, several of the pageants seem to be parodying the new mayor or the whole ritual.[13] In Norwich, the procession associated with the Company of St. George was fused with the installation of the new mayor in the early seventeenth century; while the Reformation did away with St. George, the dragon survived, but joined to a fool, so far less threatening.[14] More occasional civic processions occurred on the occasion of royal entries into towns and cities. These are particularly well documented and show that the lines we draw between processions and theatre were not yet distinct in the early modern period.[15] Whatever the occasion, civic pageants provided the opportunity to dramatize power, and in so doing they also articulated challenges to power.

Inevitably, we know more about all such events in large and wealthy cities like London and Norwich; the Wells pageants suggest that even in smaller cities these were relatively elaborate performances. They brought together large crowds of people from the surrounding countryside, to the great profit of the local publicans, and with the inevitable opportunities for disorder. It might be tempting for local malcontents to use them to criticize or ridicule prominent members of the town elite, as they often did on other occasions, by spreading crude and scandalous mocking rhymes about them. Such malcontents were especially likely to be drawn from the ill-disciplined, unmarried younger sort: mocking authority was a central part of youth culture. At Wells, in the series of events recounted here, they went even further, by acting out their superiors' alleged misdeeds in the popular modes of carnival and charivari. These were 'but the shows of their street', one of their defenders declared.[16] That they were indeed, but, as we shall see, they were a lot more besides.

The debate about the festive year is also a reminder that while there was broad agreement on the importance of patriarchal order, what actually constituted it was up for grabs. The debate on festive culture, and the larger culture wars of the period, reflected disagreements about *what* turned the world upside down. Was it young people dancing or going to alehouses without supervision? Was it festive processions? How much control should fathers have? Or was the problem the suppression of such traditional practices, which held the community together? Could you have the traditional festive culture and an orderly society? There was no one answer to these questions; instead they were repeatedly contested.[17] The debates allowed people of all points of view to point to ways the world was upside down, and helped give the metaphor its power. The events at Wells in 1607 offer us an extraordinarily well-documented opportunity to observe a direct collision of these competing worldviews in street theatre. While puritan critics of festive culture resisted most civic ceremonials, others thought civic ceremonies, including church ales, fostered community cohesion. Yet such ceremonies could be hijacked by a more populist, transgressive exercise in charivari, thus confirming the puritan mistrust of such events. The differing viewpoints of local governors in both the city and the cathedral show the multiple ways an orderly society could be understood. And they help us see how different participants used gendered inversion as a component of popular rituals, theatre and politics.

The scene: Wells, 1607

In 1607 the annual May Games in Wells included a church ale to pay for repairs to St Cuthbert's church tower. St Cuthbert's was (and is) the *townspeople's* church, the focus of a community whose history had long been marked by a love-hate relationship with the more grandiose cathedral authorities similar to the town-gown tensions familiar to anyone who has lived in a university town.[18] The 1607 celebrations featured the maypole and street dancing, but there were also processions to raise money for the church tower. Yet some Wells residents objected, and there were acrimonious divisions, ending in Hole's lawsuit that brought the city to the attention of the Court of Star Chamber at Westminster, and providing the documentation for the events.[19] The controversy was one of those typical early Stuart struggles between puritans and their enemies over festive celebrations, and several historians have mentioned it in that light.[20] But it had other significant features. A traditional civic procession accompanying an elaborate church ale was used by young rabble-rousers who organized a charivari ridiculing members of the local elite.[21] It is a complicated story, full of ambiguities and apparent contradictions. The three components of the affair – the May processions, the church ale and the charivari – illuminate not only social life and the religious and political divisions in Wells in 1607, but also the role of gender and inversion in the cultural life of the wider county of Somerset and the kingdom of which it was a part.

The May Games were more elaborate in 1607 than in previous years, but they reflected a long tradition of often raucous festive and dramatic celebration in Wells. As far back as the fourteenth century, deans had tried to clean up the plays that were put on in the cathedral at Whitsuntide, Christmas and on Holy Innocents Day, when it was the custom to elect a 'boy bishop' and turn the world upside down in unseemly parodies of the liturgy. In 1330 the dean prohibited plays 'contrary to the decency of the church of Wells'. This does not seem to have done much good, as a few years later the laity were still putting on plays containing 'obscene ravings'.[22] Some of the trouble was the fault of the vicars-choral, whose behaviour was far from the respectable decorum that we might expect to find in choir members nowadays. In 1337 they were reported to be gambling and haunting taverns, and things were no better in the seventeenth century. In 1601 a vicar-choral was ordered to do penance for fornication, and soon afterwards another singing-man in trouble with the cathedral authorities announced that 'he cared not a fart for any of the doctors of the church'.[23]

In spite of all this, the dean and chapter had permitted more decorous mystery plays, and these probably continued down to the Reformation.[24] Furthermore, by the later fifteenth century the city was developing its own festivities. We know that church ales were held in St Cuthbert's parish by 1497, because in that year the corporation investigated the embezzlement of money raised by 'the common ale of the church'; the profits of a Robin Hood play and of 'the girls dancing' had also disappeared. By 1550 there were street carnivals at midsummer, probably much like those of 1607, in which the craft guilds dressed up and processed through the town as part of a 'king's watch'. From what we know of other towns, it seems likely that such midsummer shows had existed at Wells long before 1550.[25]

Wells was in a region which had a lively festive life. Even at a small place like the nearby village of Croscombe there were annual Robin Hood plays of the kind so popular in late medieval England. These, and other pageants performed by the women of the village, raised a good deal of money for the church.[26] A bit further away, Yeovil was well known for its colourful Robin Hood plays. After 1578 there are no more references to a Robin Hood there, but occasional church ales continued, and there was a particularly noisy one, also in 1607, presided over by the 'sheriff' (presumably of Nottingham). Puritans who protested were told that if they did not shut up there would be an even bigger church ale the following year, with a Maid Marion as well, and double the amount of ale.[27] The sheriff and Maid Marion: the Yeovil church ales still involved play-acting on the Robin Hood theme. As we shall see, Robin shows up in Wells in 1607, and he also presided over the church ale at Westonzoyland in the same year. In that case the lead was played by the local parson's son, and the ritual turning of the world upside down was accomplished by putting the parson himself in the stocks; parishioners who wished to have him released had to drink 'two pots of strong ale'. Robin Hood games, which dramatized an upside down social order, were alive and well.[28]

If Robin Hood plays and games declined at all, it was due to the general hostility of the authorities to any story that celebrated resistance, and to their particular dislike of festive traditions associated with popery and paganism. By the latter part of Elizabeth's reign the Justices of the Peace (JPs) were trying to make parishes rely on equitably assessed rating systems, essentially a property tax, for the money they needed, rather than boozy church ales. At a time of rapid population growth and economic dislocation, there were fears that the whole fabric of the ordered society ordained by God was in danger of collapsing. Public occasions at which idleness and drinking were tolerated clearly contributed to the danger, and it was not only puritans who believed this: the urgent need for a 'reformation of manners' was a major preoccupation of godly people across the whole Protestant spectrum.[29] The Somerset JPs were no different from those in other counties. In 1594 they decreed that there should be no more church ales, and the order was repeated two years later. It is doubtful if the prohibitions were fully effective, although the mayor testified that until 1607 Wells had in fact obeyed, and that there had been an annual rate for the repair of St Cuthbert's.[30] Whether the guilds' midsummer processions had also lapsed is less clear. Witnesses in the lawsuits that followed the games were (perhaps intentionally) vague on this point. One man said that in 'divers years' there had been 'Pageants, May Games, morris dances and shows', another said that there had been similar shows 'three or four times within his memory', but both were old enough to have had memories going back before 1594. Defenders said the May Games were ancient customs that allowed people 'to be merry in such sort as in former time', and a witness quoted his father and grandfather as saying that the mayor's presence at them was 'according to the … usual custom'. The guild processions probably had been held, though without the church ale, fairly regularly.[31]

The festivities lasted from May Day until midsummer, and they fall nicely into two parts. Most of May was taken up with the traditional spring rituals: the maypole, the Lord and Lady of the May, the dancing in the streets. Then came the second stage, the church ale, including the guilds' processions, which went on until 25 June, just after midsummer, and which were spectacularly invaded by the subversive charivari. Linking the two parts was a Robin Hood play in the Market Place on Friday, 29 May.[32]

Dramatis personae: Wells's fractured and fractious authorities

And so in 1607, when St Cuthbert's needed to repair the tower, the churchwardens decided to ask permission to hold a church ale, which would allow them to raise the funds they needed without taking the unpopular step of increasing the parish rate. The mayor, Alexander Towse, was unwilling to defy the 1594 Sessions Orders, and a neighbouring JP, Sir John Rodney, also refused. They did better with the dean of Wells, Dr Benjamin Heydon, who like Rodney was a county JP but also had good reasons for encouraging the parishioners to look after their church. The dean and chapter owned the rectory of St Cuthbert's; they collected the tithes and paid the vicar out of them. In 1593 they had let the rectory to two Wells citizens, one of them a woollen draper named William Morgan. It was the practice everywhere for the owner of the rectory to be responsible for the chancel end of a church, the parishioners looking after the nave. Obviously both Heydon and Morgan had an interest in seeing that the parish's end of St Cuthbert's was properly maintained. Paying for it was not their problem.[33]

The churchwardens decided to combine their church ale with the midsummer pageants put on by the craft guilds. But both the city and the cathedral authorities were deeply divided. Dean Heydon was for it, but the bishop, John Still, was against it. Now that it was not his responsibility, Mayor Towse was for it, and some of his corporation colleagues even more so, but there were some influential citizens on the other side. The most prominent of these, who were all puritans, were John Yarde, a haberdasher, and John Hole, a wealthy clothing manufacturer. Neither Hole nor Yarde were natives of Wells, but they had quickly risen to prominence after they moved in. Yarde was constable in 1592, only two years after his arrival, and Hole was one of the churchwardens of St Cuthbert's the year after he arrived in 1597. He was the kind of businessman small towns liked: someone who would provide employment and thus reduce the local poor rates. He claimed to employ at least 400 poor people in 'spinning, knitting, and making of cloth and worsted hose'.[34] But Hole was a prickly character. He was soon quarrelling with other members of the corporation, and was suspended from his burgesship for speaking 'opprobrious words' against William Morgan, the lessee of St Cuthbert's rectory. But he was befriended by the more puritanically inclined JPs in the county, and they ordered that he be restored to his place. He was constable in 1607 and is therefore at the centre of our story.

Act I: May Games

So it all started early on May morning. Some twenty or so young people went 'a-maying' in the surrounding fields and woods. They brought back a maypole, had it set up in the High Street and began dancing along the street. Puritans might dislike this, but 1 May was a Friday, so there was nothing illegal about it, and trouble began only when the fun and games resumed on Sunday and Constable Hole could invoke the sabbath-observance laws. Morning service at St Cuthbert's had scarcely ended when more dancing began, to the accompaniment of fiddles and drums. The 'Lord of the May' was a gentleman named George Greenstreet, and his 'Lady' was Thomasine White, the wife of a barber-surgeon. During the dancing, a witness deposed, Greenstreet and Mrs White were 'lifted up above the ground to kiss together'. Her husband, Edmund, did not seem to mind, but it was too much for Hole, who told the dancers to disperse and go home. But Mrs White already *was* home. 'Master Constable', she shouted, 'I am at my own door and here I will stand'. Hole then tried to arrest the fiddlers, but this brought in the formidable figure of Mr William Watkins, a member of the corporation. Music and dancing were perfectly legal on Sundays, Watkins declared, as long as it was not during service time. At this point Hole lost control and told Watkins that he was 'a dog and a rebel', provoking some corresponding invective from Watkins. Eventually Hole managed to disperse the crowd and everyone left for evensong (church attendance was compulsory) – all except the musicians, who went off to a nearby house to play cards. Hole again had them

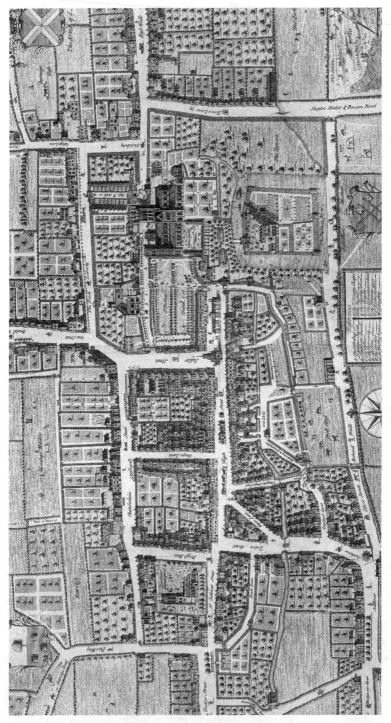

Figure 6. William Symes, Plan of the city of Wells. Southover is on the bottom left, St Cuthbert's church on the middle left; the market place is the large open square just to the left and below the cathedral. Tucker Street is the lower end of the High Street, below St Cuthbert's. Chamberlain Street runs parallel to the High Street; East Wells is at the far right, beyond the cathedral. © The British Library Board, Cartographic Items Maps K.Top.38.97.

arrested, but when the dancing resumed after church they were noisily rescued by the crowd. The dancers, some fifty to a hundred strong, were now deliberately baiting the constable. When they passed Hole's house, Edmund White urged them to make as much noise as possible, and himself took the lead, 'vehemently whooping and hallooeing and leaping'. The drummers, too, threatened Hole by repeatedly marching at him, though one of them said they were doing nothing hostile, just on their way to play their drums along by the Bishop's Palace moat to see whose were the loudest.[35]

During the following week Hole's friends the Yardes got involved in the controversy. They lived in the Market Place, and Mrs Yarde found the maypole so offensive that she could not walk by it when she went down the High Street to St Cuthbert's. The maypole, she announced, was a 'painted calf', like the one worshipped by the backsliding Israelites in the Old Testament. This comment was quickly seized on by some of the youth, providing another chance for a bit of fun. In a move that anticipates the more elaborate charivari later in the summer, they did a crude painting of a calf, 'with red and white spots on a board, suitable to the color of the summer pole', and staged a derisive procession. Young men headed by morris dancers and trumpeters paraded the 'calf' through the streets, stopping outside the Yardes' house, where one of them cried 'bah, like a calf'. During the procession they also shot at the board with muskets, saying that 'they had killed the painted calf so that Mrs Yarde could go to church'.[36] Both Mrs Yarde and her religious scruples were the focus of mockery.

Thursday, 14 May, was Ascension Day, and an excuse for further merrymaking, in which drummers and morris dancers escorted the traditional procession of children through the streets. The children were elaborately costumed; several mothers missed morning prayer because they were getting them ready. Some of the boys were wearing women's clothes. As we have seen in the theatre, puritans were particularly horrified by this kind of ungodly cross-dressing. On the following Sunday there was further trouble. A group of morris dancers went to perform at the nearby village of Croscombe. When they got back they repeated their act at the High Cross in the Market Place. Oliver Martin, one of the dancers, said that people were 'laughing, and sporting in merriment', but this changed when the constable arrived and arrested the drummer. There was some scuffling, during which Hole was pushed into the gutter and Martin got into a fight with one of the deputy constables. Later that evening other young men interrupted Hole by blowing trumpets while he was giving instructions to the city watchmen. They then went on to the moat and continued a rowdy party far into the night.[37]

The struggle was renewed every Sunday. Hole seems to have expected more serious carousing on 24 May, which was Whit Sunday, always one of the high points of the festive year. So on the Saturday he went to the mayor's house and formally read out the royal proclamation against violations of the sabbath, hoping to stir Towse into action. But the mayor was unimpressed, replying that the proclamation did not explicitly prohibit sports and pastimes on Sundays except during service time. On Sunday there was more dancing near the maypole, led by the Lord and Lady of the May, but no serious trouble. However, Hole said that on this and other Sundays he found many people from nearby villages illegally drinking in taverns and alehouses, having come into Wells for the festivities.[38]

On 29 May it was at last time for the Robin Hood play. After dinner the drums began to beat, and the Market Place was soon crowded with spectators. There seem to have been two performances: an afternoon matinee and an evening show. All that we know about the play is that a young man named Robert Prinne played Robin, and Stephen Millard, who was also the town sergeant, was one of the merry men. Hole did not intervene, and the Yardes were even willing to allow the mayor to come to their house and watch from 'a room where he might conveniently and privately' see the evening performance. This was surely a conciliatory gesture aimed at restoring civic harmony: it is remarkable that Yarde was willing to overlook the long-standing association of Robin Hood with the 'Summer Lord' common to traditional May Games, so hated by puritans of his type.[39]

Act II: church ale

After a brief interval, the second phase of the May Games, the St Cuthbert's church ale, began on Sunday 14 June, when the leading parishioners met for a breakfast of calves' head and bacon. After this gastronomic tour de force they made the final preparations for the event. Following established custom, the five traders' guilds, each associated with a particular street, would offer their pageants on successive evenings. They would process to the High Cross, down to the church house for supper, and then back to the originating street, again by way of the High Cross: five carnivals, and in summer weather! Throughout the week collectors would work the crowds. Each procession would include the mayor and corporation, other city and parish officers, and, befitting the close connection between the cathedral and St Cuthbert's, the dean and chapter. It would be a gratifying demonstration of the unity of church and city.[40] The links between politics and religion, civic duty and festive culture – each often fraught – were central to the success of the church ale.

And it was a huge success. Crowds attending the suppers at the church house were so big that they often spilled out into the churchyard. The mayor and his colleagues took the lead in giving 'their benevolence for the benefit of the church'. Others needed a bit of pressure. A man who offered four pence was told in effect, come on, you can do better than that: 'divers had given twelve pence a piece'. Besides the corporation, those present at the feasts included Sir John Rodney (who must have forgotten his earlier refusal to license the affair), Dean Heydon, several of the cathedral canons and 'all the best sort of the town'. Hole, needless to say, was nowhere to be seen, but although his puritan friends also stayed away, some were reported to have contributed to the fund for the church tower 'very liberally'. It was the merrymaking that they objected to, not the repair of the tower.[41]

Most of the pageants were based on familiar themes. The Tucker Street cloth workers built theirs around George a' Green, the legendary Pinder of Wakefield, with his men 'singing a song of Wakefield Green'. The Pinder was one of those familiar plebeian heroes, comically playing tricks on the authorities, and eventually joining Robin Hood's band.[42] High Street was allowed to display the city's silver plate, which was escorted by cathedral choir-boys in their white surplices, singing psalms and anthems. The choirmaster had refused to allow the boys to perform, but was overruled by Dean Heydon: a further sign that the cathedral community, like the city, was not united.[43] The most elaborate pageant was put on by the affluent Mercers' Company, based in Chamberlain Street. They had Hole's enemy, William Watkins, as their parade marshal, and there were two principal tableaux: one based on St George and the dragon, and the other on the classical theme of Diana and Actaeon. Mayor Towse himself took part, accompanying St George on horseback. After the church house supper there was a dramatic enactment of the dragon story, which was reasonably respectable. The Diana and Actaeon pageant was more offensive to puritans, as the goddess was inevitably a boy, accompanied by six 'nymphs' played by cathedral choristers – another sinful example of cross-dressing; in addition, the link between the story of Actaeon and the horns worn by cuckolds undoubtedly caused some sniggers.[44]

So far, if one could overlook the cross-dressing and the fact that the church ale was in itself illegal, the midsummer shows sound relatively harmless. But on 18 June the proceedings were taken over by Hole's enemies, who used the Southover show to ridicule the constable and his allies.[45] The skimmington tradition was, as we have seen, particularly strong in the West Country, so it was natural for defenders of the May Games to adapt it. The Southover show needed no less than five horses. The rider of the first one carried a collection of old hats; he had, he shouted, 'as good hats to sell as Mr Yarde in his shop'. The second horse carried a scene directly reminiscent of the skimmington. A young man named Matthew Lancaster was 'disguised in women's apparel like a spinster', Hole reported, 'holding a ... spinning wheel upon the horse before him and worsted wool upon a distaff turning the said wheel'. Asked whose wool it was, he answered 'it was Hole's'. The skimmington allusion – the man in women's clothes using a spinning wheel – was an obvious slight on Hole's masculinity: only an effeminate man could object to the red-blooded male diversions of the May Games.[46] Next came a man playing a pewterer, that being the trade followed by another of Hole's puritan friends, Hugh Mead. He had a pewter pot and a skimmer at his waist, and insisted that his product was 'as good as any was in Mead's shop'. Again we have a skimmington reference, the skimming ladle, an essential part of the familiar ritual. Another local puritan, a grocer named Humphrey Palmer, was the target of the fourth skit. Two men, representing a grocer and his assistant, rode on the same horse. They had a pair of scales and a basket of grain from which they threw handfuls at the bystanders – the skimmington ritual again – announcing that Palmer 'had no such raisins in his shop as they had'. The procession ended with a scene in which two men rode facing each other on the same horse, this time with a desk and inkwell between them; one of them represented a usurer or moneylender, the other a notary. They had been asked to lend money to the haberdasher, clothier, pewterer and grocer, but were refusing to do so because the credit of the four tradesmen was not good enough, thus implying, Hole spluttered, that he and his friends were poor men and of no account in the city. But the whole show was even more offensive because it so obviously employed the familiar symbols of the skimmington: the 'husband' in women's clothes holding the distaff, the riding backwards, the skimming ladle, the scattering of grain. Political disputes were framed through gendered insults.

After supper, a short play at the church house re-enacted the scene with the moneylender. The cast of characters had changed, however, and of the five principals two were women, one of them the wife of a local gentleman named Edward Wadham – a further provocation to the puritans, who regarded the presence of women on the stage as even worse than cross-dressed boys. The procession then reformed and moved on to the High Cross, where Dean Heydon and Mayor Towse benignly presided. Mead was also there and was so enraged by the parody of his trade that he seized the pewterer's hammer and tried to pull him off his horse. Later that evening he lodged a formal complaint with the mayor. Even Towse thought that the Southover pageant went too far; he was heard to remark that 'there was knavery in it'.[47]

The next morning Hole and Mead brought several of the young men from Southover before the magistrates. The players had a powerful friend in court, however: Edward Wadham, husband of the lady who had performed in the skit the previous evening. 'They were but the shows of their street', he told the mayor, and 'he would bear them out therein, whatever it cost him'. Angry words were exchanged between Wadham and Hole, but the constable did not renew his complaint when the case was sent to the two county JPs, Rodney and Dean Heydon. Recognizing that he was not likely to get much support in that quarter, Hole referred the charges to the bishop, who was away in London.[48]

The last of the pageants, a week later, came from the Hammermen, who included carpenters and masons, as well as blacksmiths. They were based in East Wells (the modern St Thomas Street), which was outside the city boundaries but within St Cuthbert's parish. Exempt from the jurisdiction of the mayor and his officers, East Wells had a reputation for disorder and violence. The Hammermen's contribution was even more offensive than the Southover one. They did present one conventional, and for them appropriate, tableau, depicting Noah building the Ark. But the high point of their parade was the 'Holing Game', described at the beginning of this chapter. The board was that used in the game of nine holes, or marbles. As we saw, the upright was decorated with painted figures recognizably representing Hole, Mead and John Yarde's wife, and it was carried by William Gamage, riding on horseback behind the usual drummers. The streets were packed and not everyone could see the Holing Game very well, but they could all hear the exchanges between Gamage and people in the crowd as he rolled a ball towards the holes in the board. The game reflected widespread rumours that Hole was having an affair with Mrs Yarde. Such stories of hypocritical sexual misconduct were part of the standard repertoire of anti-puritan satire, and we find them in many other towns in England. True or false, the invitation to inversionary sexual punning – *Master* Hole and *Mistress* Yarde – was too good to miss. Gamage was soon enjoying a raucous dialogue with the bystanders. 'He holes it for a crown' (the Yardes lived at the sign of the Crown); 'he holes it not within a yard'; 'if you will hole it, it must be in a mead': the sexual puns were unmistakable. The chants of 'he holes (or holes not) for a crown' were repeated time after time outside the Yardes' house, and the phrase was soon reported to be 'a common proverb in the town and county'.[49]

Act III: the libel

Young Gamage was so pleased with his Holing Game that he wrote a libellous poem about it. Like the similarly defamatory verse libels discussed in Chapter 2, it was both performed and circulated in writing. It contained descriptions of each of the shows, but its main theme was the affair between Hole and Mrs Yarde. It began:

> My loving friends that love to play,
> Use not my culver holes [pigeon holes] by day,
> But in the night I hold it best,
> When all these birds are in their nest.
>> Yet do I live in quiet rest,
>> And hold my Holing Game the best.[50]

The poem was a great success. Its distribution gives a sense of the way verse libels travelled. Gamage's friends were not able to get it printed in London as they had wished, but, like other libels, it circulated widely in Somerset, sung by 'idle boys' at the grammar school, for example. It was recited by adults too, in Wells shops and at a nearby village church ale. Gamage's friend Oliver Martin regularly sang it in alehouses, to the customers' 'great delight'. When he was reproved for it by a pious visitor from Stoke St Michael, Martin angrily turned on him: 'A turd in [his teeth] and all those who took Hole's part'. These were not very elevated surroundings, but the Holing Game was also heard in the more respectable precincts of the Deanery. One day in July a local scrivener named Richard Bourne was with Heydon in the dean's study. Their conversation was disturbed by laughter in the next room, where the dean's wife and several other women (one of them Thomasine White, the erstwhile Lady of the May) were reading Gamage's verses to each other amid much hilarity.[51]

At least one other verse libel was produced by the local wits. In the absence of newspapers, such scurrilous verses, transmitted orally or in writing, were one of the most effective ways by which criticism of authority figures – clergy, local government officials and the like – could be circulated.[52] The other Wells one, 'Tell Me of Flesh', had more literary sophistication than Gamage's crude doggerel, even quoting a line from Christopher Marlowe's *Tamburlaine*. It was written by the younger William Morgan, son of the lessee of St Cuthbert's rectory, and seems to have been intended as a dramatic monologue. The poem said little about the actual content of the May shows, but it was full of satirical wordplay on the constable's hypocrisy, culminating in a slur upon his virility:

He's grown so impotent he cannot wield

His lance, nor pike, nor scarce can bear his shield.

Most of Morgan's satire was far too complex and allusive to rival Gamage's rough ribaldry in the popular repertoire, but it too circulated widely in cathedral circles.[53]

Act IV: revenge

Hole was soon out for revenge. Legal proceedings began at Somerset Assizes in August 1607, when the St Cuthbert's churchwardens were bound over for holding an illegal church ale, and several of the other perpetrators were fined. Mayor Towse was at first among those in trouble, though he managed to get out of it. Hole's enemies had him indicted for assault at the same Assizes, though he was evidently not convicted. The constable received further vindication the next year, when the Quarter Sessions renewed the prohibitions against church ales. The campaign against them was not confined to puritans; mainstream Protestant gentry shared the same dislike of popular disorder. The JPs' order was signed by Bishop Still and eleven others, one of whom was the fence-straddling Sir John Rodney.[54] But Star Chamber was the proper venue for a case involving both libel and contempt of lawful authority, and there the case dragged on until November 1609.

We should not exaggerate the extent to which puritans at this time were seen as necessarily subversive of authority, though it is probably true that Hole's religious stance did not endear him to some of the judges. Still, as constable he represented the king's government in Wells, and open contempt of law and order could not be tolerated, particularly at a time of widespread popular violence against enclosing landlords in the Midland Rising of that same year. Those riots had themselves started on May Day – another reason for anxiety about such festivities. Hole's Bill of Complaint to Star Chamber specifically noted the possible connection, stressing that the events in Wells had taken place just when there were 'great insurrections and unlawful assemblies' in Northamptonshire; and when the court began its hearings, Lord Chancellor Ellesmere, always concerned about possible threats to public order, listed it among the cases 'specially appointed to be heard this sitting day'.[55] But in the end Star Chamber was more inclined to punish Hole's lower-class enemies than it was to reprove the town elite. Gamage and the younger Morgan received the full shaming ritual, the punishment-fitting-the-crime treatment, that was common in cases of this kind. They were to ride 'two and two upon a horse … their faces one towards another' from the Fleet Prison to Westminster, where they were to stand in the pillory, with a repeat performance from the Fleet to the pillory in Cheapside. Then at Wells they were to 'ride in like manner through the chief streets in the city and be set in the pillory', in addition to paying Hole £100 damages. They were also heavily fined. Yet the corporation, several of whose members had actively encouraged the disorders, got away scot-free, with the exception of Edmond White. One clue to this leniency is a letter from the Earl of Hertford, a powerful figure both at the royal court and in the West Country, written a few days before the sentencing, to Lord Chancellor Ellesmere, who presided over the case. Hertford was careful not to condone the mocking of authority by the Wells lower orders. But he implied that Hole's conflict with the corporation was driven by his connections with Somerset's puritan gentry, who wished to undermine 'the government and authority of that town, and the magistrates there' for their own ends. The result of punishing the city fathers, Hertford pointed out, would be that 'the baser and inferior sort of people there will ever be ready to have them and their government in contempt'. The Wells authorities should be let off, so as not to hand Hertford's gentry enemies an easy triumph that might undermine his influence in Wells. Mayor Towse's son, it might be noted, was on Hertford's payroll, and the city's recorder, Thomas Southworth, was also one of his clients.[56]

Epilogue

The Earl of Hertford's letter suggests that we ought to be careful before we conclude that the 1607 May Games simply amounted to a conflict between a handful of intolerant puritans and virtually the whole of the rest of the population. The city was in fact deeply split, and even the corporation admitted that Hole had some support. In a Star Chamber counter-suit brought in retaliation for the constable's original one, they noted that 'some others of his faction' had persuaded him to refuse an offer of arbitration, and had also contributed to his legal expenses.[57] Obviously Wells contained many people who liked the traditional festivities, and saw Hole and his friends as killjoys. But if that was all there was to it, why should Hertford have worried that a Star Chamber reproof would undermine the corporation's authority? If local opinion had been virtually unanimous, it would surely have increased their popularity, making them appear the victims of an unjust sentence for standing up for

the ancient customs of the place. Hertford's anxiety suggests that a substantial number of Wellensians had no great liking for the disorderly church ale
processions (and possibly for the cathedral authorities who promoted them),
even if they had no great liking for Hole's party either. They do not appear in
the Star Chamber records because there was no particular reason why they
should. Hole wanted to create a record in which the virtuous opponents of
disorderly street festivities could show that they had been wronged by a group
of drunken youth. The defendants wanted to show that, on the contrary, they
were respectable citizens, just out to enjoy themselves, acting only 'in merriment' (their favourite phrase), and that there was trouble only because Hole
and his friends wanted to impose their version of public morality upon a city
that for centuries had managed very well without it. Neither side wanted to
muddy the waters by introducing evidence from people in the middle: those
who might be tolerant of traditional customs and even church ales, but were
not very keen on noisy drumming and roistering going on in the streets far
into the night.

The real problem in Wells, which led to the level of interest in Star Chamber,
was the way festive life was used to comment on politics. The final procession by
the Hammermen portrayed both Constable Hole and John Yarde as failed patriarchs, calling into question their ability to be good governors of the city as well
as their households. By reading events in Wells through the lens of inversion,
what becomes evident is that the reason this case generated as much interest in
Star Chamber as it did was not because it was yet another episode in the culture
wars of early modern England, but because of the ways in which familiar patterns of inversion were invoked against members of the local government. It was
the very familiarity of charivari and the image of the failed patriarch that made
the performances at the Wells May Games so effective. The familiarity of these
images also illuminates the cultural complexities of the situation. The city, the
cathedral authorities, the county governors and the rulers of the kingdom were
all divided by the culture wars. After all, the bishop was on one side, the dean
on the other, a situation that will not surprise anyone familiar with Trollope's
Barchester; the corporation and the local bench were both divided. Few of the
Somerset JPs were puritans, but they believed in law and order and prohibited
church ales for precisely that reason. Anyone could be the target of the kind of
mockery that took place in Wells. When in the 1630s Charles I and Archbishop
Laud insisted that the prohibitions should be lifted, there was widespread resentment, and in Somerset future Cavaliers were just as indignant about it as future
Roundheads.[58]

The young men of Wells were not the only ones who used the language of skimmington as a criticism of those in authority. Nor was the 1607 Midland rising the only episode of disorder in the early seventeenth century. In a series of riots in the late 1620s and early 1630s, inhabitants of forests in the west of England protested the enclosure of land by courtiers. The forests were primarily undeveloped waste land, known for mining, the production of charcoal and grazing; enclosure deprived residents of access to resources. The leader of the rioters in Gloucester's Forest of Dean in 1631–2 was John Williams, a miner, but he was known as 'Skimmington'. The three leaders of the riots in Braydon Forest called themselves 'Lady Skimmington', and dressed in women's clothes. In using the language of skimmington as part of political protest and calling themselves 'Skimmington' they invoked not only gender inversion, but the communal disapproval that a political charivari represented. Because skimmington was a widely shared tradition, the government feared that skimmington was everywhere.[59] Such political uses did not engage the debate about festive culture but show how the ritual language of festivity could be deployed in festive contexts.

The issues did not go away in Wells. Disorders during the summer festival months continued to erupt occasionally. There was dispute about taking down a maypole in Chamberlain Street in 1610, 'after the maygaming did grow out', which reveals the survival of street organizations for maintaining the old traditions. Chamberlain Street had a 'Cuckoo Lord' who took charge of such matters. Ill-governed East Wells was still the site of disorderly celebrations: there was violent affray there on Midsummer night in 1612, in which one of the participants narrowly escaped with his life.[60] Elaborate pageants, similar to those of 1607 but without the controversial elements and the charivari, were put on for the visit of Anne of Denmark, who we have seen as a notable theatrical patron in her own right, in 1613. With memories of 1607 still fresh, the corporation prudently appointed a committee to vet the companies' shows and decide 'whether they be fit or not'. This helped to ensure that they passed off without incident, even though several involved – like Anne's court masques – female performers, and were full of sexual innuendo. The fact that the entertainment was in honour of the queen, and that criticism would thus be seen as disloyal, may account for the puritans' silence.[61]

It may also be relevant that John Hole was no longer in Wells; his vacant place on the corporation was filled shortly before the queen's visit. The constable won at least part of his case in Star Chamber, but his enemies must have made his life distinctly uncomfortable. In September 1609 the St Cuthbert's churchwardens went to the ecclesiastical court and accused him of adultery with Mrs Yarde. It is not clear whether the constable had to undergo the humiliating ritual of

penance: standing in a white sheet in church before the congregation and con-
fessing his sin. But he soon left the city, and when he died in 1618 he was living
at North Cadbury, near the house of his protector Sir Francis Hastings, the most
powerful of the Somerset puritan gentry. His will shows that he had not severed
his connections with Wells: he endowed a fund for a sermon at St Cuthbert's, left
a small bequest to the cathedral and named as overseers of the will his puritan
friends, Mead and Palmer. And lest we should think of him simply as a puritan
killjoy, the will suggests that he was fond of music; he owned a pair of virginals.[62]

* * * *

What does this story tell us about gender and inversion? We can start with the
culture wars of early modern England. While these conflicts are not explicitly
about inversion, puritans mistrusted popular festivities and pastimes precisely
because of the ways their inversionary character supported social, gender and
sexual disorder. Revels, particularly dancing and maypoles, attracted young
people and challenged the familiar order. The Cheshire magistrate Sir Richard
Grosvener argued that alehouses are 'the very bane of this country; ... Here
are you deprived of the obedience of your sons, of the duty of your servants'.[63]
Popular festivities, in other words, undermined the well-governed patriarchal
household by creating an alternate centre of activity.

The culture wars in early modern England were also part of a debate on
how much play there could be in an ordered patriarchal society. Traditionalists
thought that patriarchal order could be maintained along with festive life; puritans thought order required a suppression of traditional culture. Puritans also
thought that festive life turned the world upside down, so they were willing to
use inversion to turn the world right side up. Equally, traditionalists used the
performance of inversion as part of a critique of what they saw as puritan hypocrisy. While gendered patterns of inversion were one way in which at least some
early modern English men and women thought that popular festivities undermined patriarchal authority, they were also used to point out the failures of local
leaders. Here the attention to the rumoured affair between Mistress Yarde and
Constable Hole is a classic piece of festive truth telling. But it took place within
a larger context of inversion: the young people who led the shows suggested
that Hole, Yarde, Mead and Palmer were failed patriarchs. Rather than being
on the receiving end of discipline, the performers used their tableaux to call out
misbehaviour of their superiors. The references to cuckolds, to financial insol-
vency and to skimmington remind us that failed patriarchs took many forms.

The libels put these allegations into writing, giving even more publicity to the inversionary claims of the local youth.

There was only one way to fix the disorder that the church ale had let loose: since the young men of Wells had turned the world upside down with their pageants, it had to be turned right side up. Whatever charivari the actors performed, the punishment of Gamage and young Walker re-enacted it to affirm the expected order.

An early modern community could have a strong sense of identity and yet be beset by divisions both institutional (town/cathedral) and cultural (traditional/puritan). In Wells in 1607 there were still efforts to bridge the cultural divide: Mayor Towse thought there was 'knavery' in one of the anti-puritan skits; puritans contributed money for the repair of St Cuthbert's tower while boycotting the church ale that was the main source of funding; and John Yarde was even willing to let the mayor watch a Robin Hood play from his window. The youthful architects of the most provocative charivari – the painted calf, the holing game – were not held back by any such political constraints. They were able to use the rich and shared vocabulary of popular culture that was at the heart of early modern charivari performance. While older Wellensians might not have participated in the performance, some at least supported it. The shared festive language, understood by all onlookers, is a reminder of the shared features of early modern culture. Most beliefs about the upside down world were shared. Everyone knew that unruly women and failed patriarchs were a problem. In witchcraft, another form of inversion, we also find shared assumptions joined to conflicting interpretations of actual behaviour.

5

Witches, Magicians and the
Upside Down World

In the play *The Lancashire Witches*, by Thomas Heywood and Richard Brome, when the servants in the Seely household rule their masters, and the children their parents, it is the first step on the downward path into the dark world of witchcraft. Soon the whole community is infected. 'This is quite upside down', a scandalized visitor exclaims, 'sure they are all bewitch'd'.[1] Witchcraft not only involved the use of satanic powers which turned the entire moral order upside down, but it also provided an explanation for unruly women's actions. This double inversion helps account for the ways in which the study of witchcraft resists simple explanation: witchcraft beliefs were shaped by elite demonological theory, theology, popular culture and ideas of gender; they also responded to social and economic conflicts. The traces of witchcraft beliefs which have survived illuminate these multiple contexts. But all forms of witchcraft, at least as described at the time, involve an inversion of the natural order and are shaped by assumptions about gender. The witches who are the subject of Heywood' and Brome's play add a twist to these forms of inversion: witchcraft by unruly women made other women disorderly. Here witchcraft turns the world upside down in three ways: in the alliance with the devil made by the witches, in their rebellion against authority and in the effect of witchcraft on its victims.

Belief in witchcraft and, more generally, the belief that the natural world could be manipulated by people for their own ends were near universal in the early modern period. Then as now, people generally assumed that witches were women. While popular views of witchcraft regarded the maleficent power of witches as inherent in women and inherited through the female line, elite writers on the subject were often puzzled by this presumption. As many scholars have noted, there is no apparent reason why witches should be women; though Eve's sin was offered as an explanation, sceptical voices suggested that women were not worth the Devil's attention. In his *Treatise against Witchcraft* Henry Holland had one character in the dialogue assert that witches could not be women because a witch is 'one that wittingly & willingly useth devilish arts to attain that he purposeth, & therefore women are no witches, for they have no such arts, alack, poor fools they are no seducers, but rather poor seduced souls'. While they commit crimes, the sceptic continued, they could not conjure the devil. Evoking a commonplace image of the aged as pitiable in their physical and mental frailty, or dotage, he argued that 'our poor doting old women (which are commonly called witches)' could not be compared to the powerful witches presented in the Bible, whose practices guided theological speculation on the subject.[2]

Witchcraft was part of a continuum of practices which sought to manipulate the natural world; alongside witches were a range of magical practitioners, most of them less threatening and some fairly reputable. Both elite sorcerers and village cunning folk were frequently asked to help with challenges of daily life, from finding lost goods to promoting love, enhancing fertility, or provoking impotence; they might recite spells or provide charms or potions. When things went wrong, however, these very people could be described as witches. Men were more common among the magicians and cunning folk, because they depended on books as part of their work; women dominated among the white witches. It was women who were most likely to disrupt the order of nature, usually with help from Satan or other malicious spirits. By giving power to the powerless, they overturned the social order just as they violated the natural one.[3] The link between women and witchcraft was particularly visible in the legal system: some 90 per cent of surviving English indictments for witchcraft between 1560 and 1700 are of women.[4]

Witchcraft was a criminal offense, but the related practices of magic and cunning (for healing, or finding lost goods, for instance) were widely accepted and practiced, though after 1604 they too were illegal. Dr Lambe, who was consulted by Lady Purbeck, had clients at court, but his practice had much in common with that of village cunning men and women. Conversely, non-elite practitioners were known for such magical activities as finding lost or stolen goods, inducing love, telling fortunes and identifying and countering witches. Magicians and cunning folk claimed and even advertised their skill; similarly, some people confessed to being witches, even as they denied using their powers to harm others. While legally distinct, magic and witchcraft can be seen as mirror images of each other. In the popular mind, magic and sorcery were not as directly linked with the satanic pact as witchcraft. The work of magic was seen as benign, yet even such seemingly benign activities could have malicious consequences, as Frances Howard's employment of Simon Forman to render her husband impotent suggests.[5]

The boundaries between science and magic were equally porous. The noted astrologer and mathematician John Dee practiced alchemy and held séances with angels. Simon Forman practiced medicine as well as astrology, alchemy and magic. Richard Napier, a clergyman, alchemist and astrological physician who studied with Forman, treated upwards of 60,000 patients, from all social ranks, over the course of almost forty years. Astrological physicians assumed a correspondence between microcosm and macrocosm; physicians who practiced it kept careful records so that they could refine their interpretation of horoscopes. As a result of this empirical bent, they may have been more successful than conventional physicians of the day.[6] Such practices did not, like witchcraft, turn the world upside down, but they did depend on a belief in the ability to control nature. The ordinary village cunning man or cunning woman lacked the education of such doctors, but was often employed to heal both humans and beasts. They might be used in conjunction with other healers. When Ferdinando Stanley, the Fifth Earl of Derby, was desperately ill, his family summoned two physicians from Chester; but when they arrived, a local cunning woman was also in the sick room. Mary Woods of Stratton Strawless, Norfolk, who was consulted by Frances Howard, is an example of such a cunning woman: she found lost goods, foretold the future and provided medicines. It is telling that Howard consulted both an elite practitioner and a village one.[7] In sum, belief in witchcraft and resort to magical practices crossed class lines, and those who sought out practitioners to protect them from their enemies or accomplish their own nefarious ends might employ cunning women and magicians simultaneously.

Witchcraft suspicions and prosecutions

The century between 1550 and 1650 was the great age of anxiety about witchcraft in Britain, as well as in continental Europe. Preachers like the great William Perkins thundered against it, the king had written a book about it, witches were repeatedly portrayed on the stage (*Macbeth* is the best known example) and ordinary villagers worried about it when their children or cattle were ill or when they encountered inexplicable misfortunes. Prosecutions peaked in the late sixteenth century, with a later panic, exploited if not inspired by the witchfinder Matthew Hopkins, in East Anglia in 1645–7. The theological understandings of witchcraft that informed preachers and lawyers differed from the beliefs within popular culture that informed local accusations. Witchcraft beliefs, practices, accusations and prosecutions connect to virtually all dimensions of early modern society. Yet, while witchcraft accusations are illuminated by ideas about gender, motherhood, religion, politics and social hierarchy, among others, witchcraft cannot be mapped simply on to any one of these. Ideas about witch-craft were embedded in popular literary culture and in the practices of local communities, but they were also employed in political debates. Furthermore, concepts of witchcraft were not fixed, for the learned discourse about pacts with the devil joined popular ideas about familiars, the animals who were thought to help witches carry out their work. Witchcraft thus shows us how ideas about inversion circulated among people of all social levels.[8]

The expansion of legal prosecutions for witchcraft coincided with a pro-liferation of magicians. Indeed, what might be termed the commercialization of the supernatural led to the proliferation of professionals like cunning men and women at the lower levels and respectable astrologers at the upper lev-els. The more respectable practitioners were men, but both women and men who engaged in magic might invert the gender order. At both levels there was a grey area between what society regarded as legitimate activities, such as helping to find missing articles or people, or giving advice on prospective courses of action, for example, and the illegitimate resort to more sinister magical methods. Sometimes practitioners strayed across it, often in ways that supported the inversion of the gender order, as Simon Forman appar-ently did in advising Frances Howard and Anne Turner, and John Lambe did in helping Lady Purbeck. They were asked for help on every conceivable problem – personal, pecuniary, political. Their clients came from across the entire social spectrum. This could be good business: at his peak, Forman was dealing with over a thousand customers a year, and his successors attracted at least as many, probably more. They included wealthy people who could afford high fees, so there was money in it: Forman left a fortune of £1,200 when he died in 1611.[9]

The connection between cunning men and women and magicians, on the one hand, and witchcraft, on the other, rested on the assumption that both could manipulate the natural world; and when things went wrong, those who were reputed for their skills in helping people were often accused of causing harm. When examined by a JP in 1589, Margaret Love said that she had learned how to 'unwitch' from a woman who had died twenty years earlier, and had practiced her 'trade' as 'white witch' for sixteen years. While she had helped unwitch many people over those years, she admitted that she also knew how to bewitch, but promised 'to amend and never do the like again' – a telling admission.[10] Others staunchly maintained that they had never used their knowledge for anything but good. Joan, the wife of Thomas Guppy of South Perrot, Somerset, had long been known to 'cure such as have been bewitched and was and is notoriously known to have cured many that have been hurt by such ill means as well Christian Creatures as Beasts'. When a local woman's illness – a swelling in her body – could not be cured by physicians, the frustrated doctors suggested she had been bewitched, and Guppy was accused of bewitching her. One witness described her as 'a forward neighbour'. She and her husband sued those who had attacked her on the way to the market in Crewkerne; using a familiar folk remedy against witchcraft, they wanted to scratch her to break the spell on the sick woman.[11] In 1614, Elizabeth Smith, of Codford St Mary, Wiltshire, was presented for practicing medicine without a license and for 'witchcraft, calculating of nativities [astrology], fortune telling and such like'. Though she had 'read in a book' about how to bring a 'familiar spirit' into a ring, she denied doing it, and as for medicine, 'she doth sometimes give people some kind of purgation for agues or fevers'.[12] Cunning men and women played important roles as local medical practitioners, but their practice – at least from the perspective of their neighbours – could easily slip into witchcraft, particularly when such healing involved unwitching. Some people confessed to magical powers in part because they could use their reputation as a source of material support. In casual conversation, Mary Midgeley of Heptenstall, Yorkshire, boasted that 'she did a little witching', though she claimed that Elizabeth Crosley did more.[13] The people of the Pendle Forest in Lancashire paid bribes to suspected witches and resorted to counter-witching to avoid harm.[14]

As imagined by theologians and demonologists, both witches and magicians were able to do things that should not happen in nature; indeed, it was the very unnatural quality of an event that marked it as caused by witchcraft or magic. Elite theories of witchcraft assumed that witches did everything backwards, adapting the spirit of festive misrule that prevailed in carnival and giving it a demonic new twist. Their practices, including riding on broomsticks (an allegation that was rare in English witchcraft accusations), obscene satanic rituals which parodied those of the familiar religious ones and alliance with the devil, were signs that witches were a serious threat to the divinely ordained moral order. The explicit pact between the witch and the devil was 'the natural inversion of the biblical covenant between God and the Christian believer'. The *believer*, we should note: in the eyes of many people, witches were not true believers. Joan Flower, strongly suspected of being a witch and the mother of two more, was observed by neighbours to be 'full of oaths, curses, and imprecations irreligious, and for anything they saw by her, a plain Atheist'.[15]

The history of witchcraft is difficult to reconstruct both because beliefs changed in the ongoing dialogue between elite and popular culture, and because there were multiple local variations in belief and practice. The persecution of witches in Europe became more common in the fifteenth century, as the church turned its attention from heretics to witches; theological views began to define long-standing magical practices as a problem. Late medieval ideas were summarized in the *Malleus Maleficarum*, a theological treatise published in 1487, which served as a guide for secular authorities on how to try witches. The Reformation did not change the fundamental theological ideas about witchcraft, though witchcraft became a focus of significant concern later in England than elsewhere in Europe. The English treatises on witchcraft that appeared from the late sixteenth century onward emphasized Satan's ability to tempt humans to forsake God, putting a pact with the devil at the centre of witchcraft.[16] The documents we have – pamphlet accounts, ballads, plays and court records – sit at the intersection of elite theories and popular beliefs, but each gradually adopted elements from the other. The surviving pamphlets and legal records show changes in both language and thinking over the course of the sixteenth and seventeenth centuries. These shifts reflect the fact that a broader range of offences was subject to prosecution after 1604, but to a greater degree they register changing ideas. Elite demonology was more concerned with the satanic pact, while the witch's familiar, the animal who helped her do her work, was a creature of English popular culture. Theologians writing on witchcraft gradually accommodated the familiar, while from the early seventeenth century popular understandings of witchcraft incorporated the pact with Satan. However, the popular distinction between good witches and bad witches was never successfully challenged by the theological view that any and all forms of witchcraft were necessarily evil; the practices of 'good witches' and cunning folk were too close to those of physicians to allow a clear line to be drawn. The test of swimming a witch – where she was submerged in water, and judged guilty if she floated – was a continental import in the early seventeenth century that rapidly became a staple of popular practice. Indeed, as elite scepticism hampered legal prosecutions later in the seventeenth century, the swimming of the witch became a popular informal punishment for suspected witches.[17]

Our knowledge of witchcraft is largely shaped by the legal system in which it was defined and prosecuted. Witchcraft had, until the mid-sixteenth century, been policed by the church courts; even after there were criminal penalties available, accusations of witchcraft often came to the church courts rather than the criminal ones. The first statute against it, passed in 1542, targeted all 'invocations and conjurations of spirits' that were used either to 'get knowledge for their own lucre' or 'to the destruction to their neighbours persons and goods'. In addition to conjurations, it forbade the making of 'images and pictures' that give 'faith & credit to such fantastical practices'. Anyone who engaged in such practices was to be henceforth guilty of felony, and therefore subject to execution and forfeiture of all property. It does not appear that the statute was much used, and it was repealed within six years, perhaps because it made no distinction between different types of magical activity.[18] The next statute, passed in 1563, was narrower, and it focused not on the satanic compact of demonological theory, but on the harm done. It made it a felony punishable by death to cause death by witchcraft, but lesser harms resulted in imprisonment for the first offence, and execution for a later one. The statute also criminalized using magic to find treasure or lost or stolen goods and to 'provoke any person to unlawful love', offenses punishable by imprisonment. The only addition through the remainder of Elizabeth's reign was a provision in a 1581 statute against sedition, which outlawed consulting a witch to determine the time of the queen's death. The 1563 statute was expanded in 1604, most likely under the influence of James I, who had written a treatise on the subject and prosecuted witches in Scotland. The 1604 statute extended the death penalty to those guilty of wasting people or goods by means of witchcraft; it also made it a felony to 'entertain employ feed or reward any evil and wicked Spirit' or to use a corpse for purposes of conjuring. The 1604 statute thus moved away from the exclusive focus on the *maleficium*, or harm, done by the witch, and attempted to criminalize *being* a witch. Yet, while the 1604 statute widened the possible grounds for punishment, in practice it seems to have changed little about witchcraft prosecution. There were ongoing legal debates about the nature of evidence and proof in witchcraft cases.[19]

Witchcraft and its prosecution have received more attention from historians than the work of cunning folk because they have left records both in the courts and in a variety of pamphlets, ballads and plays which described events, trials, confessions and executions. England executed far fewer witches than many continental countries. The difference was sufficiently noticeable that Thomas Platter even alleged (wrongly) that they were not punished with death. The total number of executions for witchcraft in England during the whole period was well below 1,000, and possibly not much more than half that number. While suspicions of witchcraft were common, actual trials and executions were not. For the southeast counties, for which the best records survive, less than half of those indicted were convicted, and only half of those 104 witches, or only 22 per cent of those indicted, were hanged, a rate that works out to one a year across all of south-eastern England. Whatever the statute, witchcraft was very hard to prove in court. While belief in witchcraft was almost universal, individual accusations were often met with scepticism. Even King James, who had no doubts about the existence of witchcraft, would question it in particular cases.[20]

Witchcraft and social change

One of the most influential interpretations of witchcraft has argued that witchcraft was embedded in the social polarization of early modern society. In the classic case, an old woman had come and requested some kind of help and been refused; she went away mumbling, and when some misfortune occurred she was blamed for the misfortune. The accusation was thus a projection of the victim's guilt for refusing charity.[21] The catalogue of complaints brought against Katherine Brand of Ketteringham, Norfolk, in the 1590s is typical of such cases. Soon after Brand asked Margaret Pell for three eggs and was refused, Pell was tempted (temptations she resisted) to throw her child into a well and to kill her mother; when Brand and another suspected witch were brought before Sergeant Flowerdew by Francis Kett, he was seized with pain, and could not follow through; Margaret Chambers's final illness began after 'earnest speeches' with Brand, and she always blamed Brand for her illness; Philip Bese 'could not in conscience' do something Brand requested, and within a week he had hanged himself, to which Brand reportedly said 'she cared not & though there were twenty more of them hanged'.[22] This social dynamic is certainly visible in many cases, but tensions over charity were not the only ones expressed by witchcraft cases. Prosecutions and cultural representations of witches reveal tensions over other issues as well: How could women carry out their roles in the family and community? What kind of political power did they have? What were the expectations of age?[23] But these social tensions do not explain witchcraft itself; they explain only why certain accusations came to the attention of authorities. In many surviving cases, there was a long history of suspicion that an individual was a witch before she was formally accused. More people were suspected of witchcraft than were actually charged with it.

Witches were understood to be rebelling not only against God, but also against their social subordination by trying to control their own or their neighbours' lives, revenging themselves for the deprivations and oppressions that were normally women's lot. Equally, any woman who was thought to be 'maliciously disposed' towards her neighbours could be accused of witchcraft to bolster complaints against her or her husband.[24] The typical witch had all the features of the scolding woman, and so was often consigned to the cucking-stool by exasperated local magistrates, but with a much more sinister character. The 'chief fault' of witches 'is that they are scolds', suggested the sceptical Elizabethan writer on witchcraft, Reginald Scot.[25] Elizabeth Busher of Henton, Somerset, made this link between a troublesome woman and a witch visible. In 1612 her neighbours complained to the justices about her, because she had not only borne several illegitimate children but was 'the suspected maintainer of incontinency in her own house, the continual disturber of her neighbours quietness and threatening mischief against them'. At the same time, she was also 'reputed and feared to be a dangerous witch through the untimely Death of men, women and children, which she hath hated, threatened and handled'.[26]

Allegations that the accused had resorted to improper supernatural assistance were often used to bolster other stories of criminal behaviour, particularly in marital cases, where the possible use of illicit potions to inflame or inhibit sexual desire had an alluring plausibility. In a Star Chamber case brought by Richard Davy of Hemsworth, Dorset, the plaintiff claimed that the family of Joan Kellett, a clergyman's widow whom he had expected to marry, successfully used 'enchanted potions and drinks' to divert her affection to their own candidate, William Cumber.[27] The Suffolk lawyer Lionel Edgar, involved in a dispute over a piece of land, accused his enemies of resorting to conjurors and magicians, who raised up spirits and devils to terrify him; they also used fireworks for the same purpose.[28] Sometimes the attempt to obtain magical assistance was even more sinister. Nicholas Humphrey of Wimborne Minster allegedly tried to poison his brother so that he could inherit the whole family estate, and when this plan failed, he went to a 'witch or cunning woman' who (unsuccessfully, it appears) uttered mysterious incantations against the victim.[29]

Just as we need to remember the context of witchcraft accusations, it is important to remember that not all those who were suspected of sexual misconduct or verbal aggression were accused of witchcraft. Women were not accused of witchcraft just because they scolded; instead, they had to exhibit other disruptive behaviours. The puritan magistrates of Dorchester were convinced that self-assertive women were a threat to the peaceful godly community that they were trying to create, sending scolds to the cucking-stool with monotonous regularity. Given that the two most witch-conscious parts of the English-speaking world (at least if we go by the frequency of prosecutions) were the notably puritan regions of Essex and New England, we might have expected the Dorchester authorities to be similarly vigilant about witches. Yet in the 1630s (the decade

Figure 7. A cunning woman, linking magical practices with gendered inversion: 'The brideling, sadling and ryding, of a rich churle in Hampshire, by the subtill practise of one Iudeth Philips, a professed cunning woman'. RB 62881, The Huntington Library, San Marino, California.

for which we have detailed records), whenever Dorchester people denounced others as witches, it was invariably the accuser rather than the accused who was taken before the magistrates and given a stern warning not to cause divisions in the town by making such allegations.[30] The attitude of the municipal elite can be explained by two things: first, these incidents occurred in the 1630s, when official opinion was more cautious about the evidence in witchcraft cases and prosecutions were nationally at their lowest level during the entire 1550–1660 period; and second, the fact that the town's powerful preacher, John White, who set Dorchester's moral tone, did not apparently dwell much on the prevalence of witchcraft in his teachings.[31] The practice of Dorchester governors is a useful reminder of the choices that could be made in response to accusations of witchcraft. Even when the world was turned upside down, both those who saw it and local authorities had choices about how they could respond.

Still, for much of the period in which we are interested, most people, including most educated people from the king on down, *did* believe in witchcraft. James wrote one of the most influential works on the subject, *Daemonologia*, first published in 1597. The book was the result of anxieties awakened by a recent plot against him which involved the use of witchcraft. The connection between treason and witchcraft was often noted, as both resulted from a rejection of proper authority: of divinely ordained monarchy in the one case, of the natural hierarchy ordained by God in the other. The biblical text associating rebellion with 'the sin of witchcraft' was widely quoted. Yet James's own behaviour reminds us that belief in witchcraft in general was perfectly compatible with scepticism about particular cases. From quite early in his reign in his southern kingdom, James seems to have been more cautious about invoking the power of the state to deal with witches and more sceptical about evidence against them than he had been in Scotland. When seditious intent was absent, James was inclined to take a critical look at the evidence presented against accused witches, and to require courts to follow due process. On multiple occasions he intervened to ensure that witches received fair trials, and in 1616, judges who had hanged nine witches at Leicester – accused by a young boy whose evidence James determined to be fraudulent – were described as 'in disgrace'. He took a distinctly sceptical stand in a prominent English case concerning the alleged bewitching of Anne Gunter. James was unwilling to prosecute witches on anything less than the most secure evidence, but he never denied the existence of witchcraft itself. The expanded definition of witchcraft in the 1604 statute, and the severe punishments it included, reflected his views. The tension between James's beliefs in general and his practice in particular cases is better documented than most, but it is not unique.[32]

Several of the most famous cases of witchcraft in the period featured spectacular evidence of demonic possession. In such cases, there were two kinds of inversion: the use of demonic power to harm the person; and the symptoms of possession, where a young woman (or, less often, a boy or young man) behaved out of character in striking ways thought to typify the effects of bewitchment. The first of these cases, which served as the template for later ones, took place at the home of Robert Throckmorton, in Warboys, Huntingdonshire, from 1589 to 1593. Over the course of four years, five of Throckmorton's children were taken by signs of possession that worsened when their neighbour Alice Samuel was present.

Sometimes they fell into in a trance, but they often shouted and described creatures that were tormenting them. For instance, the first daughter to be bewitched, Jane,

> would sneeze very loud and thick for the space of half an hour together, and presently as one in a great trance and swoon lay quietly as long: soon after she would begin to swell and heave up her belly so a none was able to bend her, or keep her down: sometime she would shake one leg and no other part of her, as if the palsie had been in it.

In addition, Alice Samuel was accused of bewitching Lady Susan Cromwell, a neighbour who had visited the afflicted family in 1590; she died, allegedly from witchcraft, in 1592. In 1593, Alice Samuel, as well as her husband and daughter, were charged with witchcraft and executed, which effected the immediate recovery of the Throckmorton children. The pamphlet recounting the story, vouched for by the judge in the case, provided a detailed account of possession.[33] In later possession cases, many of the behaviours reported mirrored those of the Throckmorton children.

Cases of possession usually involved women as the accused, and young women as the possessed. In 1602, London was abuzz with the case of Mary Glover, the daughter of a London shopkeeper, who claimed to have been bewitched by Elizabeth Jackson, an older woman. Glover found herself unable to swallow and sometime blind and dumb; in the days that followed, she was at times unconscious, at other times writhing uncontrollably. Yet the case demonstrates disagreements about how to interpret such behaviour. When Jackson was tried as a witch, doctors testified both for and against her. Jackson was found guilty and imprisoned, and Glover was eventually cured by an exorcism which involved both prayer and fasting. Even more important than the legal outcome, however, was its outcome in the medical literature. One of the doctors who testified on Jackson's behalf was Edward Jorden, who argued that Glover's disease was natural. He then published a treatise, *A Briefe Discourse of a Disease called the Suffocation of the Mother*, which described hysteria. Hysteria was a particularly female disease, which connected the brain and the uterus; Jorden suggested that the source of hysteria was in the blockage of the uterus, or mother. While it was generally caused by either 'the want of due and monthly evacuation, or the want of the benefit of marriage', Jorden argued that it could be caused by external factors and 'the perturbations of the mind'.[34] The cure, in general, was marriage, as sexual activity would open the womb. Jorden saw it as a natural disease and argued it should not be attributed to witchcraft.

The ways possession enabled young women to engage in 'licensed misbehavior' are even clearer in cases that were determined to be in some way fraudulent, or at least not a result of witchcraft. Two of these involved young women of well-connected families, who thus received extensive attention. The case of Anne Gunter in 1605 is especially interesting because it engaged leading intellectuals, churchmen and the king as both supporters of Gunter and sceptics about her claim. In a world based on appearances, it could be difficult to decide what was 'true'. Before the allegations of possession, there were quarrels between Gunter's father Brian, a wealthy gentleman recently settled in the village of North Moreton, Berkshire (now Oxfordshire), and long-established villagers. Gunter held the Rectory of North Moreton, which meant he collected the tithes and paid a vicar to carry out the work of the church; he also owned tithes in several other parishes, so he made money not from farming his own lands but from 'creaming off wealth from local farmers'.[35] There had been a fight at a football match in 1598, in which two men died after being assaulted by Gunter. An attempt by the victims' friends and relatives to have Gunter charged at the Assizes came to nothing, but it angered him so much that he sought revenge. So in 1604, when his daughter, Anne, fell into spasmodic fits, he announced that this was the result of witchcraft being practiced by women of the village against his family. Anne quickly achieved local fame by regularly spitting or vomiting pins and showing other symptoms of bewitchment, attracting spectators from miles around to her performances. In 1605 the alleged witches were brought to trial at Abingdon Assizes. After an eventful trial, in which Anne Gunter dramatically failed to demonstrate these or any other symptoms of her bewitchment, they were acquitted.[36]

Those who supported the accusations of witchcraft and those who doubted them were all members of the elite; neither credulity nor scepticism was universal. Anne Gunter's sister had married the eminent Oxford theologian, Thomas Holland, Regius Professor of Divinity and Rector of Exeter College. This connection gave Anne, and more importantly her father, access to an impressive number of university dons who witnessed Anne's fits, either at North Moreton or when she moved into Holland's rooms at college, and were willing to testify that she was the victim of witchcraft. These supporters included Bartholemew Warner (Regius Professor of Medicine), John Prideaux (who was to be Holland's successor as rector of Exeter and Regius Professor, as well as a future vice-chancellor and a bishop), Thomas Winniffe (another future bishop), and an assortment of lesser-known divines and medical men. For many of them, Anne Gunter seems to have been simply a convenient case study, though they all started from the assumption that witchcraft was a widely occurring phenomenon.[37]

Other members of the educated elite, including Oxford undergraduates, became suspicious of the genuineness of Anne's fits. And rightly so, because it later emerged that the whole affair was an elaborate deception orchestrated by her father, who used printed accounts of earlier witchcraft cases to coach his daughter to exhibit symptoms that would get his North Moreton neighbours into serious trouble. The first to be suspicious was Thomas Hinton, a Wiltshire gentleman and distant kinsman of the Gunters, who had originally come to North Moreton out of concern for a relative after he heard of her apparent afflictions. Having started with an open mind, he soon caught Anne out in several deceptions and played an important part in securing the acquittal of the alleged witches in the subsequent trial at Abingdon Assizes.[38] A number of Oxford students later admitted that they saw some of her sleights of hand. Three members of the Royal College of Physicians who had been asked to investigate the case came to the same conclusion, and although their report was completed only after the trial had ended, the conduct of both the judges and the Assize jury (an unusually socially prominent one) showed that they shared similar scepticism. Here, as in other cases, they believed in the reality of demonic possession, but demanded persuasive evidence in a particular case. So did the Bishop of Salisbury and his chancellor, who conducted further tests on Anne after the trial, in the process showing an almost total incredulity about her claims.[39] So did James I after Anne Gunter's father foolishly presented her to the king when he visited Oxford in August 1605. James handed her over to the Archbishop of Canterbury, Richard Bancroft, a known sceptic as to witchcraft, and he initiated the investigations which led to Anne's confession that her performances had been orchestrated by her father. Brian Gunter was brought to trial in Star Chamber in 1606 for fraud and perversion of justice.[40]

Anne Gunter's illness was initially diagnosed as 'the mother', the same illness which Edward Jorden diagnosed in Mary Glover. When the deception was finally revealed, she admitted that after her initial fit, her father had trained her to have fits and to accuse women from families he was at odds with. The symptoms she displayed were modelled on those displayed by the Throckmorton children, and the family owned a copy of *The Witches of Warboys*. Her alleged possession gave her great freedom, however, and even as she complied with her father's instructions she might well have enjoyed taking liberties with others while acting as if she were possessed. While she was in Oxford, Frances Stewart, the son of the Earl of Murray, met her; later, when he was examined in court, he described how she would 'untie her own garters though they were tied of many knots, and would throw off her shoes though the shoestrings were tied, and sometimes she would untie this examinants garters and closely convey them away, pretending that the witch had conveyed them away'. Stewart and his friends 'well perceived the sleight whereby she did untie her own garters', but a well-born young woman would never have been able to untie her garter in public – or that of a marriageable man – without the excuse of possession. Students would hold her around her waist, and she would sit on their laps – another familiarity that would otherwise have been unthinkable.[41]

The case of Anne Gunter clearly could fit into the general picture of seventeenth-century witchcraft as an expression of social tensions. According to Brian Gunter, the village women revenged themselves for his murderous violence at the football match by bewitching his daughter, thus stepping outside of their divinely assigned roles as docile, obedient females in an inversionary scheme concocted, as usual, by the devil. In fact they had done no such thing, but Gunter's chosen strategy used familiar ideas of a world turned upside down by women in league with evil. But Gunter's own actions were equally those of a failed patriarch. Instead of being content with turning things right side up, as he would have done if he had genuinely believed that this was a case of witchcraft, he went further and turned the world upside down by coaching his daughter in her fraudulent fits and by perverting the course of justice. From the king and archbishop downwards, members of the elite who intervened in the case or took part in the trials, both, of the alleged witches and of Brian Gunter, exhibited an ambivalent attitude toward witchcraft; they believed that it was a crime worthy of investigation but were sceptical when the evidence turned out to be uncertain. That attitude was becoming increasingly common, at least among the elite, in the early seventeenth century. It is interesting to discover that Anne Gunter's eventual confession, according to one account, was obtained by methods that took full advantage of the lack of sexual self-control that so often, it was believed, led women into inversionary behaviour. During her weeks under Bancroft's care, she was approached by a good-looking young page in the archbishop's household who worked on her desire for affection to the point where she pursued him, in James I's words, 'most importunately and immodestly'. He was then able to extract the whole story of her father's deception from her and pass it on to the authorities.[42] While Anne Gunter may have been the star of the show, it was her father who was held responsible: he had not just failed to maintain an orderly household, he had actively created one that disturbed local order.

The first sign of possession for Edward Fairfax's daughter Helen in 1621, as with Anne Gunter, was a fit which was first thought to be the mother. In one of her early fits, she reported seeing 'a young gentleman, very brave', who told her 'he came to be a suitor unto her, if she were minded to marry'; this figure forbade her to speak God's name, and she quickly decided he was the devil. Ultimately not only Helen, but Fairfax's younger daughter Elizabeth, and Maud Jeffray, the daughter of a neighbour, were also possessed. Like Anne Gunter, Helen Fairfax and her companions engaged in behaviour that would otherwise have been unacceptable, on one occasion 'bunching' or kicking the witches. Fairfax's account of his family's sufferings, however, records that the family discussed resorting to a cunning man to use counter-magic against the witches, although they eventually rejected this option in favour of a pious reliance on God's providence and the legal system. The case was brought to the Assizes, but there it turned out that Jeffray was performing her possession at her father's behest, so the witches – who also had a certificate from neighbours that they were of 'good fame' – were released. Fairfax wrote his account of the case to defend his daughters and himself from charges of fraud. His older daughter, who was 21, was 'educated only in my own house, and therefore not knowing much', but her 'speeches in trances are far above their capacities'; the younger daughter was only 'an infant of scarce seven years'. His implication was clear: his virtuous and innocent daughters behaved and spoke in ways they could not have otherwise known. The visions they described ranged from the more or less ordinary ones to one in which a baby was nursing on the girl's breast, so that her 'heart's blood was sucked out'.[43] Fairfax described multiple ways in which the world was upside down: not only were his daughters bewitched, but the witches refused to admit their responsibility, and he and his daughters were not believed. To this was added the ways in which possession led his daughters to step out of their expected behaviour and patterns of speech. Fairfax is best known as a scholar and translator, but his account of his daughters' experience shows that he not only believed in witchcraft, but continued to believe that his own daughters were bewitched.

In these cases of possession, whether real or fraudulent, fathers took the lead in pursuing the alleged culprits. In this, they were acting as good fathers.

Yet on some level they had already failed, because they had not protected their children from the witches. The need to prosecute the witches marked, in some ways, patriarchal failure. It is most obvious in the Gunter's case, where Brian Gunter's lack of self-restraint after the 1598 football match had provoked the enmity that followed; Elizabeth Gregory, the main target of his accusations in 1604, was related to two of the men who had been killed. Edward Fairfax, who was adamant that his daughters were *not* feigning possession, was careful to recount all the steps he had taken to care for them. Indeed, in following cases of witchcraft, we repeatedly find multiple layers of inversion. The witch turned the world upside down not only through her alliance with Satan, but also by undermining normal rules of behaviour. When, as was generally the case, the witch was from a more humble background than the victim, she had also inverted the social order, just as women claiming power through witchcraft challenged the gender order. These multifold inversions can become dizzying, but the instability created by those interlocking challenges to order explains the power of witchcraft over the social imagination of early modern England.

Playing witchcraft

Much of our surviving knowledge of witchcraft comes not from formal legal records, which are sparse for the period before 1640, but from popular literature. Some of the prosecutions of Essex witches in the sixteenth century, for instance, were reported in a series of pamphlets that provides considerable detail on the social contexts of village witchcraft.[44] The Warboys case was recorded in a published pamphlet, which proved quite influential. A similar pamphlet described the prosecution of a large group of witches in Lancashire in 1612. There were three pamphlets about the Mary Glover case.[45] Our ability to tell stories about witches, and not just count prosecutions, is shaped by publishers' marketing decisions. These have provided historians with rich tales and images, but their powerful narratives represent a distinct interpretation of events. These pamphlets demonstrate the kinds of stories that were thought to be plausible about witches and highlight the widespread interest in them; but they never tell the whole story.

The best known dramatic witches today are Shakespeare's witches in *Macbeth*. These witches, who prophesy like the Delphic oracle, seem distant from most English witches: on stage, the witches foretell, and they only report the kinds of activities usually associated with witches. They have supernatural knowledge, and the contents of the cauldron reflect beliefs about the witches Sabbath, but any *maleficium* by the witches is off stage, and the bad things are done by people.[46] Two other plays, however, are based on contemporary witchcraft cases. *The Witch of Edmonton*, a 1621 play by Dekker, Ford and Rowley, was loosely based on a case described by Henry Goodcole in a pamphlet that same year. In his preface, 'Apologies to the Christian Readers', Goodcole describes the numerous ballads written in the subject as 'base and false'. His criticisms suggest the place of witchcraft in the popular imagination: 'I was ashamed to see and hear such ridiculous fictions of her bewitching Corn on the ground, of a Ferret and an Owl daily sporting before her, of the bewitched woman braining herself, of the Spirits attending in the Prison: all which I knew to be fitter for an Ale-bench then for a relation of proceeding in Court of Justice'.[47] The second play, Heywood and Brome's *The Witches of Lancashire*, performed in 1634, was based on a case which, at the time the play was performed, had resulted in convictions of several women for witchcraft, but was currently under reconsideration by the Privy Council.

The Witch of Edmonton is a dark play; as in the revenge tragedies discussed in Chapter 3, the viewer watches people caught up in a world they cannot control. The play has two plots that function largely in parallel. The witch of the title, Elizabeth Sawyer, matches all the criteria of the stereotype: she is old, poor and at odds with her neighbours. She curses them and harms the crops and animals of Old Banks. But the tragedy of the play is not a result of her action. At its centre is the story of Frank Thorney, who at the beginning of the play has secretly married Winifred, with the assistance and encouragement of his master Sir Arthur. Winifred, it emerges, had been Sir Arthur's mistress, but after her wedding she will no longer have anything to do with him. Frank and Winifred do not enjoy their marriage for long, as Frank is summoned to his father; in order to rescue the family fortunes a marriage has been arranged for Frank with Old Carter's daughter Susan. As we know from the revenge tragedies, secret marriages never turn out well. Having married secretly, Frank finds it impossible to resist this second, bigamous marriage. Both marriages reflect patriarchal failure by men who should have had his interests at heart. Frank says as much to Winifred when escaping from his marriage to Susan (ostensibly by travel, in fact by murdering her). 'He would not bless, nor look a father on me, / Until I satisfied his angry will. / When I was sold, I sold myself again'[48]. Frank's guilt for Susan's murder is eventually discovered; at the same time, his prior marriage to Winifred is acknowledged by all. As Frank is led off to his execution, Sir Arthur is commanded by the justices to provide 1,000 marks (a considerable sum) for Winifred's support, as a penalty for his role in starting the disastrous train of events.

And what of the witch? She was not involved in Susan's murder, though some of her neighbours accuse her of responsibility. She is a poor old woman who is abused and hated by her neighbours, and who responds with curses. The dog that serves as her familiar notes that he cannot kill, but can harm; many of his actions suggest mischief more than hurt. Sawyer wishes harm on Old Banks, who ends up kissing his cow's behind, and on Ann Ratcliffe, who goes mad and beats out her brains; but she is accused of *all* the harms that happen to anyone in the village. When neighbours (including Old Banks) accused her of witchcraft before a justice, he first mocked them for using the folk divining method of setting fire to some of the thatch from her house: 'Unless your proofs come better armed/ Instead of turning her into a witch, / You'll prove yourselves stark fools'. She denies she is a witch, but ties witchcraft to social inequality, as she remarks that for every old woman who was daily, like her, 'trod on thus by slaves, reviled, kicked, beaten', the only hope for revenge was witchcraft. She even argues with the justice that the true witches are the unruly women at court and in the city, 'painted things in princes courts / Upon whose eyelids lust sits blowing fires / To burn men's souls in sensual hot desires'; and lawyers 'whose honeyed hopes the credulous client draws'.[49] She posits a moral universe where the witches are not beleaguered poor women like herself, but those whose sins involve the exploitation of others. In responding to those who abuse her, she, like Frank, seems pushed into action by a lack of alternatives; after Ann Ratcliffe's death, her death is the expected punishment, and she precedes Frank on the way to the gallows. Even while offering a critique of witch accusations, *The Witch of Edmonton* underlines the powerful association between witchcraft and an upside down world. The failed patriarchs whose actions led to Frank's bigamy are parallel to the villagers who abuse Sawyer. Her argument with the justice articulates an alternative moral universe, suggesting that the current society is upside down. The failure of good government, in family and community, traps people into evil that they cannot escape.

The Lancashire witch case of the early 1630s provided dramatic copy: a young boy, Edmund Robinson, reported that he had seen a witches Sabbath, and he was then taken around the churches of Lancashire pointing out the witches. Some twenty appear to have been charged and condemned at the Lancashire Assizes in spring 1634, but the judges sent the women first to the Bishop of Chester for additional interrogations, and then four, along with Robinson, were sent to London to be examined by the Privy Council. Robinson ultimately confessed that the story of the witches Sabbath that had started the whole thing was 'false and feigned, and has no truth at all, but only as he has heard tales and reports made by women'. He made up the story because he had been sent to fetch the cattle, but instead 'went to play with other children'.[50] The play was only one representation of the case at the time; there was a puppet show in Oxford, and the multiple manuscript accounts of the case attest to the widespread public interest.[51]

The play, while it presents the prosecution's account of the case, presents the witches more as tricksters than doers of harm. Moreover, it is obsessed with the inversionary nature of witchcraft. It starts with a group of young gentlemen out hunting, who find that the hare disappears right before it is caught.[52] But soon there are more obvious signs of witchcraft: the household of one Seely, a gentleman, 'a man respected / For his discretion and known gravity / As master of a govern'd family', is all 'now turn'd topsy-turvy'.[53]

> The good man
> In all obedience kneels unto his son;
> He with an austere brow, commands his father.
> The wife presumes not in the daughter's sight
> Without a prepar'd curtsy. The girl she
> Expects it as a duty, chides her mother,
> Who quakes and trembles at each word she speaks.
> And, what's as strange, the maid she domineers
> O'er her young mistress who is aw'd by her.
> The son to whom the father creeps and bends
> Stands in as much fear of the groom his man.
> All that in such rare disorder that, in some
> As it breeds pity and in others wonder,
> So in the most part laughter.[54]

There were multiple inversions here, of gender, age and status. The only explanation is that this upside-down situation is the result of witchcraft. Yet Master Generous doubts it: 'For my belief is no such thing can be'. Needless to say, as the play progresses, it turns out that not only is Seely's household bewitched, but Master Generous's wife is one of the witches. The witches are proud of their 'feat' at the Seely household:

> The father to the son doth cry
> The son rebukes the father old,
> The daughter at the mother scold,
> The wife the husband check and chide.[55]

Seely and his wife Joan act as 'steward and cook' for the wedding feast for their servants, Lawrence and Parnell, but when the wedding bells ring, Joan remarks that 'They ring them backwards'.[56] When the wedding feast is served, the food is transformed into inedible things: the cake falls apart and turns into bran, the leg of mutton first is cold, and then turns into a ram's horn, and pie is opened and birds fly out. The ram's horn is a sign that the new husband is destined to be a cuckold and a failed patriarch. But one of the guests, Doughty, sees the truth: 'Witches, live witches! The house is full of witches!'.[57] As the play continues, there are more signs of witchcraft: the newlyweds come to blows because Lawrence is impotent, though Parnell notes that this was not the case before the wedding! 'What he were when he were a bachelor, I know better than the best maid i'th'town'. The neighbourhood stages a skimmington to mock them, but Doughty realizes that 'the poor fellow is bewitched' . When the skimmington procession enters, however, Parnell and Lawrence are united in attacking it; they pull Skimmington and Skimmington's wife off the horse and beat them, and Lawrence claims that he beat Skimmington's wife 'with her own ladle'.[58]

Meanwhile, the Generous household is equally upside down. Mistress Generous, her husband discovers, has been riding out at night several nights a week to join the witches' feasts. He forbids the groom to allow her to ride the horse. At the same time, he asks his groom to go to Lancaster to replenish his supply of wine. He and his groom Robert happily reminisce about a great wine they had enjoyed in London, and regret that Robert will be unable to get such good wine in Lancaster. Robert is happy to go on this errand, however, knowing that he can visit his sweetheart, Moll, on the way. Moll, it turns out, is another of the witches. She manages to transport him to London to fill up his bottles with the best wine, and still get him back in eight hours, with an interlude of love-making along the way. But when Robert refuses to bridle the horse for his mistress at night, she turns him into a horse and rides him to the Sabbath. He breaks away, and manages to bridle his mistress for the ride back. She promises her husband that she will turn away from witchcraft, but does not. Witchcraft is not allowed to flourish unremarked, however. A boy who was taken against his will to the witches' feast identifies them to Doughty, who begins to take them into custody. At the same time, a soldier who had taken over the local mill fights with the imps who have tortured him, and cuts off Mistress Generous's hand, thus identifying her as a witch. As soon as all the witches are in custody, life returns to normal. While the play suggests that the witches will meet their death at the Assizes, the Epilogue also suggests that 'while the witches must

expect their due / By lawful justice ... Perhaps great mercy may / After condemnation give them day / of longer life'.[59] The play would not work if the real
outcome were included.

While the events described in the play are fantastical, they illuminate the
role of witchcraft in the popular imagination. This is a topsy-turvy world, where
bewitching turns the household order upside down, but witchcraft is also enabled by a failure of patriarchal government: Master Generous has not, it turns
out, ensured his wife's good behaviour. Yet Master Generous's predicament also
reflects on the general problem of failed patriarchs: they are expected to control
a wife who is, in fact, an independent person.

Sorcery and aristocratic scandal

The Privy Council's engagement with the 1634 Lancaster witches case is a
reminder that fascination with witchcraft extended far beyond the lower orders.
Aristocrats, like everyone else, were vulnerable to local witches: in 1619, the
children of Francis Manners, the Earl of Rutland, were bewitched, and one of
them died. Two sisters, Margaret and Philippa Flowers, and their mother Joan,
were accused of the crime. Joan had received relief from the earl's household at
Belvoir, then the sisters were hired as charwomen, with Margaret 'a continual
dweller' there. However, they were fired when it was discovered that Margaret
was stealing food from the castle, 'provision as they thought was unbefitting
for a servant to purloin', presumably food that was rarely part of the diets of
the poor. The young women allegedly turned to witchcraft to support themselves, as their mother, a 'monstrous malicious woman, full of oaths, curses, and
imprecations', was already suspected as a witch. First several of Rutland's cattle
died; then Rutland and his wife began to suffer mysterious illnesses; then the
children fell ill, and the oldest son, Henry Lord Roos, died. Rutland had the case
investigated by local JPs, though since he was one of them, the panel was hardly
neutral. When the three suspects were being carried to Lincoln Jail, Joan Flower
asked for bread and butter, and 'wished it might never go through her if she were
guilty'; she ate a little, then fell down and died. After a trial at Lincoln Assizes,
Margaret and Philippa were duly executed.[60]

More often, elite engagement with witchcraft was not with such 'ordinary
witchcraft'. Instead, witchcraft and the supernatural were central to many of
the aristocratic scandals of the period. Its traces in the Essex nullity and the
Overbury murder scandals of 1613–16 fascinated many. Frances Howard was

herself seen as a witch, at least after the trial of Anne Turner in November 1615.[61] The wax images, the magical charms and other sinister objects which Simon Forman had provided to make Essex impotent and arouse Robert Carr's love were sensationally introduced at the trial, and evidence about the use of sorcery also figured in the trials of some of the other conspirators. The image of Frances Howard as a witch was deployed in the many libels inspired by the affair and may even have preceded the discovery of Overbury's murder and the disclosures at the trials.[62] Less anonymous commentators made much of the witchcraft allegations, as Chief Justice Coke did at the trials. In his lengthy poem about the affair, Richard Niccols refers to Forman as 'that fiend in human shape'.[63]

The early accounts of the Overbury affair often reflect a belief that witchcraft attempted to invert the entire moral, social and gender order. No wonder, then, that Jacobean playwrights saw the dramatic possibilities of the subject. Francis Howard's connection with the supernatural was picked up by Thomas Middleton in several plays, especially *The Witch*, performed (possibly for the only time) in 1616. In some ways the witch of the title is marginal to the play: like the witches in *Macbeth*, she gathers exotic ingredients, but she offers magical remedies like a cunning woman more than she acts against others. However, each of its three plots mirrors some aspect of the Howard case: in one, the witch provides a potion that makes a husband impotent only with his wife; in the second, a 'maid', Francesca, who is pregnant, seeks revenge against her sister-in-law; and in the third, a wife tries (unsuccessfully, it turns out) to have her husband murdered. Poisons and potions are used by everyone. The play apparently encountered immediate problems, and the text remained unprinted for over a century; in the dedicatory epistle attached to the only surviving manuscript, made at some time before Middleton's death in 1627, the author speaks of having lost possession of it soon after it was performed at Blackfriars, recovering it only years later. He describes it as 'this (ignorantly ill-fated) labour of mine', which might be a possibly intentionally ambiguous reference to the play having been suppressed after its first performance because it was so dangerously topical.[64]

The role of witchcraft and magic in the collapse of the Howard-Essex marriage was mirrored in other cases of aristocratic family breakdown. One such case, as we saw in Chapter 2, was that of the Earl and Countess of Sussex. In duelling Star Chamber suits in 1622, the earl and the countess each accused the other of employing sorcerers to harm them. The countess's suit was motivated by her fear that the earl would marry Mrs Shute and deprive her children of their inheritance – or what was left of it. Sussex was incensed that his wife had used the money he had reluctantly settled on her and the children to pay for the services of several people (of both sexes) who practised astrology, and 'the unlawful and damnable arts of witchcraft, charms and enchantments'. Her intention, Sussex charged, was to feed him 'poisonous powders, potions, broths, etc', and use the charms to win 'the unlawful loves and affections of others'. The accusations, perhaps deliberately, echo those against Frances Howard in the previous decade. The cases also link up with later stories involving the Duke of Buckingham. Frances Shute, Sussex's second wife, alleged that the countess, her 'heavy enemy', had hired the sorcerer Edward Frodsham to harm her and members of her family. Frodsham was an associate of another well-known sorcerer, Dr John Lambe; in 1625 they were both being employed by Lady Purbeck to bewitch her brother-in-law, Buckingham.[65]

The accusations against the most notable and politically important person to be suspected of involvement in witchcraft, the Duke of Buckingham, and his astrologer, Dr Lambe, were more spectacular. Accusations of witchcraft and sorcery against Buckingham were not just political. For instance, on 12 June 1626, London was struck by a tornado – a rarity in England's temperate climate. It began at about three o'clock, during a furious thunderstorm, when a waterspout erupted in the Thames, 'near the garden in Lambeth marsh'. The 'whirlwater' was about thirty yards across and ten feet high, with the typical empty centre. It raced downstream, creating havoc for the watermen, and eventually smashed into the bank against the walls of York House, at the very place where Buckingham was building his new watergate. That ended its life as a waterspout; instead it became its land-based equivalent, a 'tempest whirling and ghoulish', as one Londoner described it. Courtiers watching anxiously from Whitehall saw 'a thick smoke like that of a brewer's chimney ascending from it as high as a man could discern' – an apt description of a tornado. A couple of churchyard walls were knocked down, and several graves of victims of the previous year's plague epidemic were opened, or flung into London's 'town ditch'. Rumours quickly spread that the storm had been caused by the enchantments of Dr John Lambe, the Duke of Buckingham's personal astrologer. The story spread that 'one of the Duke's devils did arise in it'. Three days later Charles I dissolved parliament, and thus put a stop to the impeachment proceedings against the powerful favourite. But the fateful decision to do this, it was believed, had been made on the 12th, that 'terrible Monday'. Lambe's suspected motives for raising the storm were not entirely clear: Was it a celebration of the forthcoming dissolution, or simply a demonstration of the old magician's continuing power? Perhaps, some thought, Lambe had nothing to do with it; instead, it was 'a sign against the Duke'. But however they interpreted it, the smashing of the waterspout against

Buckingham's watergate had a powerful symbolic meaning for his contemporaries.[66] The inverted world of witchcraft was never far from discussions of Buckingham and his family.

Dr Lambe, accused of raising the storm, warrants our attention here. He was an old man in 1626, having been born around 1545. In the late sixteenth century he made a living, apparently innocently enough, as a tutor to children of the local gentry, but he then became more ambitious and began fraudulently passing himself off as a physician. Strongly attracted to the occult, he earned a little money through fortune-telling. In 1608 he was indicted for having used enchantments to make a local peer, Lord Windsor, impotent; this use of witchcraft is similar to Simon Forman's employment by Frances Howard against the Earl of Essex for the same purpose. At Worcester Assizes he was arraigned on another occasion for having invoked 'evil and impious spirits'. In prison awaiting trial, he gave demonstrations of his magical skills to the people who flocked to see him. Judgment had not been finally reached when there was an outbreak of gaol fever, which killed the sheriff, several JPs, and others who had been present at the trial. The worried authorities quickly transferred the prisoner to London, where he lived comfortably in the King's Bench prison for many years. As prisons were open to the world, he was frequently consulted by people who needed surreptitious solutions for marital or other personal problems.[67]

Lambe's life in prison took a new turn in 1623, when he was indicted for the rape of an eleven-year-old girl and was sentenced to death. After intervention by (presumably) one of his clients, there was an investigation by the Lord Chief Justice, who found enough inconsistencies in the evidence to justify a pardon, which was issued in June 1624. Living as he did in Westminster, Lambe had easy access to influential people, and was soon being employed by Lady Purbeck, Buckingham's sister-in-law, who had decided that the duke was the cause of all her misfortunes and sought Lambe's assistance. She supposedly got powders and potions 'to intoxicate her husband's brains', and also for use against Buckingham himself: a wax effigy of the duke, of the sort thought to be commonly used by witches, was found in her possession. There were even reports of a sexual relationship between the lady and the sorcerer, though charges of adultery were quickly dropped. James I's law officers did not think there was actual proof of sorcery by either of them against Buckingham or Lord Purbeck, though they noted that Lady Purbeck 'did resort often to Lambe ... and we verily think with evil intention to [Lord Purbeck]'.[68] Buckingham, anxious about his brother's symptoms of insanity, himself consulted Lambe, but at first was concerned that the doctor's claims to cure Purbeck by laying hands on him might involve a sorcery that would rebound against himself. In January 1625 he asked his spiritual adviser, William Laud, then Bishop of St. David's, about it: Laud's diary records a 'discourse which L.D. [Buckingham] had with me about witches and astrologers'. Laud was sceptical about the curative effects of the laying-on of hands by anyone but a monarch, and the duke was still uneasy about it. His mother was also worried, so she too went to Lambe, who chillingly predicted that her son would be murdered within two years of the dissolution.[69]

Buckingham soon decided that it was safer to have a magician working for him than one working against him. For the remaining two years of their lives, Lambe was in his employment, a fact given wide publicity by the duke's enemies. 'Foul Lambe, that lewd imposter', as one of the libels described him; Buckingham's source of 'philters to incite / Chaste ladies to give my foul lust delight', another sneered. The sexual inversion caused by witchcraft was part of the problem.[70] Popular hatred was strikingly reflected in the violence of the mob which lynched the old man after an ill-timed visit to the Fortune Theatre in June 1628.[71] Everyone involved – Buckingham, Lady Purbeck and the London street population – took it for granted that malign supernatural forces could be deployed in ways that did the devil's work by turning the natural order upside down. This belief is so far from present-day assumptions that we find it hard to take seriously these and other instances of the impact of magical and witchcraft beliefs on the public as well as the private behaviour of educated people in the early seventeenth century. Yet inversionary thinking loomed large in the mental world of that time.

Other astrologers, sorcerers, wizards, or magicians (contemporaries often used the terms interchangeably) were consulted by members of the elite. Earlier in the century, Simon Forman was the most successful London practitioner. In addition to Lambe, Lady Purbeck and her husband both resorted to the astrological healer Richard Napier for help against each other. Lady Purbeck and the Countess of Sussex consulted Edward Frodsham, who seems to have been well known and turns up several times in court records. Another Frodsham, Humphrey, who was in King's Bench prison on a charge of murder, professed 'to have skill in conjuration and magic'. According to the nephew who was accused of blackmailing Lady Tresham while her husband was abroad on the king's business, when Lady Tresham was pregnant from adultery, she had consulted with Frodsham and received advice as to how to induce a miscarriage. She was convinced that Frodsham, 'by his skill', already 'knew all her thoughts and actions'. Dr Lambe, a fellow-prisoner at the time, was also consulted.[72] In all these cases, consultation with witches or sorcerers was accepted as a common behaviour, not an extraordinary one.

Magic was sufficiently normal that some members of the elite wanted this kind of knowledge for themselves. The career of the Earl of Northumberland, known as the 'wizard earl', underlines the links between science and magic, and demonstrates that such studies were not always malicious. Northumberland, a notable book collector, was interested in medicine and the related field of alchemy; while imprisoned in the Tower after the Gunpowder Plot, he continued to study. Among the books dedicated to him was one on the 'judgment of nativities', an activity that fell within the scope of witchcraft. Frances Howard's mother, the Countess of Suffolk, and her friend Mrs Thornborough, wife of the Bishop of Bristol, were both alleged to be enchantresses. A gentleman named Whithead was accused of travelling to Germany 'for learning of the magical art, and received instruction in conjuration'. Among other inversionary activities, he baptized a dog, and made a girdle out of human skin, and with these he could 'command all spirits and rolls and books', an interesting combination. He could also turn rushes from the floor of a house into 'spirits and serpents'. But he also forged letters from the Earl of Salisbury so that he could have an enemy dismissed from the Commission of the Peace in Essex, and it was the forgery that did him in: he was sentenced to stand in the pillory, to have his ears cut off and to suffer perpetual imprisonment.[73]

* * * *

However widespread the scepticism in individual cases, most people in early modern England believed that witches and other magical practitioners employed satanic power to overturn the divine natural order. Because the natural order was gendered, so too was witchcraft. It is not just that most ordinary witches were women who stepped out of their familial and social roles to wreak havoc in their communities. Witches were themselves scolds, linked to the unruly women who were such a source of concern for early modern villagers. In addition, witchcraft disrupted the family. The Seely family in *The Late Lancashire Witches*, where children ruled their parents, servants their masters, makes this most evident. But it was also true in less spectacular and fraudulent cases. Young women who were possessed gained a freedom from usual restrictions on their behaviour. Furthermore, fathers whose children were bewitched had failed in their role as patriarchs by being unable to protect their children from harm. Similarly, women whose children fell ill failed to be good mothers. Yet while witchcraft was expected to reflect the witch's animosity rather than solicitation by others, the widespread consultation of magicians and cunning women, and the fuzzy boundary between medicine and magic, meant that many people consulted magicians or cunning men and women at some point in their lives. Witchcraft and magic were by no means fringe activities; we are as likely to find people who believed that the devil was actively trying to turn the moral order upside down in the upper reaches of society as in the lower ones. The ways in which witchcraft figures in local communities, theatre and politics is a reminder of the profound ways in which concern about the world upside down was manifested in early modern England.

Conclusion

In the 1640s, women and men in England were provided irrefutable evidence that the world was turned upside down when civil war broke out between the king and parliament; war had also broken out in Ireland in 1638 and Scotland in 1639. Just as failed patriarchs were the flip side of disorderly women, civil war represented both a failure of the king as governor of the realm and parliament as subordinate to the king. Gender inversion was joined to social and political inversion in a wide range of political abuse and propaganda. This began even before war broke out in England. In 1640, as Richard Brome published his version of an upside down world in *The Antipodes*, a satirical pamphlet was published called *The Parlament of Women*; its subtitle described the inverted world caused by women's political engagement, where the laws had the goal of allowing them to 'have superiority and domineer over their husbands: with a new way found out by them to cure any old or new cuckolds, and how both parties may recover their credit and honesty again'. While the events described ostensibly took place in Rome, the concerns – with power within the household, cuckolds and honour – were based on contemporary English issues.[1] And while *The Parlament of Women* was satire, over the course of the 1640s, women were more engaged in political activity, including several formal petitions to parliament. Outside such formal activities, the disruptions of the war allowed and even required many women to take a broader role in their households and the wider society.[2] For many people, as in *The Antipodes*, everything was indeed opposite to what it should be.

The sense of the world upside down was not limited to the author of *The Parlament of Women*. In 1642, John Taylor, who we met when he wrote about Cuckold's Haven, wrote a pamphlet called *Mad Fashions, Od Fashions, All out of Fashions, or The Emblems of Our Distracted Times*. The cover illustration was used in a slightly revised pamphlet that appeared in 1647, *The World Turn'd*

Upside Down (frontispiece). In both cases, the author lamented that 'All things are turned the clean contrary way'. After a long description of things that were wrong, mostly focused on religion, Taylor wrote, 'this shows men's wits are monstrously disguis'd / or that our country is Antipodis'd'; indeed, by the time he published the revised version in 1647, even his initials were upside down.[3] The flying fish, the cart pulling the horse, the man walking on his hands – all these visual images describe the upside down world. There are no women, though: with the political issues clear, gender was no longer a necessary mask for other issues. The context for Taylor's pamphlets – civil war – was new, but the concern with the upside down world should not surprise us. Civil war is by definition an inversion of the political order: rebellion replaced obedience. Who was up and who was down was changing: one of the popular songs of the time, with both royalist and Parliamentarian versions, was 'Hey then, up go we'. And while Taylor's pamphlet focused on political and religious inversion, much of the writing about the upside down world continued to focus on gender. Accusations of sexual impropriety were levelled at both sides. For instance, late in 1643, the news book *Mercurius Britanicus* refuted a story in a royalist paper that accused an imprisoned Parliamentarian of bestiality. After all, the author wrote, this was on offense of the court, where 'ladies of honour may keep stallions and monkies, and their Bishops She-goats and ganymedes, for they make nothing of such prodigious fornications, they make nothing of sodomy and Gomorrahism'.[4] Earlier that same year, the *Scottish Dove* had denounced a report that 'the Parliament is ruled by the Citizens, and the Citizens by their wives'; in fact 'the citizens obey Parliament, and the men command their wives'.[5] According to participants on both sides of the conflict, political virtue and the proper patriarchal household were aligned.

Inversion was visible also in the proliferation of stories and accusations of witchcraft that appeared during the war. Some of these accusations were explicitly tied to battles and warfare, with witches as either omens or orchestrators of outcomes; furthermore, there are numerous stories of soldiers attacking women as if they were witches. There was also a spike in the prosecution of witches: after decades of decline, between 1645 and 1647 almost 250 people were accused of witchcraft in East Anglia, with over 200 investigations and trials in the second part of 1645 alone. The trials that followed had a relatively high rate of conviction and execution, with at least 100 witches hanged. The trials are the only English trials which feature a witch finder, Matthew Hopkins. Yet the descriptions of the witches and their actions are aligned with earlier cases; the only difference is that there is greater emphasis on the witch's inversionary alliance with Satan than in earlier trials. At a time when both sides in the war suggested that the other was in league with the Devil, it is not surprising that people turned to witchcraft. The trials, and particularly the high rate of conviction, reflected a world that was quite obviously upside down.[6]

The language of gendered inversion was used in the 1640s by those on both sides of the conflict between king and Parliament because it was already a familiar component of the social and political vocabulary of early modern England. Unruly women and failed patriarchs had long been visible in court scandals, in towns and villages and on the stage. They were visible because the world upside down was a foundational concept in early modern society. The very familiarity of the concept allowed it to be used as both a positive and negative symbol. It framed the gap between the expectations of a fixed gender order, and the reality of one that could never be fully realized. The ubiquity of the idea provides us with a way of reading political, social and cultural developments in relation to each other. It helps us see early modern England as a coherent whole, rather than a set of separate analytical problems.

The ultimate inversion of the political order, the execution of the king, brought out gendered language, as we might expect given the parallels between the family and the state. In the weeks before the execution, Elizabeth Poole, a radical preacher, spoke to the High Court of Justice, and an account of her vision and testimony was published. Her vision situates her as a gendered speaker, noting that she was in labour, 'the pangs of a travailing woman was upon me'. She then goes on to affirm that kingly power had fallen into the army's hands; however, the king was still their 'father and husband', though he had forgotten his own 'subordination to divine father-hood and headship'. Vengeance belonged to God, not to them; for while 'you may hold the hands of your husband, that he might not pierce your bowels with a knife or sword to take your life. Neither may you take his'.[7]

After the king's execution, the underground royalist newspaper/jestbook, *The Man in the Moon*, played broadly with ideas of inversion, calling London 'Nodnol', as it too was upside down. *The Man in the Moon*'s satire was often sexual and definitely gendered; it called General Thomas Fairfax 'Tom Ladle' and described an imagined skimmington against him at Smithfield, where a man representing Fairfax wore a ladle, and his 'doxie' rode backwards on the donkey. This imagined skimmington referred to the popular rumour that Lady Fairfax ruled her husband, rather than the other way around; at the trial of the king, she (wearing a mask) had several times interrupted the proceedings with abuse. *The Man in the Moon* itself performs a literary charivari to try to turn the world right side up again.[8] Fairfax may have been a general, but he was a failed patriarch. Allegations of unruly women and failed patriarchs were ubiquitous in the voluminous political commentary of the period.

The gender order of early modern society was, in theory, clear, yet it embodied a whole series of structural contradictions, as men and women balanced subordination in some relationships with authority in others. These contradictions were particularly strong within the household, where men's authority as a husband had to be balanced with a collaborative relationship with their wife, who played a significant role in household management. The internal contradictions of patriarchy made it almost impossible for men not to fail as patriarchs. These tensions were especially evident in the late sixteenth and early seventeenth centuries, as England experienced rapid demographic change, accompanied by an expansion of the number of poor and vagrants. Those with property were being pulled more firmly into the market, and patterns of agricultural production changed at the same time. The debate on women, while it surfaced familiar ideas about women's virtue and vice, was one response to the tensions in the system and the social and demographic challenges of the period. That debate placed disorderly women and failed patriarchs into a moral universe, with a significance far beyond their actual behaviour. This was not just an abstract issue: it echoed concerns about real events and real women.

Disorderly women and failed patriarchs were present at all levels of society. The village scold might be lowly, but reactions to her help us understand the reactions to unruly aristocratic women like Frances Howard. Howard's engagement of magicians and cunning women linked her to another model of the world upside down, that of witchcraft. Similarly, the cuckolds who were mocked with horns on their doors provided tools for understanding reactions to the failed patriarchy of James I and Charles I. The political echoes of these tensions were amplified by the patterns of analogical thinking which modelled the state on the family. If the family could not be orderly, then perhaps the state too lacked the requisite order. If the king, who was the head of state, could not manage his family, could he manage the state?

When the household is a model for the state, all thinking about gender is in some way political. Gendered thinking, and particularly thinking about unruly women and failed patriarchs, provided a central way of conceiving politics and articulating political conflict. Yet these ideas served political debate precisely because the gender order was not stable; the competing demands on women and men mirrored competing demands in the political order. One could use these competing ideas to see an upside down or right side up world. The sexual scandals of James I's court were not just the subject of titillating gossip. The Howard-Carr marriage was managed by the king, and when the murder of Thomas Overbury was discovered, James was harmed. Equally, resentment about the corrupt behaviour of the Duke of Buckingham and his family had a profound impact on how both James and Charles were seen by their subjects. The scurrilous verse libels about the Howard-Carr marriage, the Overbury scandal and the Duke of Buckingham remind us that sexual language provided a coded way of talking about politics.

The ubiquity of failed patriarchs and unruly women extends to the early modern stage. Plays directly – in the case of *Swetnam the Woman Hater* – or indirectly – in the case of *The Duchess of Malfi* – referenced political scandals. Tragedies provided an ongoing commentary on the nature of politics and political virtue, and on the risks posed by failed patriarchs. Comedies reminded their viewers of the costs not only of the failure to maintain the social order, but even of imagining that failure. Failed patriarchs and disorder on the stage reminded viewers of the political and social consequences of personal choices.

Inversion's role in comedy meant also that humour was a central component of inversion. The laughter about cuckolds or uppity women was broadly visible. The festive laughter of charivari and verse libels played an important role in maintaining patriarchal order. Yet that laughter was anything but light-hearted. Laughter ensured that the costs of stepping too far outside expected roles was not acceptable. Jokes were a tool for maintaining patriarchal equilibrium.[9] But they were also a key to the mocking laughter of political satire.[10] At the very time that economic changes might have provided women with more autonomy, such festive and mocking laughter ensured that they knew their place.

Yet over time, and particularly after the Restoration of Charles II, the world turned upside down lost some of its resonance. In part this was because the social and demographic stresses that marked the period from 1560 to 1640 were reduced: the population stopped growing, and even shrank a little; as a result, there was less concern about disorder in general, and the upside down world in particular.[11] In addition, the Restoration political settlement began the process of resolving structural political tensions.[12] The dynamics of gender changed in multiple ways as well. While women remained active participants in the economy – and particularly the emerging financial economy – they played a more limited role in production and marketing. At the same time, there were changes in ideas about women's sexuality and women's nature. By the early eighteenth century, ideas about women's sexual passivity were becoming more common; women were no longer assumed to be disorderly and managing. By the middle of the eighteenth century, when Henry Fielding wrote *Joseph Andrews*, Lady Booby's aggressive sexuality was seen as strange, a throwback to an earlier era. Skimmingtons were increasingly directed not at men beaten or abused by their wives, but at men who beat their wives.[13] The Restoration court was famously one of sexual license, but that license involved men being free to have mistresses; while several of Charles II's mistresses were married, the king and his friends having mistresses was not seen as a particular inversion of the gender order. And while the theatre continued to engage with gender, sexuality and marriage, the employment of women actors took away one dimension of inversion. While the restoration theatre has its share of cross-dressing and disguised characters, its most common genre was the comedy of manners, which turned a satirical eye on morals and manners. There might be challenges to the gender order, but they were not so serious that one could not make them the subject of laughter.[14] Political debates still engaged with gender but not with women turning the world upside down. While the familial metaphor for the state remained important, neither society nor the state seemed as insecure. Political writers after the Restoration could debate whether fatherhood or marriage was the appropriate familial metaphor, but both upheld a version of the patriarchal family. Order was not in question as much as which order.[15]

Our understanding of the world of early modern England has grown in depth over the past thirty years. Yet that depth has often come by separating out narrow strands of history from each other. The study of gendered inversion, of disorderly women and failed patriarchs, reminds us that the women and men who attended the theatres of early modern London also paid attention to political events, and policed each other's behaviour through a range of tools. They could see failed patriarchs and unruly women in all these areas, and their understanding of each was influenced by their experience of the others. When we focus too narrowly on one aspect of society, whether it be political, social or cultural history, we lose the broader contexts in which our subjects are understood.

The world turned upside down was a critical concept in structural analyses of early modern society. We are now aware of the many limitations of a structural analysis, and of the many ways subordinate people, as individuals and groups, claimed and exercised agency. Cultural approaches to the history of the period illuminate the ways in which meaning was made. But paying attention to the upside down worlds of early modern society offers a useful reminder that there was not endless freedom, and that options, especially for women and the poor, were constrained by the structures within which they lived.

It is important that gender provides the lens for making these connections. Patriarchy itself was almost never directly challenged in the period, so the gender order provided a shared language across other divisions, political and religious. Debates about gender took place around the edges: What constituted good behaviour? When could a wife disobey her husband? What constituted failures of patriarchy? The stability of patriarchal ideas, in spite of the changes in actual experiences of women and men, made it a critical vehicle for thinking about many kinds of conflict.

Uncovering the centrality of gender has required crossing between multiple areas of knowledge. If this book constitutes an argument to give gender far more attention particularly in political history, it is also a plea for all of us to recover a more integrative approach to the study of the early modern period. The integration of political, social and cultural history provides a richer understanding of the early modern world, one that comes closer to giving us tools to think about the ways in which early modern women and men experienced their world.

Notes

Introduction

1 Cranmer, 'An Exhortation Concerning Good Order', sig. I 6v–I 7 (sigs I 5–7 not numbered).

2 Coignet, *Politique Discourses*, p. 163.

3 For an overview of these issues, see Amussen, 'Social Hierarchies', and Shepard, 'Family and Household'; for a theorization, Braddick and Walter, 'Introduction. Grids of Power'.

4 Rowlands, *The Bride*, sig. C4v; according to Geoffrey of Monmouth, Merlin's mother was pregnant by an incubus, so by a spirit and not a man.

5 Davis, "Women on Top", *Society and Culture*, chap. 5; Clark, *Thinking With Demons*, pp. 26, 281; for a different reading of such ideas, see Lake, *Antichrist's Lewd Hat*, esp. chaps 2 and 3: my approach is an inversion of Lake's: while he acknowledges gender, he focuses on the ways sin is deployed as an explanation of the world turned upside down; I acknowledge that there are religious readings of these developments, but focus on gender.

6 Hill, *World Turned Upside Down*.

7 Underdown, 'Language of Popular Politics'; Cranmer, 'Exhortation Concerning Good Order', sig. I7. The view that this official view was widely accepted is argued by Marsh, 'Order and Place'; Amussen, *An Ordered Society*, esp. chap. 2.

8 For widows, see Mendelson and Crawford, *Women in Early Modern England*, pp. 174–84; remarriage seems to have been much more common in London: Hubbard, *City Women*, chap. 7; detailed information on the lives of mothers of bastard children is primarily from a later period, but the outcomes depended on their location: see Crawford, *Parents of Poor Children*, chap. 1, esp. pp. 48–59; Amussen, 'Elizabeth I and Alice Balstone'; Capp, *When Gossips Meet*, pp. 36–42; Mikalachki, 'Women's Networks and the Female Vagrant'; such tensions leave aside the frequent complexity of households that included remarried adults who frequently had children from multiple marriages: Chaytor, 'Household and Kinship'.

9 For scolds, see Underdown, 'Taming of the Scold'; for updated discussions, see Weil, 'Politics and Gender in Crisis' and Amussen, 'Turning the World Upside Down'; for charivari in England, Thompson, '"Rough Music": Le Charivari Anglais' and 'Rough Music'; Ingram, 'Juridical Folklore', esp. pp. 75–8; and idem., 'Charivari and Shame Punishments'.

10 Clark, *Thinking With Demons*, p. 13. There was an additional peak in prosecutions
    during the 1640s, but after that both prosecutions and convictions declined
    rapidly: Gaskill, 'Witchcraft Trials in England'; Sharpe, *Instruments of Darkness*,
    esp. p. 109; for the links between witchcraft and other forms of gender disorder, see
    Underdown, 'Taming of the Scold', p. 118; Underdown, *Freeborn People*, pp. 16–17.

11 *The Poetics and Poems of Rachel Speght*, pp. xxi–xxii; Peters, 'Religion, Household-
    State Authority, and the Defense of "Collapsed Ladies"', shows recusant women
    arguing for independence from spousal authority in matters of religion.

12 Sowernam, *Ester Hath Hang'd Haman*, p. 19; Mikalachki, 'Taking the Measure
    of England', esp. pp. 134–42; Mossman, 'Holinshed and the Classics' focuses on
    Holinshed's 1577 edition rather than the 1583 one; Frye, *Elizabeth I*, p. 11; Lee, 'A
    Bodye Politique to Governe'; Jardine, *Still Harping on Daughters*, pp. 70–7, 93–8;
    Hutchinson, *Memoirs of the Life of Colonel Hutchinson*, p. 72.

13 Underdown, *Freeborn People*, pp. 27–39 and 'Yellow Ruffs and Poisoned Possets'.

14 Shepard, *Meanings of Manhood*, 'Swil-bols and Tos-pots', esp. p. 114, and 'From
    Anxious Patriarchs to Refined Gentlemen'; Amussen, 'The Part of a Christian Man';
    Richardson, *Household Servants*, chap. 7, esp. pp. 148–50; Lake, *Antichrist's Lewd
    Hat*, pp. 78–94.

15 The Introduction to Burke, *Popular Culture*, 3rd ed., provides a useful overview
    of the most recent historiography on the subject; a useful guide to multiple
    perspectives on popular culture is Hadfield, Dimmock and Shinn, *Ashgate Research
    Companion to Popular Culture*.

16 Taylor, *Mad fashions, od fashions, all out fashions* (1642), republished with minor
    revisions as *The World Turn'd Upside Down, or A Briefe Description of the Ridiculous
    Fashions of these Distracted Times* by 'T.J.' in 1647.

17 'Hey Then Up Go We', in *Collection of National English Airs*, pp. 33–4: this version
    is mostly the Parliamentarian one, but with Cavalier verses added at the end.
    'The World is Turned Upside Down'; Hughes, *Gender and the English Revolution*,
    pp. 102–6, and 'Gender and Politics in Leveller Literature'; Underdown, 'Language
    of Popular Politics'; Mack, *Visionary Women*.

18 For carnival, see especially Bakhtin, *Rabelais and his World*; Burke, *Popular
    Culture*, esp. chap. 7; for Robin Hood plays, Underdown, '"But the Shows of their
    Street"', esp. p. 9; Le Roy Ladurie, *Carnival in Romans*; Cressy, *Bonfires and Bells*,
    esp. p. 105; see also Hutton, *The Rise and Fall of Merrie England*, chap. 3; Guynn,
    'The Wisdom of Farts': I am grateful to Professor Guynn for allowing me to cite
    his unpublished work; Archer, *Pursuit of Stability*, pp. 1, 3; Scott, *Domination
    and the Arts of Resistance*; Scott's theorization undergirds Braddick and Walter,
    'Introduction: Grids of Power'.

19 Davis, 'The Reasons of Misrule', chap. 4 in *Society and Culture*; Amussen, 'The Part
    of a Christian man', pp. 220–1; Bucholz and Ward, *London*, pp. 279–80.

20 In addition to the citations in n. 9, see Underdown, *Revel, Riot, and Rebellion*, pp. 99–103, 110–11; Ingram, 'Ridings, Rough Music, and Mocking Rhymes' and 'Ridings, Rough Music, and the 'Reform of Popular Culture''. For a fuller discussion of charivari, see chap. 4.

21 Wrightson, *Earthly Necessities*, pp. 22–4, 116–21; Wrigley and Schofield, *Population History*, pp. 161–2 and Table A3.1, p. 528; Hoyle, 'Rural Economies'; Fumerton, *Unsettled*, esp. part I.

22 Whittle, 'Housewives and Servants'; Stretton, 'Women', esp. pp. 343–4; Bennet, *Ale, Beer and Brewsters in England*, esp. chap. 8, for the way this pattern worked in an earlier period and different industry.

23 For an overview, see the essays in Whittle (ed.), *Landlords and Tenants in Britain*; Wrightson, *Earthly Necessities*, pp. 141–4; for the social conflict consequent on changes in landholding, see, e.g., Wrightson and Levine, *Poverty and Piety*; Amussen, *An Ordered Society*, esp. chap. 4.

24 For a general overview, see Coffey and Lim, *The Cambridge Companion to Puritanism*, esp. Walsham, 'The Godly and Popular Culture'; also Ingram, 'Who Killed Robin Hood', esp. pp. 470–5; for cultural puritanism, see Wrightson and Levine, *Poverty and Piety*, esp. chap. 7; Underdown, *Fire From Heaven* explores these conflicts in a puritan town.

25 Lake, *Antichrist's Lewd Hat*, p. 713; the literature on religious life in this period is vast, but MacCulloch, *Reformation* provides a good starting point: in addition to specific sections on England, his discussion places these developments in a wider European context.

26 Harris, *Rebellion*, pp. 23–7; Houston, *James I*, pp. 13–16, 28–9; Kishlansky, *A Monarchy Transformed*, chap. 2.

27 Herrup, 'The King's Two Genders'.

28 Fox, *Oral and Literate Culture in England*; Watt, *Cheap Print and Popular Piety*; Boys, *London's News Press*; Randall, 'Joseph Mead, Novellante'; Cogswell, 'Published by Authoritie'; Cust, 'News and Politics'.

29 See, e.g., essays by Palmer, White, and Manley in Ostovich, Syme and Griffin, *Locating the Queen's Men*; Johnston and Hüsken, *English Parish Drama*; Greenfield, '"The Actors are Come Hither"' and 'Touring'; Knapp, 'The Academic Drama'.

30 For this, see Lakoff and Johnson, *Metaphors We Live By*, chap. 4; also Kovecses, *Metaphor*, p. 40; the underlying framework of a conceptual metaphor is represented in capital letters.

31 Ortman, *Winds from the North*, p. 206.

32 Abbot, *An Exposition Upon the Prophet Jonah*, p. 71.

33 Abbot, *The Reasons which Doctour Hill Hath Brought . . .*, p. 228.

34 Perkins, *A Golden Chaine*, p. 168.

35 Nicholson, *Acolastus His After-Witte*, sig. H4.

36 Knolles, *The Generall Historie of the Turkes*, pp. 994, 1142.

37 Dekker and Middleton, *The Patient Man and the Honest Whore*, in *Middleton Works*, 12.69.

38 Quoted in Donaldson, *The World Turned Upside Down*, p. 45.

39 Ingram, 'Charivari and Shame Punishments'.

40 Brome, *The Antipodes* 1:3, speeches 164, 166, 172; Traub, in *Thinking Sex*, chap. V, uses Martha Joyless, Peregrine's wife, to explore knowledge of sex and pedagogy.

41 Brome, *The Antipodes*, 3:1, speech 556, 4.1, speeches 740, 759.

42 Dyson, *Staging Authority*, pp. 112–20; Richard Cave, 'The Antipodes: Critical Introduction'.

43 Babcock, *Reversible World*, esp. pp. 16–23.

44 Babcock, *Reversible World*, esp. p. 15; Donaldson, *World Turned Upside Down*, p. 6; Guynn, 'Wisdom of Farts'.

45 Babcock, *Reversible World*; Davis, 'Rites of Violence'; Underdown, 'But the Shows of their Street', pp. 6–7.

46 Greenblatt, *Renaissance Self-Fashioning*; Butler, *Gender Trouble*, esp. pp. 171–80; Amussen, 'Social Hierarchies'; Cressy, 'Gender Trouble and Cross-Dressing'; Howard, 'Cross-Dressing, the Theatre, and Gender Struggle'.

47 Jardine, *Still Harping on Daughters*; the classic study of what he calls the 'one-sex' body is Laqueur, *Making Sex*. While his account provides an incomplete account of the medical theories, stories about sex changes were well known in the period – suggesting that while the one sex body was not the dominant conception of sex, medical thinking made room for changeability: King, *The One Sex Body on Trial*; Breitenberg, *Anxious Masculinity*, esp. pp. 151–2.

48 For this, see especially Dolan, *True Relations*. For purposes of clarity, I have not hedged every statement with the uncertainty I know is there.

49 For patriarchal equilibrium, see Bennett, 'Patriarchal Equilibrium', in *History Matters*; for women's work, in addition to the references in n. 22 above, Capp, *When Gossips Meet*, pp. 42–7.

1 Unruly Women

1 Swetnam, *Araignment*, pp. 25–6; it was entered in Stationers' Register 8 February 1615. Van Heertum, *Swetnam's The Araignment* discusses the printing history on pp. 93–109; the comment on sales is from Sowernam, *Ester Hath Hang'd Haman*, p. 32.

2 Swetnam, *Araignment*, p. 15.

3 The three responses are Speght, *A Mouzell for Melastomus*, modern ed. in *Polemics and Poems*, pp. 1–41; Munda, *The Worming of a Mad Dogge*; and Sowernam, *Ester*

Hath Hang'd Haman; for a modern edition of the play, Crandall (ed.), *Swetnam the Woman-Hater*; Gouge, *Of Domesticall Duties*. For Gouge's discussion of the complaints about his treatment of the wife's duties, see 'Epistle Dedicatory', pp. 4–5: his response was, 'That which makes a wives yoke heavy and hard, is an husband's abuse of his authority: and more pressing his wives duty, then performing his own'.

4 Shepard, 'From Anxious Patriarchs to Refined Gentlemen?', pp. 293–4; Rowlands, *A Crew of Kind Gossips*, sig. E2. For the 'Querelle des femmes' more generally, see Kelly, 'Early Feminist Theory'; Woodbridge, *Women and the English Renaissance*; Malcolmson and Suzuki, *Debating Gender*.

5 Swetnam, *Araignment*, p. 64.

6 Perks, 'The Ancient Roots of Humor Theory'; Carroll, *Humour*, chap. 1.

7 Shakespeare, *Taming of the Shrew*, 5.2.152, 161–2.

8 The most recent review of scholarship on the play is in Hodgdon's edition of *The Taming of the Shrew*, esp. pp. 4, 35–6: citations to the play are to this edition; Boose, 'Scolding Brides and Bridling Scolds', esp. pp. 181–3; for a more recent reading that places the play in dialogue with other shrew pamphlets and plays, see Bayman and Southcombe, 'Shrews in Pamphlets and Plays'. While the play has traditionally been dated to the early 1590s, both Bayman and Southcombe, and Leah Marcus, 'The Shrew as Editor/Editing Shrew' suggest that it might better be dated to the early Jacobean period.

9 Hodgdon, 'Introduction', pp. 35–6 sees *A Shrew* and *The Shrew* 'as representing different stages of an ongoing theatrical "commodity" that was formed some time in the early 1590s and has been undergoing mutations ever since'; *A Shrew*, li. 1619.

10 Fletcher, *Woman's Prize*, 1.1.47–8, 5.4.45–6.

11 Fletcher, *Woman's Prize*, 5.4.91–98.

12 Fletcher, *The Woman's Prize*, pp. 25–6; Amussen, *An Ordered Society*, pp. 120–1; Mendelson and Crawford, *Women in Early Modern England*, esp. chaps 5 and 6; Hubbard, *City Women*, pp. 125–35, suggests that *Shrew* had it wrong, and that wives had to tame spendthrift husbands who were reluctant to take up the burdens of adulthood.

13 Van Heertum, *Swetnam's The Araignment*, chap. 1, esp. pp. 3–4, 8, 10; Sowernam, *Ester Hath Hang'd Haman*, sig A2R; the tradition is discussed in Woodbridge, *Women in the English Renaissance*, part I; the Swetnam controversy is discussed on pp. 81–112; Woodbridge suggests that while Swetnam 'plundered the formal controversy', he 'neither respects nor understands the genre' (p. 87); Boleyn, 'Because Women are not Women'.

14 Crandall, *Swetnam the Woman-Hater*, p. 62; for the Red Bull, see Griffith, *Jacobean Company*, Introduction; her discussion of *Swetnam the Woman Hater* is pp. 130–45; she finds more humour in Swetnam than I do.

15 Speght, *Polemics and Poems*, pp. xx–xxii: Lewalski connects Speght to the proto-feminist circle around Queen Anne; Luckyj, however, suggests she and Swetnam were part of a Protestant network critical of court corruption, arguing primarily about how to respond to corruption: 'A Mouzell for Melastomus in Context'.

16 Speght, *Polemics and Poems*, p. 92; Lewalski suggests Swetnam as a possible annotator, but the hand suggests a literate reader accustomed to writing; she reprints and numbers the annotations, pp. 95–106; the original is Beinecke Library, Yale University, Ih Sp 33 617m; they are also discussed, with numerous excerpts, in Van Heertum, *Swetnam's The Araignment*, pp. 74–7: she also notes (p. 75) the author's apparent dislike of Swetnam in Lewalski annotation #12. Annotation was a common practice in early modern reading: see Sherman, *Used Books*, pp. 3–5; for the complexities of the relationships between writers and readers, Zwicker, 'What every literate man once knew'.

17 Van Heertum, *Swetnam's The Araignment*, pp. 74–7, Speght, *Polemics and Poems*, pp. 95–106, annotations # 46, 47, 50, 52, 66, 7, 73, 20, 27, 67, 68, 76, 11, 18, 80, 63 (in order of quotation).

18 There are multiple modern editions of these texts: in addition to Lewalski's edition of Speght, see the facsimile edition by O'Malley, Travitsky and Cullen, *Defenses of Women*; also Benson, ed., *Texts from the Querelle*; and Simon Shepherd, *The Woman's Sharp Revenge*, which reprints the three responses to Swetnam. The scold arguments are Sowernam, *Ester Hath Hang'd Haman*, p. 46; Munda, *Worming*, pp. 25–6. While Speght's pamphlet was published by Swetnam's publisher (although very different from his usual wares) Sowernam and Munda were published by those who usually published more learned works.

19 Underdown, 'Taming of the Scold', p. 119; Amussen, *Ordered Society*, p. 122; Underdown was criticized in Ingram, 'Shame and Pain' and 'Scolding Women Cucked and Washed', p. 51. Weil, 'Politics and Gender in Crisis', p. 386; both Weil and Amussen, 'Turning the World Upside Down' survey the evidence and debate: in different regions there are different chronologies and different social profiles of scolds, but there are also epistemological questions in play. *Wiltshire County Records*, p. 59 (1580); in the visitation of the Diocese of Bath and Wells in 1594, scolding represents just over 1 per cent of prosecutions, but 62 per cent cover absence from church, incontinence, and standing excommunicated: *Bishop Still's visitation*, p. 19.

20 *Oxford Quarter Sessions Order Book*, pp. 5, 61, 72.

21 *Worcester Quarter Sessions*, vol. II, p. 105.

22 North Riding, *Quarter Session Records*, vol. 1, p. 180.

23 Griffiths, *Lost Londons*, pp. 133, 394; as Laura Gowing has shown, accusations of scolding often encoded other conflicts: *Domestic Dangers*, esp. p. 118.

24 TNA STAC 8 249/19, Nicholas Rosyer v. James Quarry, Thomas Hammond et al., 1604: the use of the 'next neighbour' is typical of these processions. See Ingram, 'Juridical Folklore in England Illustrated by Rough Music'.

25 Hawarde, *Camera Stellata*, pp. 316–18; Macfarlane, *Marriage and Love in England*, p. 138; Cressy, *Birth, Marriage and Death*, pp. 324–5; TNA STAC 8/282/12, Turner v. Humphrey, Constable, Reynoldes alias Gattes and others. For more about Ludlowe's daughter, see Chapter 2.

26 5 Eliz cap. 4.3, 'An Acte touching dyvers Orders for Artificers, Laborers, Servantes of Husbandrye and Apprentises', in *Statutes*, vol. IV, part 1, p. 415; the classic work on the European marriage pattern is J. Hajnal, 'European Marriage Patterns in Perspective'.

27 *Southampton Court Leet Records 1550–1624*, vol. 1, part 2, pp. 186, 197, 236; *Assembly Books of Southampton*, vol. 1, pp. 53, 70; vol. III, p. 30; vol. IV, pp. 10–11, 42, 67; Froide, *Never Married*, pp. 2–3, 19–22; Kowaleski, 'Singlewomen in Medieval and Early Modern Europe', pp. 38–81 and Appendix, pp. 325–44. For a recent review of vagrancy statutes and enforcement, see. Beier, 'A New Serfdom'; Carroll, 'Vagrancy'; for female vagrants, Mikalachki, 'Women's Networks and the Female Vagrant'; Amussen, 'Elizabeth I and Alice Balstone'.

28 Griffiths, *Lost Londons*, p. 134; Griffiths, 'Masterless Young People in Norwich'; Wales, 'Living at their own hands'.

29 The idea of a 'crisis in gender relations' was first proposed in Underdown, 'Taming of the Scold'; it has been criticized (for different reasons) especially by Ingram in 'Scolding Wives', as well as Gowing, *Domestic Dangers*, pp. 28–9; for the earlier history of female disorder and scolding, see McIntosh, *Controlling Misbehavior*, pp. 58–65, 149–50; Jones, *Gender and Petty Crime*, pp. 95–101; Bardsley, *Venomous Tongues*, pp. 10–13, 113–17, and chap. 6. For recent analysis of this work in relation to the idea of crisis, see Weil, 'Politics and Gender' and Amussen, 'Turning the World Upside Down'. *An Act against Conjuration, Witchcraft and dealing with evil and wicked spirits* (2 Ja. I c. 12) and the *Act to Prevent the Destroying and Murthering of Bastard Children* of 1623 (21 Jac I cap. 27) in *Statutes*, vol. IV, part II; for more on witchcraft, see chap. 5; for infanticide, see Amussen, *Ordered Society*, pp. 113–15; for a recent survey, Ingram, 'Infanticide in Late Medieval and Early Modern England'.

30 HMC *Downshire*, II, p. 328; for an account of the marriage arrangements, and what is known about its progress, see Lindley, *Trials*, pp. 13–18, 43–4.

31 Ingram, *Church Courts, Sex and Marriage*, p. 145.

32 *CSPD 1611–18*, pp. 134, 161, 172–3. The first of these examinations were taken by JPs in Norwich, and presumably been sent to the Council later when Woods was examined in relation to the Essex case; they detail her activities as a cunning woman, and an allegation of theft, but there was no suggestion of activity outside the Norwich area. The last two were taken in Suffolk, after (apparently) Woods had been in London and left; for the links between cunning women and witches, see below, Chapter 5, and also Gregory, *Rye Spirits*.

33 TNA SP 14/74, f. 6, 14 June 1613; *CSPD 1611–18*, pp. 172–3, 183, 187.

34 *CSPD 1611–18*, p. 182; *Chamberlain Letters*, I, pp. 444–5, 449. Winwood, *Memorials of Affairs of State*, vol. III, 453–4. Lindley, *Trials*, pp. 45, 49–51, 80–1, 95–101, 116–18. On the transmission of news in the early seventeenth century, see Bellany, *Politics of Court Scandal*, chap. 2, and references there. For a popular libel commenting adversely on the annulment that obviously dates from 1613 (when nothing was known about the full extent of Howard's crimes), see BL, Add.MS 34218 (Fane MSS), f. 165. The King's and Abbot's views are recorded in 'The proceedings wch happened touching the divorce between the lady Frances Howard and Robert Earle of Essex' (1613); HL, Ms. HM 1553, ff. 5v, 13.

35 *Early Stuart Libels*, F, nos. F 1, 2, 4, accessed 9 June 2011; Bellany, *Politics of Court Scandal*, chap. 2, esp. pp. 97–8 considers the way the scandal played out in public; see below, chap. 3, for more on this phase of the scandal.

36 Bellany, *Politics of Court Scandal*, pp. 6, 71–2; *Early Stuart Libels*, no. F 10.

37 Bellany, *Politics of Court Scandal*, pp. 71–2.

38 For the poisoning and subsequent trials, see Bellany, *Politics of Court Scandal*, pp. 71–3, 76–9, 145; Lindley, *Trials*, chap. 5, esp. pp. 145–50: as Lindley shows, the evidence is problematic, so the extent of Howard's involvement is unclear.

39 *Araignment*, sigs. A2v, C3 and F3v.

40 Marston, *The Insatiate Countess*, see esp. p. 17. The 1613 and 1616 editions of the play were both published by Thomas Archer, who also published Swetnam's *Araignment*, Speght's *Mouzell*, Webster's *White Devil*, and Middleton and Dekker's *Roaring Girl*, all works that deal with dangerously strong women: Van Heertum, *Swetnam's The Araignment*, p. 96.

41 Scot, *Philomythie*; the second part of the volume, *Certaine Pieces of thie Age Paraboliz'd* is dedicated to Essex, signed by Scot; 'Aquignispicium', pp. 106, 107f.; the dedication to Essex and the reference to two marriages is missing in the second edition, but that edition includes more explicit descriptions of female lust, including 'Vice growes so common, that it is far more/Opprobrious to be chaste then to be a whore', K7–K7 v (the copy in EEBO has 4 unnumbered signatures between K 4 and L); The dating of the two editions is difficult, but the first edition is entered in the Stationer's Register on 4 July 1615, the second part of the second edition in April 1616: *Transcript of the Registers of the Stationers Company*, vol. 3, pp. 262, 271; there are several Thomas Scots writing at this time, which makes identification difficult, but the *ODNB* links this Thomas Scot to the author of a later far more politically incendiary pamphlet, *Vox Populi, or Newes from Spayne* (1619): Kelsey, 'Scott, Thomas (d. 1626)'.

42 BL, Add.MS (Trumbull MSS), 72377, f. 46. HMC, *Downshire*, vol. V, p. 268. For other contemporary issues, Bellany, *Politics of Court Scandal*, p. 72 and n. 222; Bellany does not mention Trumbull's suspicions about the existence of a plot, or say anything about the mysterious Bonajuti.

43 BL Add. MS 72377, f. 52; TNA SP 77/11 (Trumbull's dispatches), ff. 351–80; HMC *Downshire*, vol. V, pp. 257–8, 268; for Coke's mysterious warnings, see Bellany, *Politics of Court Scandal*, chap. 4, esp. pp. 181–3. Bellany argues (p. 183) that suspicions of the Overbury affair being connected with this alleged plot date only from late October 1615, although Trumbull informed Winwood about the plot (without connecting it to the murder) as early as 20 June: BL, Add. MS 72377, f. 46.

44 For Howard's mother, see Lindley, *Trials*, pp. 45–6; for the prosecution of the Earl and Countess of Suffolk, see Payne, 'Howard, Katherine' and Croft, 'Howard, Thomas' in *ODNB*; Stone, *Family and Fortune*, chap. 9, esp. pp. 276–81.

45 *Chamberlain Letters*, I, pp. 85, 97–8, 139, 369: another Boughton brother was a member of Archbishop Whitgift's household, and was killed by a fellow page after a game of bowls: p. 139; *CSPD* 1598–1601, p. 296, 17 August 1599; for the account of the sentencing, see HL, EL 2690, 12 June 42 Eliz.; Ingram, 'Charivari and Shame Punishments', p. 369.

46 Notestein, *Four Worthies*, pp. 123–66, esp. pp. 132–6; Clifford, *Diaries of Lady Anne Clifford*, esp. pp. 36–47. Lady Anne outlived her uncle and cousin, thus inheriting the lands in question in 1643; from 1649 until her death in 1676 she lived on her Westmoreland estates and held sway over tenants and minor gentry. Spence, 'Lady Anne Clifford, 1590–1676' *ODNB*, accessed 22 June 2011; for another woman fighting for her honor in the form of property, see Heal, 'Reputation and Honour'.

47 Peck, *Court Patronage and Corruption*, pp. 181–4; Rubin, 'The Traffic in Women', esp. pp. 171–7; for the decline of morality at James I's court, see Stone, *Crisis of the Aristocracy*, pp. 664–8.

48 Stone, *Crisis of the Aristocracy*, p. 596; Fraser, *The Weaker Vessel*, pp. 12–16; *Chamberlain Letters*, II, pp. 32–3, 77, 88–9. Longueville, *Curious Case of Lady Purbeck*, p. 44. See also Aughterson, 'Hatton, Elizabeth', *ODNB*.

49 *CSPD, 1623–5*, pp. 474, 476–7. *Chamberlain Letters*, 2, p. 601. HMC, *Mar and Kellie*, 2 (Supplement): 220; HMC *Hodgkin*, pp. 284–5: the case came to light when Lady Purbeck charged the servant with threatening her life. *The Works of . . . William Laud*, vol. 3, pp. 154–7. *CSPD 1625–6*, p. 363. Goodman, *The Court of King James the First*, vol. 2, p. 377; *Curious Case of Lady Purbeck*, pp. 70–101, passim; see also Macdonald, *Mystical Bedlam*, p. 199.

50 Stone, *Crisis of the Aristocracy*, p. 667; *Chamberlain Letters*, II, pp. 80, 217–18. *CSPD 1611–18*, p. 488; *1619–23*, p. 13. TNA SP 14/105, ff. 121–9; STAC 8/24/19 (Att-Gen v. Chapman, 1617); STAC 8/111/26, 27 (Exeter v. Lake, 1618); STAC 8/196/24 (Lake v. Exeter, 1618).

51 *Chamberlain Letters*, II, p. 214. Akrigg, *Jacobean Pageant*, p. 212, quotes a different version of James's language.

52 Dympna Callaghan rightly points out that a central theme of *The Duchess of Malfi* is the problem of female sovereignty: Callaghan (ed.), *The Duchess of Malfi*, pp. 2, 8–11;

Loomis, *The Death of Elizabeth I*, chap. 2, esp. pp. 49–52; Amussen, 'Elizabeth I and Alice Balstone' pp. 221–2; Clapham, *Elizabeth of England*, esp. pp. 114–15.

53 *Chamberlain Letters*, II, pp. 92, 100, 145, 601. Fraser, *Weaker Vessel*, p. 18.

54 For Rich, see Wall, 'Rich, Penelope', *ODNB*; also Rickman, *Love, Lust and License*, chap. 3.

55 Thomas Scott, 'Meditations', c. 1626–7, Kent Library and History Centre, U951/ Z17, f. 78: I am grateful to Thomas Cogswell for this reference; *Tom Tell-Troath*, (Holland: 1630?): even this was published after James' death. For the framing, see Campbell, *The Puritan*, p. 218; an anonymous writer in 1720 referred multiple times to Queen James, as well as to 'Mother William Laud' and 'Madam the Duke of Buckingham': McCormick (ed.), *Secret Sexualities*, p. 146; Young, *James I and the History of Homosexuality*, pp. 5–6: I am grateful to Professor Young for his assistance on this matter.

56 *Chamberlain Letters*, 2, pp. 214, 216; on the controversy over cross dressing and fashions of dress, see Woodbridge, *Women and the English Renaissance*, pp. 139–51; and Howard, 'Crossdressing, the Theatre, and Gender Struggle'; for an alternate view, see Cressy, 'Cross-Dressing'.

57 These were among the charges when Buckingham was impeached by the House of Commons in 1626: see Lockyer, 'Villiers, George', *ODNB*, accessed 30 June 2016.

58 *The Diary of Thomas Crosfield*, pp. 7, 109; Wilson, *History of Great Britain*, p. 149. *Chamberlain Letters*, 2, p. 439. For the Catholic inclinations of the duke's family, see also Lockyer, *Buckingham*, pp. 58–60, 115, 258, 358, 372, 461, 469.

59 Eglisham, *The Forerunner of Revenge*, pp. 7–22; HMC, *Mar and Kellie*, 2 (Supplement): 225–6. *Calendar of State Papers, Venentian*, 18 (1623–25): 627. Bidwell and Jansson, ed., *Proceedings in Parliament 1626*, vol. 3, 57–94 and vol. 4, 260, 279, 281, 297; Bellany and Cogswell, *Murder of King James I*, part III; see also Macdonald, *Mystical Bedlam*, pp. 21–2.

60 [John Rhodes], *The Spy*. Many of the libels are printed in Fairholt (ed.), *Poems and Songs Relating to George Villiers*; for Catholic women, see Dolan, *Whores of Babylon*, esp. pp. 95–6; Bellany and Cogswell, *Murder of James I*, pp. 330–4.

61 For the Concini, Duccini, *Concini*; for Mantua, see Arnold, 'Fortifications and Statecraft', p. 225.

62 Bellany, 'The Murder of John Lambe'; Cogswell, 'The People's Love' and 'John Felton'. Filmer, *Patriarcha and Other Writings*, Introduction, pp. viii, xxxxii–xxxiv.

63 The poem's publishing history is given in Rimbault (ed.), *Miscellaneous Works in Prose and Verse of Sir Thomas Overbury*, Introduction, pp. xiii–xix; Murphy, *Bibliography of English Character-Books*, pp. 15–25; Savage, *The 'Conceited Newes' Of Sir Thomas Overbury*, Introduction, pp. xiv, xv, xxi, xxx, suggests that the first edition of 'A Wife' dates from 1611, written to support Overbury's supposed 'improper suit' to the Countess of Rutland, and only later adapted to oppose the Frances Howard match. The

1611 date rests only on a manuscript note on the fly-leaf of the fifteenth impression of *A Wife* (1632): Murphy, *Bibliography of English Character-Books*, p. 24. The allegation of Overbury's suit to the Countess of Rutland depends on Drummond's account by way of Ben Jonson, and it may have been Jonson's suit to the Countess, not Overbury's, that was improper. However, the story implies that Overbury wrote *A Wife* sufficiently in advance of his imprisonment to be able to ask Jonson to read it for him. See Herford, Simpson and Simpson, *Ben Jonson: The Man and his Work I*, pp. 54, 137–8; but cf. Donaldson, *Ben Jonson*, pp. 292–3; John Chamberlain reports the Countess of Rutland's death in August 1612, so if Jonson's story is true, Overbury must have written *A Wife*, and thus have been opposing Carr's intention to marry Frances Howard, well before that date: *Chamberlain Letters*, I, p. 374.

64 Rimbault (ed.), *Overbury's Works*, pp. 33–45. The stanza quoted is from p. 42.

65 Francis Delavale to Sir Ralph Delaval, 28 Nov. 1613, in 'Selections from the Delaval Papers', p. 138; the politics of the situation are made explicit in the next sentence, where Francis stops, saying 'thus fearing to enter too far'.

66 *Works of Thomas Campion*, pp. 269–73.

67 *Poems of George Chapman*, pp. 305–24. Chapman got into trouble for implying in the poem that Frances Howard (Andromeda) had been rescued from Essex, who was a 'barren rock', in other words impotent as charged in the nullity suit; he felt obliged to publish a subsequent *Justification* to defend himself: pp. 328–34.

68 Tuke, *A Treatise Against Painting [sic] and Tincturing*, sigs. A2, B3–B4v, 21.

69 *Egerton Papers*, pp. 472–3.

70 Bellany, *Politics of Court Scandal*, pp. 157–9, 222, and 'Mistress Turner's Deadly Sins'; Lindley, *Trials*, pp. 148, 152, 179–82; Jones and Stallybrass, *Renaissance Clothing*, chap. 3, esp. pp. 66–9, 76–7; for the scaffold performance, see Royer, *English Execution Narrative*, esp. pp. 83–4, 90.

71 Tuke, *Treatise Against Painting and Tincturing*, sigs. A3, B3, and pp. 21, 42–9, 52–3, 57, 60.

72 Van Heertum, *Swetnam*, p. 76; Lewalski, *Polemics and Poems*, annotation 39, p. 99.

73 Hawarde, *Camera Stellata*, p. 57. *Chamberlain Letters*, I, p. 97; there were multiple proclamations reminding people of the laws: see Hughes and Larkin, *Tudor Royal Proclamations*, vol. II #464, 494, 542, 601, 623, 646 and vol. III, # 697, 786, 787; *Statutes*, vol. 4, part 1, p. 239 (1&2 Philip & Mary c. 2). For cross-dressing, in addition to references in Introduction, n. 45, see Levine, *Men in Women's Clothing*; one of the striking aspects of Shakespeare's plays to a modern viewer is the apparent ease with which a woman (already a boy playing a woman) can disguise herself as a man (or vice versa) and be accepted as one: clothing marked identity; Bennett and McSheffrey, 'Early, Erotic, and Alien'. TNA, E. 178/512, 570, 733, 1052, 1077, 2004, 2096, 2473, 3058, 3299 (Special Commissions of Inquiry for Cornwall, Cumberland, Durham, Huntingdonshire, Kent, Hampshire and the Isle of Wight,

Wiltshire, Worcestershire, Northumberland, Anglesey); presumably returns from other counties have been lost. These report women who, since the previous August, have worn gowns of silk, velvet, or cloth of gold; responses typically note what a man's wife has worn, and then note 'and hath a gelding with armor and furniture for the same': E. 178/512.

74 Jansson, *Proceedings in Parliament 1614*, p. 75.

75 Scot, *Phylomythie* (1615), p. 106.

76 Rowlands, *The Bride*, sig. B.

77 Hentschell, 'Treasonous Textiles', esp. p. 113.

78 *Chamberlain Letters*, II, pp. 286–7, 289, 294.

79 *Ilic Mulier*, sigs. A3, A4, and C2; the pamphlets were both published by John Trundle, licensed on 9 and 16 February respectively: *Transcript of the Registers of the Company of Stationers*, vol. III, p. 310; for a discussion of how these pamphlets fit into more general concerns about masculinity, see Breitenberg, *Anxious Masculinity*, pp. 162–4.

80 *Haec Vir*, sigs. A3-v, A4v, B3, C3v, C4.

81 *Quarter Sessions Papers for Worcester*, vol. II, p. 161; for a fuller discussion of *The Roaring Girl*, see chapter 3.

82 In addition to sources in n. 70, see Dolan (ed.), *Taming of the Shrew*, pp. 37–8; Prynne, *The Unloveliness of Lovelocks*, sig. A3–A3v: the subtitle sums up his argument, *A summarie discourse, prooving: the wearing, and nourishing of a locke, or love-locke, to be altogether unseemely, and unlawfull unto Christians. In which there are likewise some passages collected …, against face-painting; the wearing of supposititious, poudred, frizled, or extraordinary long haire; the inordinate affectation of corporall beautie: and womens mannish, unnaturall, imprudent, and unchristian cutting of their haire; the epidemicall vanities, and vices of our age;* Denison quoted in Lake, *The Boxmaker's Revenge*, p. 43; for Prynne, see Lamont, *Marginal Prynne*, chaps 1 and 2; Kishlansky, 'A Whipper Whipped'.

2 Failed Patriarchs

1 Shepard, *Meanings of Manhood*, p. 1; Dod and Cleaver, *Godly Forme*, p. 13.

2 Dod and Cleaver, *Godly Forme*, pp. 13, 16, 34, 87; their section on the duties of husbands runs from pp. 97–218 and wives, pp. 218–42; parents, pp. 244–342 and children, pp. 342–64; on masters, pp. 364–78, and servants, pp. 378–84.

3 Gouge, *Domesticall Duties*, Treatise 8, Section 5, p. 651.

4 Fletcher, *Gender, Sex, and Subordination*, p. 112.

5 Smith, *De Republica Anglorum*, p. 45; Dod and Cleaver devote four times as much space to the duties of husbands as wives, 121 pages vs. 29.

6 Gouge, *Of Domesticall Duties*, p. 349.

7 Gouge, *Domesticall Duties*, Epistle dedicatory, sig. 2v; pp. 349, 350, 396 (and treatise 4 passim); Amussen, *Ordered Society*, pp. 37–47.

8 Accountability for church attendance changed over time, and was the subject of intense debate: Neale, *Elizabeth I and her Parliaments, 1584–1601*, pp. 396–402 for the debate in the early 1590s; Questier, 'Conformity, Catholicism, and the Law'; the responsibility of the master or mistress, or of parents, to ensure that their servants/children are catechized is enshrined in the canons of both 1571 and 1604: *Anglican Canons*, pp. 189, 349; sending children to catechism was a regular query in Episcopal Visitation articles: see *Visitation Articles*, e.g., vol. I, pp. 35, 77–8, 105, 132, 163, 183, 190, 193, 204 and vol. II, 46, 58, 79, 91, 121, 135, 176, 202 and 207, 214, 239; Dolan, *Whores of Babylon*, esp. pp. 61–4; for the way these issues shaped rethinking of women's responsibilities to their husbands, see Peters, 'Religion, Household-State Authority'.

9 *Basilikon Doron*, pp. 20, 34.

10 Osborn, *Historical Memoires* (Elizabeth), pp. 39–40, (James), pp. 2–3 (sig. G5v–G6).

11 *Basilikon Doron*, p. 35; Osborn, *Historical Memoires* (James), pp. 124–5 for examples of the excesses of James's court.

12 Osborn, *A Miscellany*, pp. 691, 694–5: 'It is the condition of those in Power to be guided by Servants'; *Early Stuart Libels*, L5.

13 Harington, *Nugae Antiquae*, vol. II, pp. 126–9.

14 Weldon, *A Cat May Look Upon a King*, pp. 52–3: Weldon follows this with a discussion of the poisoning of Prince Henry. Criticisms of Charles I's court are different, so the allegations of misconduct are not just based on political disagreement. For one example of polemical debate tied to gender ideas, see Cuttica, *Sir Robert Filmer and the Patriotic Monarch*, pp. 118–20.

15 Weldon, *The Court and Character of King James* in Smeeton (ed.), *Historical and Biographical Tracts* (Westminster, 1820), I, 42. For the gambling, see *Chamberlain Letters*, I, pp. 253, 327–8.

16 Weldon, *Court and Character*, p. 42; French ambassador quoted by Young, *James VI and I*, p. 16.

17 Quoted by Young, *James VI and I*, pp. 39, 49–50; for legal dimensions and complications, see Herrup, *House in Gross Disorder*, pp. 26–38.

18 Stanivukovic, 'Between Men in Early Modern England', esp. pp. 234, 238, 240–1; Stewart, 'A Society of Sodomites'.

19 Barnes, *Post-Closet Masculinities*, p. 21.

20 Carlson, *Marriage and the English Reformation*, pp. 62–6; Parish is less sanguine than Carlson about the Queen's attitude to clerical marriage: *Clerical Marriage*, pp. 228–33; of the six Archbishops of Canterbury from the reign of Elizabeth to the Civil War, only Matthew Parker was married.

21 Bray, *Homosexuality*, pp. 33–5, 47–51; Herrup, *House in Gross Disorder*, esp. pp. 30, 32–7; Traub points out that in *The Antipodes*, Martha Joyless recounts a sexual encounter with a fellow female servant: Traub, *Thinking Sex*, esp. pp. 104–7; for a recent overview of thinking about James I that also engages more broadly with the history of homosexuality, see Young, 'James VI and I: Time for a Reconsideration?'.

22 *Early Stuart Libels*, L 6, 7, 8. *The Diary of Sir Simonds D'Ewes*, pp. 92–3; McGee, *An Industrious Mind*, pp. 81–2; for a discussion of the evidence, and the historiography, Young, 'James VI and I: Time for a Reconsideration?'; See also Bellany, *Politics of Court Scandal*, pp. 254–5.

23 The letters were printed by Gardiner in the first edition of his *History of England ... 1603-16* (London, 1863), II, App. iv. The quotations above are from pp. 370, 373, 379. We are grateful to Michael Young for his thoughts on these letters; *Letters of King James VI and I*, pp. 337; Young, *James VI and I*, p. 43.

24 Hutchinson, *Memoirs of the Life of Colonel Hutchinson*, pp. 64–5.

25 Weldon, *Cat May Look at a King*, p. 42. *Early Stuart Libels*, L10, M.ii.4. Osborn, *The True Tragi-Comedie*, p. 34; BL Harley 646, f. 59; I am grateful to Sears McGee for sharing his transcription of this passage; Bray, *Homosexuality*, p. 49.

26 James I, *Basilikon Doron*, p. 42; l Young, 'Queen Anna bites back', esp. p. 118; Knowles, 'To Enlight the Darksome Night, Pale Cinthia Doth Arise'; Lewalski, 'Enacting Opposition'; Barroll, 'The Court of the First Stuart Queen'.

27 *Chamberlain Letters*, II, 319, 441, 446, 533–4; Sussex's extravagance led him in 1622 to sell much of his estate to Buckingham: Stater, 'Radcliffe, Robert, fifth earl of Sussex', *ODNB*; Manningham, *Diary*, pp. 97, 343–4; TNA STAC 8/245/32, (Ratcliffe) earl of Sussex v. Ratcliffe and Normanvile.

28 'An Unpleasant Declaration of thinges passed betweene Countess of Derby & me since our marriage, and some directions for my sonne', 27 July 1611, HL, EL 213; Baker, 'Egerton, Thomas', *ODNB*; Hasler, 'Egerton, Thomas I (1540-1617)'.

29 Ellesmere's notes on the case are in HL, EL 2786, and he describes the suit as 'Sir Pexall Brocas v. William Norton Ar., Robert Hyett, William Mistlebrook, John Arlatt, Richard Osborne, Luke Lessame, Mathewe Watts, Robert Wexton, John Philipps, John Crooke, William Mitten, Anthonie Denbigh, Richard Denbigh, Thomas Bloes, Goerge Godwyne'; the hearing was held in May 1612, and refers to events in a previous but unspecified summer; they appear to be based largely on depositions and interrogatories for a missing Star Chamber case. The earlier case between Brocas and Norton is TNA STAC 8/75/20, Brocas v. Ward, Norton, Smart, Newman alias Newcombe (1607), in which Brocas alleged that Norton and his allies broke down hedges and pastured their cattle on his land.

30 Burrows, *The Family of Brocas*, pp. 208–24; J.E.M., 'Sir Pexall Brocas'; TNA STAC 8 24/7, Attorney General v Brocas, and a counter suit, STAC 8/60/3 Brocas v. Truseller, Savage, Payne, Wyllmott, Cuckson and others (both 1618) result from

disputes regarding property between Brocas and Edward Savage, son of Sir Thomas Savage, who had been Dame Elinor's second husband.

31 For debt, see Burrows, *Family of Brocas*, pp. 215–16; debts, and whether they have been properly paid, is at issue in a number of cases Brocas was involved in late in Elizabeth's reign: TNA C 3/233/71, Brocas v. Worsopp (1593); TNA C 3/223/22, Brocas v. Danvers. The cases involving Tirrell (or Turrell) regarding the forged release are TNA STAC 5/N17/11; STAC 5/B106/39; STAC 5/B17/19; and STAC 5/A48/32: there are references in these cases to other cases in Chancery and Exchequer. For Tirrell at the Fleet, see, e.g., *CSPD 1581–90*, p. 21; for the quote, see STAC 5/A57/21, Bill of Complaint; for the pardon, see SP 38/7, f. 58v; Brocas is listed as Brockhurst among those knighted by James on his arrival in London: John Nichols, *The Progresses ... of King James the First* (London, 1828), vol. I, p. 118.

32 TNA STAC 5/A57/21, Attorney General v. Brocas & West; TNA STAC 8/8/11: Attorney-General v. Brocas (1605); TNA STAC 8/82/3: Sir Pexall Brocas v Thomas Brocas (1613); SP 38/7, f. 58 v, 18 Jan. 1604; *Chamberlain Letters*, I, p. 334; Burrows, *Family of Brocas*, p. 221.

33 TNA STAC 8/8/11 (Att.-Gen. v. Brocas); TNA STAC 8/8/8 (Att.-Gen. v. [Edwardes] et al.); TNA STAC 8/82/3 (Sir Pexall v. Thomas Brocas, 1613); TNA STAC 8/260/11 (Savage v. Lambert et al., 1621); for the issue with his bailiff, see TNA STAC 8/6716, Brocas v. Wilkinson, Wadloue, Morralle and others, especially demurrer by Wilkinson on sheet 3; and TNA STAC 8/10/20, Attorney-General v. Scullard, Hasker, Crooke and others, which accused the coroner of misconduct.

34 HL, EL 2786;Gouge, *Of Domesticall Duties*, pp. 651–2; Richardson, *Household Servants*, pp. 148–9.

35 For this see TNA catalogue; as many documents in STAC 5 catalogued as separate cases appear to be part of the same one, I have counted one case for each year in which there is a case; the disputes between Pexall and Sir John Savage (who married his grandfather's widow) extend as late as 1618; Burrowes, *The Family of Brocas of Beaurepaire*, pp. 208–10.

36 Heal and Holmes, *The Gentry*, pp. 359–74.

37 *CSPD* Charles I, vol. IV, 1629–31, p. 371: this entry, which apparently started the Privy Council investigation of Castlehaven, is in fact a letter from Lord Audley to his father, saying he is turning to the father of his county.

38 Herrup, *House in Gross Disorder*, chap. 1; Herrup, 'Mervin Touchet' in *ODNB*. The family trees in *House in Gross Disorder* sort out these genealogical complexities.

39 *The Casebook of Sir Francis Ashley*, p. 70; *Dorset Quarter Sessions Order Book*, pp. 22, 42, 81.

40 TNA, STAC 8/277/7 (Castlehaven v. Bishop et al.); STAC 8/210/6 (Morley et al. v. Audley et al.). Herrup, *House in Gross Disorder*, pp. 18–19, 41, 45–6, 74–5.

41 BL, Harl. MS 390, f. 529: Mead to Stuteville, 19 Dec. 1630: Herrup, *House in Gross Disorder*, esp. pp. 64–5, 70–7.

42 Herrup, *House in Gross Disorder*, pp. 14–15; Pope, 'Roman Catholics at Bewill, Dorset'; TNA SP 16/12, f. 120 (71 i), 12/28/1625: Sir Walter Erle noted that while Castlehaven's house at Stalbridge had not yet been searched, this is where his 'ancient armor' was thought to be.

43 *Cobbett's Complete Collection of State Trials*, III, pp. 410, 413. Ironically, as Herrup notes, it was Castlehaven's son who was a staunch Catholic, not Castlehaven: Herrup, *House in Gross Disorder*, p. 5.

44 'The Manner of the Arraignment of the Earle of Castlehaven': HL, EL 7976 (1), f. 12; Herrup, pp. 37, 59–60.

45 Herrup, *House in Gross Disorder*, p. 44 and n. 41; BL, Harl. MS 390, f. 529: Mead to Stuteville, 19 Dec. 1630.

46 HL, Hastings Legal Papers, Box 5, no. 1.

47 BL, Harl. MS 390, ff. 529, 534: Mead to Stuteville, 19 Dec. 1630 and 30 Jan. 1630/1; Halsey allegedly had 16 children by his first (and legal) wife; the Welshman had married his sister's son's wife, which was it was noted, in the same degree as Sir G. A. [Gyles Allington]; for Allington, *CSPD Charles I*, vol. 5, 1631–32, pp. 41–2; Perry, 'Brother Trouble', esp. pp. 295–8; Folger Lib. V.a.262, 'Poetical Miscellany Manuscript, 1630–31, 1637': I am grateful to Amanda Herbert for this reference.

48 Amussen, *Ordered Society*, pp. 123–9; Stone, *Road to Divorce*, pp. 190–4; Elizabeth Foyster, *Manhood in Early Modern England*, pp. 164–77.

49 Bruster, 'The Horn of Plenty', pp. 195–7; Machyn, *Diary*, p. 283 (25 May 1562); Taylor, *A New Discouery by Sea*, ff. A3–A4; Sugden, *Topographical Dictionary*, p. 140.

50 Shakespeare, *As You Like It*, 4.2.14–19.

51 McEachern, 'Why Do Cuckolds Have Horns', pp. 616–17.

52 Norf R.O. DEP /26, Holmes con Elmar, f. 315v; Wilts. R.O., Deans Peculiar, Presentments, 1609 no 18; TNA STAC 8/152/7, Glovier con Warren et al.; Emmisson, *Elizabethan Life: Morals and the Church Courts*, p. 127.

53 Norf. R.O. DEP 35, William Gray con Robert Nash, f. 21v. Quaife, 199;

54 TNA STAC 8/140/29, Complaint of Edward Fosse, yeoman.

55 Quoted by Gowing, 'Gender and Language of Insult', p. 17.

56 Fox, 'Ballads, Libels, and Popular Ridicule'; 'Introduction', in *Early Stuart Libels*, (accessed 23 Jan. 2014): several of these libels, most of which are political, directed particularly at courtiers, include references to horns and cuckolds: see, e.g., L10, Nv11, Oi5, Oii5, R8.

57 TNA STAC 8/153/29, Gordon, Frances v. Auncell, Owen and others, 1622/23.

58 TNA STAC 8/164/18, Harris, Robbins v. Webb alias Rawlins, Kinge and others.

59 TNA STAC 8/150/5, Gobert alias Goborne v. Brewster (1605); STAC 8/150/4: Gobert v. Brewster, 1606.

60 Ingram, 'Charivari and Shame Punishments', pp. 297–8, provides the complaint in this case: see also Underdown, 'The Taming of the Scold', esp. pp. 130–1.

61 Somerset R.O. CQ3 1/86 (2), f. 154.

62 Staffordshire Quarter Sessions, Staffordshire RO Q/SR 98/31, 32 (Trinitiy sessions 1606): I am grateful to Laura Gowing for sharing this with me; Margaret's petition is quoted in Crawford and Gowing (eds), *Women's Worlds*, p. 172; for other responses, see Capp, *When Gossips Meet*, pp. 92–103.

63 *CSPD, 1611–18*, p. 516; the statute, 1 & 2 Jac 1, cap. 11, made it a felony (therefore punishable by death) to marry when a spouse was alive; if a spouse was absent 'beyond the Seas' for more than 7 years and the remaining spouse could not know if s/he was alive or dead, it did not apply: *Statutes*, p. 1028; for Markham, see Nicholls, 'Markham, Sir Griffin', in *ODNB*.

64 Norf R.O., DN/DEP 19/20, Off. Con John Dey and wife Audrey, pp. 291–4; DN/DEP 37/40 (1617) Audrey Dey, wid., con Edmund Smyth, ff. 167–70.

65 Norf. R. O., C/S3/27, 'Articles of misdemeanors against Thomas Vyollett, Gent and one Elizabeth Hewes his woman servant'; the word used to describe Hewes which I have transcribed as 'debauch' is 'debeise', which could also be 'debased'.

66 *Two most unnaturall and bloodie murthers*; 288; Wells, 'Introduction', p. 452; for a discussion of the play, *The Yorkshire Tragedy*, see chapter 3.

67 TNA STAC 8 /83/ 1: Bolter v. Seafowle, 1615.

68 TNA STAC 8/118/ 19: Roger Day, Gent. vs. Sir Francis Ashby, Kt, JP, William Ashby his brother et al., 1619: Day brings the case alleging assault, and the backstory provides Ashby's defense.

69 Dolan, *Dangerous Familiars*, esp. pp. 39–42; Chamberlain, *Letters*, I, 440; Manningham, *Diary*, p. 122; for the challenges of 'what really happened', see Dolan, *True Relations*, esp. chap. 4.

70 Dolan, *Dangerous Familiars*, discusses *Arden of Faversham* at pp. 36, 52–8, 72–6, 79–87; for a fuller discussion of the play, see below, chapter 3.

71 TNA STAC 8/ 145/ 1:Froome v. Loope et al., 1613; while, as Dolan notes in *True Relations*, in any specific case, the 'truth' of any account is questionable, taken together the patterns in court cases allow us to understand what constituted plausible stories – though whether plausible because they represent common occurrences or because they represent common anxieties is always a question.

72 Wrightson and Levine, *Poverty and Piety*, p. 128: they group adultery between a married man and single woman with master/servant cases, and these together make up 31.7 per cent of their cases; Quaife, 'The Consenting Spinster' finds that most cases of illegitimacy recorded in the quarter sessions involve those living in the same household: 65 per cent of those cases involve either the master or his son; unfortunately his figures are impressionistic.

73 Norf R.O., DEP/28, Ex Offic. Con Robert Dey, Rector of Cranwich, ff. 235–42, 244v–5, 247–50v, 251v, 2536; DEP 28, Robert Dey, cler. con Leonard Poole,

Richard Dey, Robert Bate and Elizabeth Purkey alias Bate, ff. 89–91, 3–11, 25–27. Cf. Richardson, *Household Servants*, p. 204.

74 Oxfordshire Archives, Ms. Oxf. Dioc Papers c.2, ff. 103, 114, 117v, 131v.

75 Hawarde, *Camera Stellata*, pp. 316–18.

76 Goodfellow, *Tarltons Newes out of Purgatorie*, pp. 21–4. For the role of credit, see Amussen, *Ordered Society*, pp. 152–5; Shepard, 'Manhood, Credit and Patriarchy'; for an economic focus, Muldrew, 'Interpreting the Market'.

77 Jonson, *Volpone*, 1.5.105, 109–12.

78 Jonson, *Volpone*, 1.5.118, 4.673, and 5.12.137–8.

3 Performing Inversion: Theatre, Politics and Society

1 For an example of this interaction, see Cogswell and Lake, 'Buckingham Does the Globe', esp. pp. 262–3, 278; this is a form of 'local reading' advocated by Marcus, *Puzzling Shakespeare*, esp. chap. 1.

2 Holland, 'Shakespeare, William (1564–1616)', *ODNB*; for Middleton, this is visible in the range of his writing in *Middleton Works*: the pamphlet attributed to James I is *The Peacemaker*; for Jonson, his varied employment is clear in Donaldson, *Ben Jonson*; Middleton's *Game at Chess* packed the theatres for nine performances before being shut down by the government: Taylor, 'Introduction', p. 1825; for Webster and Overbury, see Forker, *The Skull Beneath the Skin*, p. 122.

3 For recent overviews, see Hackett, *Short History of English Renaissance Drama*; Kinney, *Companion to Renaissance Drama*, esp. part II; and Dutton (ed.), *Oxford Handbook of Early Modern Theatre*.

4 Jonson, *Bartholemew Fair*, Induction, li. 104–5.

5 Webster, *Duchess*, 1.3.6–9.

6 García points out that the problem of the Duchess's marriage could be seen as both its secrecy and the status difference between the Duchess and Antonio: *Secret Love and Public Service*, pp. 122–4.

7 The evidence on dating is summarized by Gunby et al., *Works of John Webster*, vol. I, pp. 379–80: for the play's sources, see Carnegie, *John Webster: The Duchess of Malfi*, pp. 95–104; Webster, *The Duchess of Malfi*, ed. F. L. Lucas, p. 13. The most extensive list of Webster's borrowings from other authors is to be found in Brown's edition of *The Duchess*, App. III, pp. 214–16; and see also Intro., pp. xvii–xviii. Lucas argues (*Duchess*, Intro., pp. 14–15) that Webster made further revisions for a revival in 1617, Antonio's speech about the French Court in the first scene being a reference to the Concini affair in that year. For reasons given below this is unlikely.

8 *Duchess*, 1.1.8–9, 12–15, 19–22. Earlier literary scholars took the references to France literally, and thought that the speech must refer to the Concini affair in

1617, thus arguing either that the play should be assigned to that year, or that Webster revised the text at about that time for a revival: Lucas (ed.), *Duchess*, pp. 14–15.

9 Callaghan, 'The Duchess of Malfi and Early modern Widows'; Panek, *Widows and Suitors*, p. 10; Marcus, 'The Duchess's Marriage'.

10 Webster. *Duchess*, 1.1.126. The term 'fratriarchy' is from Allman, *Jacobean Revenge Tragedy*, chap. 4, esp. p. 148; Luckyj, 'Great Women of Pleasure'.

11 Quoted by Dolan in 'Can this be certain?', p. 122.

12 *The White Devil* was not a success, possibly because it was produced at the more plebian Red Bull theatre; *The Duchess of Malfi* was moved to the more upmarket Blackfriars theatre. David Gunby et al. (eds), *Works of John Webster*, I, pp. 10–11. Ranald, *John Webster*, p. 40. Griffith, *Jacobean Company*, pp. 204, 208, notes that the Red Bull was not automatically the playhouse for *The White Devil*, and argues that the evidence is suggestive rather than definitive.

13 *Overbury's Works*, pp. x, xiii–xix; For the relationship between Webster and Overbury, see Forker, *Skull Beneath the Skin*, pp. 110, 121–2; for the Middle Temple Wits of the 1590s, see Winston, 'Literary Associations of the Middle Temple', esp. pp. 160–2.

14 *Overbury's Works*, pp. 33–45. The stanza quoted is from p. 42.

15 Scholars have disagreed on the likely responses of Jacobean audiences to a play in which a woman overturns convention by (a) remarrying, and (b) marrying beneath her. Among those who have argued for a sympathic response are Forker, *Skull beneath the Skin*, esp. pp. 297–301; and Goldberg, *Between Worlds*, chap. 5. Examples of those taking the opposite position – that audiences would have believed that the Duchess was wrong to remarry, and wrong to take the initiative and marry a man of lower rank – include Peterson, *Curs'd Example*, passim and Jardine, 'The Duchess of Malfi'.

16 Peterson, *Curs'd Example*, pp. 17–18; and cf. also pp. 41–2, 52, 76.

17 Sherlock, 'The Monuments of Elizabeth Tudor and Mary Stuart'.

18 Steen, 'The Crime of Marriage'; Stuart, *Letters of Lady Arbella*, pp. 94–5; Lucas (ed.), *Duchess of Malfi*, p. 26.

19 However, there were already rumours that James I's eldest son, Prince Henry, who had died suddenly in November 1612, had been poisoned. See D'Ewes, *Autobiography*, I, 90–1.

20 Holles speech quoted by Peck, *Court Patronage and Corruption*, p. 24; *Life, Letters and Writings of John Hoskyns*, pp. 37–40; Foster (ed.), *Proceedings in Parliament 1610*, II, p. 344; Jansson (ed.), *Proceedings in Parliament 1614*, pp. 422–3. See also Peck, *Northampton*, pp. 208–10.

21 For libels, see *Early Stuart Libels*: Hoskyns is one of the authors of the parodic 'The Parliament Fart', C1a; Norfolk R.O. C/S3/17, Information of William Thompson, Cler, and Randall Cooke.

22 Webster, *Duchess*, 1.1.284–5, 296–7.

23 Webster, *Duchess*, 3.1.23–5. Bellany, *Politics of Court Scandal*, p. 98, and see also pp. 134, 169. Lindley, *Trials of Frances Howard*, pp. 129–44.

24 There are later plays – Middleton's *The Witch* (1616), Middleton and Rowley's *The Changeling* (1622), and the 'lost pastoral play', *The May Lord* – in which the Overbury murder is more clearly part of the subtext: Heinemann, *Puritanism and Theatre*, pp. 107–11, 173–9; O'Connor, 'Introduction', pp. 1124–5; Patterson, 'Introduction', pp. 1633–4; Hayes, *The Birth of Popular Culture*, pp. 59, 126–7. Jonson, *Ben Jonson's Conversations*, pp. 34–5.

25 For an overview, see Hackett, *Short History*, chap. 6; Allman, *Jacobean Revenge Tragedy*, esp. pp. 18–20, 34, 37–8.

26 Middleton, *Revenger's Tragedy*, 1. 1.33–34.

27 Middleton, *Revenger's Tragedy*, 1.3.90, 103–4.

28 Middleton, *Revenger's Tragedy*, 2.2.137.

29 Middleton, *Revenger's Tragedy*, 1.1.115, 1.2.28–29.

30 Middleton, *Revenger's Tragedy*, 1.2.73.

31 Gossett, 'Best Men are Molded out of Faults'.

32 Middleton, *Women Beware Women*, 5.1.184, 193, 195.

33 Middleton, *Women Beware Women*, 5.1.252–3.

34 Middleton, *Women Beware Women*, 4.1.30–34.

35 Middleton, *Women Beware Women*, 3.2.93; Jowett, 'Textual Introduction', esp. p. 1489.

36 Holinshed, *Chronicles* (1587 ed.), vol. 6, pp. 1062–6. Hattaway, 'Drama and Society', p. 112; Orlin, *Private Matters and Public Culture*, pp. 74–6.

37 *Arden of Faversham*, 1.101, 103; Dolan, *Dangerous Familiars*, p. 54; for a full discussion of the historical Arden/Ardern's career, see Orlin, *Private Matters*, pp. 33–50; Lake, *Antichrists Lewd Hat*, pp. 38–9, 48–9, reads the play with a focus on its religious implications, particularly understandings of sin.

38 *Arden of Faversham*, 1.475, 472.

39 *Arden of Faversham*, 1.496, 498–501.

40 *Arden of Faversham*, 1.221.

41 *Arden of Faversham*, 8.40–43.

42 *Arden of Faversham*, 8.77, 8.31, 8.11, 8.73.

43 For the authorship, and the other pamphlets, see Wells, 'Introduction', p. 452; Orlin, *Private Matters and Public Culture*, quoted on p. 212; see also her discussion of the play on 228–37. Cf. Shepard, *Meanings of Manhood*.

44 Middleton, *Yorkshire Tragedy*, 2.41–2, 3.51–55.

45 Middleton, *Yorkshire Tragedy*, 8.59–60.

46 For the play and its stage history, see Crandall, *Swetnam the Woman-Hater*.

47 *Swetnam the Woman-Hater*, 3.2.163–4, 3.3.126.

48 *Swetnam the Woman-Hater*, 3.3.259–60, 3.3.276–9.

49 *Swetnam the Woman-Hater*, 5.2.263, 5.2.320, 5.2.334, 338.

50 This dynamic is evident in many places in Treatise 4 of Gouge, *Domesticall Duties*, pp. 366–7, 372–5, 379–86, 393–8.

51 *Swetnam the Woman-Hater*, 4.4.10, 5.1.116.

52 Griffith, *Jacobean Company*, esp. pp. 141–2.

53 Lewalski, 'Old Renaissance Canons, New Women's Texts'; Woodbridge, *Women and the English Renaissance*, chap. 12; Griffith, *A Jacobean Company*, pp. 135–45: Griffith also notes (p. 145) that the title page illustration represents performance practice.

54 For a fuller discussion of these, see Carroll, *Humour*; and Perks, 'The Ancient Roots of Humor Theory'.

55 Amussen, 'Cuckolds Haven'.

56 William Shakespeare, *Merry Wives of Windsor*, 1.3.42, 56–7; 5.5.110. Weiser, 'The Shamings of Falstaff'.

57 *A Chast Maid in Cheape-side*, in *Middleton Collected Works*; the discussion in this and the following paragraphs has been influenced by Woodbridge, 'Introduction'; and Howard, *Theatre of a City*, esp. pp. 135–40; Hume, 'The Socio-Politics of London Comedy' focuses on the satirical nature of such plays.

58 *Chast Maid*, 1.2.49–50, 4.1.231–2, 234; Panek, 'A Wittall Cannot Be a Cookold'.

59 Jardine, *Still Harping on Daughters*, chap. 1; Levine, *Men in Women's Clothing*, esp. chap. 1.

60 For Frith, see Griffiths, 'Frith, Mary', *ODNB*; Ungerer, 'Mary Frith, alias Moll Cutpurse'; Korda, 'The Case of Moll Frith'.

61 Griffiths, 'Frith, Mary'.

62 Middleton and Dekker, *Roaring Girl*, 4.39–41.

63 Middleton and Dekker, *Roaring Girl*, 4.186, 5.72–3, 88–9.

64 Traub, *Thinking Sex*, pp. 295–6.

65 Middleton and Dekker, *Roaring Girl*, 10.358–9.

66 Van Heertum, *Swetnam's The Araignment*, p. 96: Archer also published Middleton's *White Devil* and Marston's *Insatiate Countess*.

67 Field, *Amends for Ladies*, 2.2, 3.1, pp. 439, 447; Lady Perfect's instructions from her husband are similar to those given by Frankford to his wife in Thomas Heywood, *A Woman Killed with Kindness* (1603), 2.1.49, 2.3.78-82, though with very different results.

68 Field, *Amends for Ladies*, 4.1, p. 462; see discussion in Jennifer Panek, *Widows and Suitors*, pp. 102–4.

69 Field, *Amends for Ladies*, 5:2, p. 488.

70 Field, *Amends for Ladies* 2.2, p. 441; 4.1, p. 462; 2.1, pp. 432–4; 3.4, p. 459; 4.3, p. 470.

4 Performing Inversion in Civic Pageantry and Charivari

1 The quotations that follow are taken from the text of Hole's complaint, printed in *REED* I, pp. 261–74; the passages quoted are on pp. 264–6; spelling has been modernized and abbreviations spelled out. I have silently removed phrases like 'the aforesaid' and 'the said' for readability.

2 Underdown, *Revel, Riot, and Rebellion*, pp. 110–11.

3 Elstrack, 'All doe Ride the Asse'; the fullest analysis of the print is Griffiths, *The Print in Stuart Britain*, cat. 90, quoted in www.bpi1700.org.uk, BPI 277; the print is described in Hind, *Engraving in England*, pp. 290–2, and plate 135; also Stephens, *Catalogue of Political and Personal Satires*, vol. I, #60, p. 30: both provide the full text from the print.

4 For the ritual, Ingram, 'Juridical Folklore in England', esp. pp. 62–4, and 'Charivari and Shame Punishments'; also Wieser, 'Shaming of Falstaff'; Underdown, *Revel, Riot and Rebellion*, p. 102; Norfolk RO ANW/7/3, 1615, Faith Docking con. Alice Kemp; *Journals of Two Travellers*, p. 45.

5 TNA STAC 8 249/19, Nicholas Rosyer v. James Quarry, Thomas Hammond et al., 1604.

6 Somerset R.O. CQ3 1/86 (2), f. 154.

7 For a useful short survey of theoretical work on this subject, see Muir, *Ritual*, pp. 90–2.

8 Phythian-Adams, 'Ceremony and the Citizen', p. 79. Underdown, *Revel, Riot and Rebellion*, p. 69. For a fuller discussion of a striking case at Chester, see Tittler, *Townspeople and Nation*, pp. 150–5. Sacks, *Widening Gate*, provides a good example of the transformation of urban civic culture towards one proclaiming messages of authority and order, pp. 180–92.

9 For 5 November, see Cressy, *Bonfires and Bells*; and Sharpe, *Remember, Remember*; For the origins of Queen Elizabeth's Day, see Strong, *The Cult of Elizabeth*, chap. 4.

10 Dekker, *Shoemaker's Holiday*, 3.5: First Three-Men's Song, li. 1–4.

11 See, e.g., 'Rural RECREATIONS', and 'Love in a Maze'; Cressy, *Bonfires and Bells*, pp. 25–8.

12 There is a large literature on this subject. See especially Underdown, *Revel, Riot and Rebellion*, and Hutton, *The Rise and Fall of Merry England*.

13 Hill, 'On the most Eminent seate thereof is Gouernement Illustrated'; Munro, *The Figure of the Crowd*, chap. 2; Manley, *Literature and Culture*, chap. 5; Stock, 'Something Done in Honour of the City'.

14 McClendon, 'A Moveable Feast'.

15 Bergeron, *English Civic Pageantry*, p. 100 for the Queen's Visit to Wells; Phythian-Adams, 'Ceremony and the Citizen', esp. pp. 57–8.

16 *REED*, II, p. 946.

17 For cultural conflict, see Underdown, *Revel, Riot and Rebellion*, esp. chap. 3; Ingram, 'Who Killed Robin Hood'; Hughes, 'The "Chalk" and the "Cheese"'; Braddick and Walter, 'Introduction: Grids of Power'.

18 For city-cathedral relations in Wells during this period, see Estabrook, 'In the Mist of Ceremony'.

19 The suit is TNA STAC 8/161/1, Hole v. White et al.: the case includes more than 200 sheets, but excerpts are transcribed in in *REED*, I, pp. 261–369, and Stokes provides a chronology in *REED*, II, pp. 719–28; a summary of the chronology, and those accused, along with an index of the answers related to particular issues is provided in HL EL 2728.

20 There is a lengthy account of the affair in Sisson, *Lost Plays of Shakespeare's England*, pp. 162–85, and briefer notices in Underdown, *Revel, Riot and Rebellion*, p. 55, and Hutton, *Merry England*, pp. 158–9.

21 Charivaric outbreaks ridiculing local authority-figures were not, of course, unique to Wells; for a good example, see Hindle, 'Custom, Festival and Protest'; few if any were on the public scale of the 1607 events in Wells. Similarly, there are cases where the elite was divided: see Collinson, 'The Shearmen's Tree and the Preacher'.

22 *REED*, I, pp. 236–9, II, pp. 830–3.

23 HMC, *Dean and Chapter of Wells* 2, 341–2, 354. Estabrook, 'In the Mist of Ceremony', 144.

24 *REED*, I, pp. 241–9, II, pp. 834–8.

25 *REED*, I, pp. 251–2, II, pp. 480–1, 841.

26 *Church-Wardens' Accounts of Croscombe*, pp. 4, 10; *REED*, I, pp. 86–90.

27 *REED*, I, pp. 405–13. Stokes, 'Robin Hood and the Churchwardens in Yeovil'; Underdown, *Revel, Riot, and Rebellion*, p. 98. See also Goodchild, 'Elizabethan Yeovil Festival', pp. 84–5; Trotman, 'The Church Ale and the Robin Hood Legend', p. 37.

28 For the Westonzoyland affair, see *REED*, I, pp. 388–9.

29 For a valuable survey of this subject, see Hindle, *State and Social Change*, chap. 7; for the history of communal drinkings focused on marriage, which parallels the issues here, Houston, *Bride Ales and Penny Weddings*, chaps 1 and 2.

30 *REED*, I, pp. 327, 432–3, II, p. 480. See also Underdown, *Revel, Riot, and Rebellion*, p. 49.

31 *REED*, I, pp. 354–6, II, p. 954.

32 *REED*, II, p. 720–7; Hole's Star Chamber case states that the 29th was Trinity Sunday. But in 1607 Trinity Sunday was actually on 31 May, and it is inconceivable that anyone, even Hole's enemies, would have been permitted to put on a play at a time conflicting with Evensong on the sabbath.

33 HMC, *Dean and Chapter* 2, pp. 325, 345–6. How much Morgan paid for the lease of the rectory is not clear, but when Edward Bisse of Spargrove got a similar one for three lives in 1627, it was for £240, to be paid in eight annual instalments.

34 This account of Hole is mainly from *REED*, II, p. 933. Other information from
    Wells City Charters, pp. 116–17, 191, 193; and Serel, *Historical*, p. 53.

35 *REED*, I, pp. 282, 300–1, 320, 331–2, 339, 347, and II, pp. 720–1. In his dispute
    with Watkins Hole was presumably relying on an ambiguous royal proclamation of
    1603 regarding the lawfulness, or otherwise, of Sunday pastimes. During this whole
    period the issue of sabbath observance was shot through with ambiguities: Hindle,
    State and Social Change, p. 191.

36 *REED*, I, pp. 287–9, 351, II, pp. 721–2.

37 *REED*, I, pp. 276, 280–8, II, p. 722.

38 *REED*, I, pp. 336, 338, II, p. 723.

39 *REED*, I, pp. 321, 342, and II, pp. 713, 723, 949. There is a large literature on Robin
    Hood in early modern popular culture, which generally accepts the association
    with the Summer Lord. See, e.g., Knight, *Robin Hood: A Complete Study*; Wiles,
    Early Plays of Robin Hood; and Singman, *Robin Hood*.

40 *REED*, II, pp. 723–4.

41 *REED*, I, pp. 285, 327, 338, 355–6, II, pp. 723–4, 727, 935, 943–4, 954.

42 For the Pinder, see Horsman, ed., *The Pinder of Wakefield*; and Walker, *Wakefield*,
    pp. 106–9; the version of the Pinder presented in a 1632 chapbook goes beyond
    jests to policing those who might violate local norms; the clothworkers do not seem
    to have adopted that approach: Capp, 'English Youth Groups'.

43 *REED*, I, pp. 338, 358, II, p. 724.

44 *REED*, I, pp. 337, 358, II, pp. 724–5; for cuckolds, see chapter 2.

45 For the multiple variations of charivari of this kind in early modern Europe, see
    Thompson, *Customs in Common*, chap. 8; for the English cases, see Underdown,
    Revel, Riot, and Rebellion, pp. 99–103, 110–11; Ingram, 'Ridings, Rough Music,
    and Mocking Rhymes', and 'Ridings, Rough Music, and the "Reform of Popular
    Culture"'.

46 The account of the Southover show in this and the following paragraph is based on
    REED, I, pp. 263, 353, II, pp. 725–6, 727–8. It is also possible that Hole was known
    to be a henpecked husband and that the representation of him in women's clothes
    was an allusion to this.

47 *REED*, I, pp. 264, 328–9 and II, pp. 726, 945; Stokes, 'Women and Mimesis', pp. 176–7.

48 *REED*, I, pp. 329–30, and II, 726, 946.

49 'Yard' was a common slang term for a penis. *REED*, I, pp. 265–6, 279, 345, 354, II,
    pp. 726–7, 943, 950. For allegations of Puritan hypocrisy in sexual matters, see, for
    example, Underdown, *Fire From Heaven*, pp. 28–9.

50 *REED*, I, pp. 267–9, II, pp. 709–16, 936–7.

51 *REED*, pp. 267, 271, 269–70, 290, 303–5, 321, 345, II, pp. 937, 939, 950.

52 For different aspects of this, see, e.g., Bellany, 'Rayling Rymes and Vaunting Verse';
    Fox, 'Ballads, Libels and Popular Ridicule'; Fox, 'Rumour, News and Popular

Political Opinion'; and Ingram, 'Ridings, Rough Music and Mocking Rhymes in Early Modern England'; for another case from 1607, Walter, 'The Pooremans Joy and the Gentlemans Plague'.

53 *REED*, I, pp. 271, 294–5, 354, II, pp. 716–17, 932, 954.

54 *REED*, I, pp. 270, 273, 365, 433–4. *Quarter Sessions Records Somerset*, vol. 1, p. 7. Wells City Archives, *Wells Corporation Act Book, 1553–1623*, p. 306.

55 *REED*, I, pp. 262, 359–63; HL, MS EL 2773; for the Midland Rising, see Roger B. Manning, *Village Revolts*, 229–52; Walter, 'The Pooremans Joy and the Gentlemans Plague'; Hindle, 'Imagining Insurrection'.

56 *REED*, I, pp. 310–13, 359, 363–7; Barnes, *Fines in the High Court of Star Chamber*.

57 The counter-suit is in TNA STAC 8/145/26: Foster v. Hole, 1609. See also Wells City Archives, *Corporation Act Book*, 1553–1623, pp. 316, 321. Eight Corporation members voted against bringing the counter-suit, with Hole and Yarde either absent or not voting.

58 *REED*, I, pp. 310–11, II, p. 941. For the Somerset church ales controversy in the 1630s, see Barnes, 'County Politics'; Capp, *Puritan Reformation and its Enemies*, pp. 4–7.

59 Underdown, *Revel Riot and Rebellion*, pp. 106–12; Sharp, *In Contempt of All Authority*, chap. IV, esp. pp. 100–5.

60 *REED*, I, pp. 368–70. Bates, ed., *Somerset Quarter Sessions Records: James I*, 76.

61 *REED*, I, pp. 371–8, II, pp. 724–5, 957–8. Stokes, 'Women and Mimesis', 177. Bergeron, *English Civic Pageantry*, 100. Estabrook, 'In the Mist of Ceremony', pp. 150–1.

62 *REED*, I, p. 357, II, pp. 955, 959. *Corporation Act Book*, 1553–1623, p. 375. 'The Will of John Hole, 1618', *Somerset and Dorset Notes and Queries* 15 (1916–17), pp. 214–15.

63 Cust and Lake, 'Sir Richard Grosvenor and the Rhetoric of Magistracy', p. 45; Underdown, *Revel, Riot, and Rebellion*, pp. 47–8.

5 Witches, Magicians and the Upside Down World

1 Brome and Heywood, *Late Lancashire Witches*, 1:2, speech 139

2 Holland, *A Treatise Against Witchcraft*, Sig B2–2v, D4v–E1; also found at http://name.umdl.umich.edu/A03468.0001.001, accessed 23 Feb. 2015; the best discussion of this is in Holmes, 'Popular Culture?', esp. pp. 94–5; for the exceptions, see Kent, *Cases of Male Witchcraft*, notes that men who were accused of witchcraft were remarkably similar to the women, pp. 1–2.

3 Thomas, *Religion and the Decline of Magic*, pp. 7–9; Wilby, *Cunning Folk*, esp. chap. 2; Davies, *Popular Magic* distinguishes cunning folk by their use of books: see

esp. pp. 68–9; for links to witchcraft, pp. 13, 111–12; Gregory, *Rye Spirits*, shows that even a woman who was known as a cunning woman could write, pp. 109–10.

4 Scot, *Discoverie of Witchcraft*, p. 7; Holland, *Treatise against Witchcraft*, Sig D4v-E1; Sharpe, *Instruments of Darkness*, pp. 114–15.

5 'An Acte against Conjuration, Witchcraft and Dealing with Evil and Wicked Spirits'1 Jac I cap. 12, *Statutes*, IV, part II, pp. 1028–9; McConnell, 'Lambe, John (1545/6–1628)', *ODNB*; Kassell, 'Forman, Simon (1552–1611)', *ODNB*; Wilby, *Cunning Folk*, 31–41; Davies, *Popular Magic*, chap. 4.

6 Roberts, 'Dee, John (1527–1609)', *ODNB*; Macdonald, *Mystical Bedlam*, pp. 24–30; Andrews, 'Napier, Richard (1559–1634)', *ODNB*.

7 Sharpe, *Instruments of Darkness*, 66–70; Bonzol, 'The Death of the Fifth Earl of Derby'; *CSPD 1611–18*, pp. 134, 161, 172–3; Clark, *Thinking with Demons*, pp. 155–8; for the broader links between magic and science, see Hunter, 'Alchemy, Magic, and Moralism'.

8 The voluminous modern historiography of witchcraft is summarized in Levack, *The Oxford Handbook of Witchcraft*; for a recent argument that witchcraft prosecutions are shaped by politics, see Elmer, *Witchcraft, Witch-Hunting, and Politics*, esp. chaps 2, 3; particular works will be cited as necessary. My discussion is particularly indebted to feminist scholarship on the subject by Roper, *Witchcraft in the Western Imagination* and *Oedipus and the Devil*; Purkiss, *The Witch in History*; Willis, *Malevolent Nurture*; while some scholars have suggested the persecution of witches in general is a panic, the term is useful applied only to occasions when multiple prosecutions take place in a relatively short span of time.

9 For all this, Thomas, *Religion and the Decline of Magic*, pp. 300–22.

10 Norf. R.O. AYL/17(80), Examination of Margaret Love by William Blennerhassett, Esq., 12 May 1589. For similar examples, see Sharpe, *Witchcraft in Seventeenth Century Yorkshire*, esp. pp. 11–12; in the case studied by Gregory, *Rye Spirits*, a woman initially suspected of entertaining fairies was later accused of witchcraft.

11 TNA STAC 8/149/24, Thomas Guppye of South Perrot and Joan Guppye his wife v. Robert Gybbes, Margaret late the wife of Andrew Abington gent, and others (1605), quotes from 'Answer of Robert Gibbs and Richard Newman', f. 4, and Interrogatories of Richard Newman, f. 9.

12 Wilts, R. O., Bishops Act Book Office 7 (1613–15), f. 90v; her literacy connects her to cunning folk: Gregory, *Rye Spirits*, 110.

13 TNA ASSI 45, 1/5, 38–9 (1646); Gibson, *Cunning Folk*, pp. 31–7.

14 Holmes, 'Women: Witnesses and Witches', p. 52.

15 Clark, *Thinking with Demons*, chap. 2, esp. p. 13; Sharpe, *Instruments of Darkness*, p. 85. *Wonderful Discoverie of the Witchcrafts*, p. 1619.

16 Sharpe, *Instruments of Darkness*, pp. 19–23, 80–8.

17 Holmes, 'Popular Culture', pp. 104–5.

18 'The Bill Against Conjuracions and Wichecraftes'33 H VIII cap. 8, in *Statutes*, III, pp. 837; discussion in Notestein, *A History of Witchcraft in England*, pp. 10–12.

19 For the statutes, Ewen, *Witchhunting & Witch Trials*, pp. 15–21; Sharpe, *Instruments of Darkness*, pp. 89–90. Gibson, 'Applying the Act of 1604'; for the legal context and debates, see Darr, *Marks of an Absolute Witch*: Darr uses the pamphlets to focus on legal understandings of proof.

20 *Journals of Two Travellers*, p. 54; for a useful review of recent thinking on these matters, see Sharpe, *Witchcraft in Early Modern England*; Sharpe, *Instruments of Darkness*, pp. 110–14; for purposes of comparison, felonies in general have a conviction rate of 58 per cent in early seventeenth-century Sussex: see Herrup, *Common Peace*, Table 6.2, p. 144; for the comparison to European countries, see Davies, 'Superstition and Witchcraft', esp. pp. 325–6.

21 The two works that provide the basis for this view are Macfarlane, *Witchcraft in Tudor and Stuart England* and Thomas, *Religion and the Decline of Magic*.

22 Norf. RO AYL/180, Articles Against Katherine Brand of Ketteringham, n.d. 1590s.

23 Amussen, 'Punishment, Discipline, and Power', esp. pp. 27–31; Gregory, 'Witchcraft, Politics and "good neighbourhood"'; Purkiss, *The Witch in History*, Willis, *Malevolent Nurture*, and Roper have each in different ways located witchcraft in tensions around motherhood.

24 For example, the wife of Richard Martyn of Bletchingley, whose husband was unpopular locally: TNA, STAC 8/ 17/6, Attorney-General Hobart v. Turner (1607).

25 Scot, *Discoverie of Witchcraft*, p. 34.

26 *Quarter Sessions Somerset*, I, p. 96.

27 TNA, STAC 8/122/17; Davy v. Window et al. (1606).

28 TNA, STAC 8/133/13; Edgar v. Wythe et al. (1621).

29 TNA, STAC 8/169/8; Aldington Humphrey v. Nicholas Humphrey (1610).

30 Underdown, *Fire From Heaven*, pp. 78–9; Elmer, *Witchcraft, Witch-Hunting and Politics*, pp. 85–6, suggests that the position of those who made accusations affected the attitude of the Dorchester governors.

31 Underdown, *Fire From Heaven*, passim. Few of White's sermons have survived, but it is significant that the Dorchester diarist, William Whiteway, makes no mention of White's interest in the subject.

32 James VI and I, *The First Daemonologie*: two editions were published in England in 1603, the year of James's accession. See also Sharpe, *Instruments of Darkness*, pp. 48, 91. Thomas, *Religion and the Decline of Magic*, pp. 458–9; *CSPD 1611–18*, p. 398. Sharpe, *Bewitching of Anne Gunter*, esp. pp. 173–8.

33 The Warboys case is recorded in *The Most strange and admirable discoverie*, the quote from sig. A3v; the case is accessibly summarized in Almond, *The Witches of Warboys*, which creates a clear narrative from the pamphlet and related documents; for the death of Lady Susan Cromwell, see pp. 66–7; for possession more generally, see French, *Children of Wrath*, chap. 3.

34 Macdonald, *Witchcraft and Hysteria*, pp. x–xi, xviii; he reprints Jorden's *Brief Discourse of the Disease Called the Suffocation of the Mother* (1603), quote from 22v;

Glover's case also emphasizes the religious dimensions of these cases: she was from a family with a long history of Protestantism, and her grandfather was one of the Marian martyrs; as the demon left her, Glover was alleged to have spoken the same words as her grandfather did as he died at the stake: French, *Children of Wrath*, pp. 89–93; for the role of exorcisms in religious argument, see Freeman, 'Demons, Demoniacs, and Defiance', esp. pp. 56–59.

35 Sharpe, *Bewitching of Anne Gunter*, pp. 39, 156.

36 For the trial, see Sharpe, *Bewitching of Anne Gunter*, chap. 6.

37 Sharpe, *Bewitching of Anne Gunter*, pp. 99–104.

38 Sharpe, *Bewitching of Anne Gunter*, pp. 108–10.

39 Sharpe, *Bewitching of Anne Gunter*, pp. 131, 137–8, 169–73.

40 Sharpe, *Bewitching of Anne Gunter*, pp. 179–94.

41 Sharpe, *Bewitching of Anne Gunter*, esp. p. 156; HL, EL 5955, 'Interrogatories and Answers to Frances Stewart'; this is evidently copied from the large Star Chamber case that is the basis for Sharpe's work.

42 Sharpe, *Bewitching of Anne Gunter*, pp. 186–7. Anne Gunter seems to have welcomed the attentions of young men: Francis Stewart recalled that when he visited her during her original stay at Oxford she had 'put her head into his neck, and used him very gently': HL, EL 5955, 'Interrogatories and examination of Francis Stewart, 1607.

43 Fairfax, *Daemonologia*, pp. 32, 37, 38–9, 46, 77, 123–4, 125, 127–8; Sharpe, *Instruments of Darkness*, esp. pp. 199–202.

44 Court records demonstrate that there were far more cases, but only provide the names, place of residence, and a brief description of the crime; Macfarlane, chap. 5.

45 See Gibson, *Reading Witchcraft* for the issues raised by our reliance on the stories from pamphlets.

46 Purkiss, *Witch in History*, chap. 8.

47 Goodcole, *The Wonderfull Discouerie of Elizabeth*, sig A3v.

48 Rowley, Dekker and Ford, *Witch of Edmonton*, 3.2.25–7.

49 Rowley, Dekker and Ford, *Witch of Edmonton*, 4.1. 42–4, 83, 113–15, 139.

50 Ewen, *Witchcraft and Demonianism* 244–51; *CSPD* 1634–5, pp. 141, 152–3; the second examination of Edmund makes clear how suspicions of witchcraft can exist without prosecution.

51 Purkiss, *Witch in History*, p. 233.

52 Brome and Heywood, *Late Lancashire Witches*, 1.1, speech 6.

53 Brome and Heywood, *Late Lancashire Witches*, 1.1, speech 88.

54 Brome and Heywood, *Late Lancashire Witches*, 1.1, speech 92; Brome reused this language to describe Anti-London in *The Antipodes* four years later.

55 Brome and Heywood, *Late Lancashire Witches*, 2.1, speeches 201, 205.

56 Brome and Heywood, *Late Lancashire Witches*, 3.1, speeches 362, 369.

57 Brome and Heywood, *Late Lancashire Witches*, 3.1, speech 414.

58 Brome and Heywood, *Late Lancashire Witches*, 4.3, speeches 735, 752, 774.

59 Brome and Heywood, *Late Lancashire Witches*, Epilogue, Speech 1084.

60 The story is told in *Wonderful discouerie of the witchcrafts*, esp. sig. C2(v)–C4(v), D1(v)–D3.

61 Bellany, *Politics of Court Scandal*, p. 149.

62 *Early Stuart Libels*, F2. Bellany comments brilliantly on the many other references to witchcraft in the libels, in *Politics of Court Scandal*, pp. 150–2.

63 R.N., *Sir Thomas Overburies Vision*. See also Bellany, *Politics of Court Scandal*, p. 151.

64 O'Connor, 'Introduction' explores the parallels with the Howard/Overbury scandal in some detail, as well as the publication problems, pp. 1124–8; Purkiss, *The Witch*, esp. pp. 216–20 is particularly useful on how Middleton uses contemporary witchcraft theory. Bellany, *Politics of Court Scandal*, pp. 152–3.

65 TNA, STAC 8/245/32 (Earl of Sussex v Countess of Sussex, 1622); STAC 8/255/23 (Shute v. Poulton et al., 1623). [Longueville], *Curious Case of Lady Purbeck*, pp. 93–6. Lambe was subsequently hired by Buckingham and assassinated a few weeks before the Duke was, in 1628. See above, chap. 2; Stater, 'Radcliffe, Robert, 5th Earl of Sussex (1569–1629)'.

66 Underdown, *Freeborn People*, p. 35. *Proceedings in Parliament 1626*, IV, 293, 343. Mead's newsletters containing fuller notices of the storm are in BL Harl. MS 390, fols. 79–84: Mead to Stuteville, 17, 12 June, and 1 July 1626.

67 McConnell, 'Lambe, John (1545/6–1628)', *ODNB*.

68 Goodman, *The Court of King James the First*, vol. II, p. 377.

69 *Chamberlain Letters*, II, 605; HMC, *Mar and Kellie*, II (supplement), p. 220. *CSPD 1625–1626*, p. 363. Laud, *Works*, III, pp. 154, 156–7; VII, p. 623; *Proceedings in Parliament 1626*, IV, 345.

70 *Early Stuart Libels*, Oii, 11; Oiii, 5. There are several libels celebrating Lambe's death (Oiii, 6–9), and many other references to him in libels against Buckingham in section Pi.

71 Bellany, 'The Murder of John Lambe'.

72 TNA, STAC 8/29/10: Attorney-General Coventry v. Greene.

73 Hawarde, *Camera Stellata*, p. 251: there is no other record of this case, and Whitheade's first name is never mentioned. Northumberland's relation to the Gunpowder Plot was limited: *CSPD* 1603–10, p. 262 (vol. XVI, 112a); Nicholls, 'Percy, Henry, ninth earl of Northumberland', *ODNB*; Batho, 'The Library of the "Wizard" Earl'.

Conclusion

1 *The Parlament of Women* (1640); the pamphlet was reprinted in 1646 (Wing P505) and 1656 (Wing P506); in addition, in 1656, a new pamphlet was also published, *Now or Never: or, A New Parliament of Women Assembled and Met Together*

(Wing N1434); by 1674, the ballad tune known as 'Digby's Farewell' was renamed 'The Parliament of Women' for a ballad about 'The Gossips Meeting, or the Merry Market Women of Taunton' (Wing G1317); such accounts reappeared in times of political conflict: in 1679, there is 'A List of the Parliament of Women'(Wing L2481); in 1683 there is *An Account of the Proceedings of the New Parliament of Women* (Wing A370), and the following year, a *Cuckold's Petition to the Parliament of Women* (Wing C7455A); 1684 also saw the publication of 'The Parliament of Women; or *A Compleat History of the Proceedings and Debates, of a Particular Junto, of Ladies And Gentlewomen, with a Design to Alter the Government of the World by Way of Satyr* (P506A).

2 Hughes, *Gender and the English Revolution*, esp. pp. 49–71.

3 John Taylor, *Mad Fashions, Od Fashions*, sig A2, A3; T.J., *The World Turn'd Upside Down*.

4 *Mercurius Britanicus*, 19 (28 Dec. 1643–4 Jan. 1643/4); 'Hey Then Up Go We', in *Collection of National English Airs*, pp. 33–4.

5 *Scottish Dove* no. 10, 15–22 Dec. 1643.

6 The data on the trials are summarized in Sharpe, *Instruments of Darkness*, chap. 5; he also points out the costs that communities were willing to pay to prosecute witches. See also Macfarlane, *Witchcraft*, chap. 9; for the stories of witchcraft during the war, Purkiss, *Literature, Gender and Politics*, chap. 8, esp. pp. 210–12.

7 Poole, *Alarum of War*, pp. 1, 3, 5–6.

8 Crouch, *Man in the Moon*, Issue 40, 23–31 Jan. 1650, p. 314; for more on the *Man in the Moon*, see Underdown, 'The Language of Popular Politics'; Raymond, *The Invention of the Newspaper*, esp. pp. 180–3; McElligott, 'The Politics of Sexual Libel'; Underdown, *Freeborn People*, pp. 102–3.

9 Bennett, *History Matters*, chap. 4.

10 Curelly, '"Ha, ha, ha": Modes of Satire'.

11 Wrigley and Schofield, *Population History*, Appendix 3, pp. 532–3.

12 The key word is began – they were not finally resolved until after 1688: Harris, *Restoration*, chap. 1, esp. pp. 60–1.

13 The best overview of this is Fletcher, *Gender, Sex and Subordination*, chap. 19; Thompson, '"Rough Music": Le Charivari Anglais', and 'Rough Music', in *Customs in Common*, pp. 466–531.

14 Gill, 'Gender, Sexuality, and Marriage'.

15 Weil, *Political Passions*, shows the varied ways in which gender was used in argument, but finds that none of them engage with the idea of the world upside down.

Bibliography

All works cited in the text are listed in the bibliography. Whenever possible, I have used editions that are freely available through such online collections as the Hathi Trust or Internet Archive.

Printed Primary Sources

The Anglican Canons, 1529–1947. Edited by Gerald Bray. Church of England Record Society, Vol. 6. Woodbridge, 1998.

Arden of Faversham. In *Norton Anthology of English Renaissance Drama*. Edited by David M. Bevington, Lars Engle, Katharine Eisaman Maus and Eric Rasmussen, 421–81. New York, 2002.

Abbot, George. *An exposition upon the prophet Jonah Contained in certaine sermons, preached in S. Maries church in Oxford*. 1600: STC 34.

Abbot, George. *The reasons which Doctour Hill hath brought, for the upholding of papistry, which is falselie termed the Catholike religion: unmasked and shewed to be very weake*. 1604: STC 37.

Ashley, Francis. *The Casebook of Sir Francis Ashley J.P. Recorder of Dorchester 1614–35*. Dorset Record Society, Vol. 7. Edited by J. H. Bettey. Dorchester, 1981.

The Assembly Books of Southampton. Southampton Record Society, vols. 19, 21, 24–25. Edited by J. W. Horrocks. Southampton, 1917–25.

Benson, Pamela Joseph (ed.). *Texts from the Querelle, 1616–1640*. Aldershot, UK, 2008.

Bishop Still's visitation 1594 and the 'smale book' of the clerk of the peace for Somerset 1593–5. Somerset Record Society, vol. 84. Edited by Derek Shorrocks. Taunton, 1998.

The brideling, sadling and ryding, of a rich churle in Hampshire, by the subtill practise of one Judeth Philips, a professed cunning woman. 1595: STC 19855.

Brome, Richard. *The Antipodes*. Edited by Richard Cave for 'Richard Brome Online'. http://www.hrionline.ac.uk/brome.

Brome, Richard and Thomas Heywood. *The Late Lancashire Witches*. Edited by Helen Ostovich for 'Richard Brome Online'. http://www.hrionline.ac.uk/brome.

Calendar of State Papers, Domestic, 1547–1625. 12 vols. London, 1856–72.

Calendar of State Papers, Domestic, 1625–1649. 23 vols. London, 1858–97.

Calendar of State Papers, Venetian. Vol. 18: *1623–25*. London, 1912.

Campion, Thomas. *The Works of Thomas Campion*. Edited by Walter R. Davis. New York, 1970.

Chamberlain, John. *The Letters of John Chamberlain*. 2 vols. Edited by Norman McClure. Philadelphia, 1939.

Chapman, George. *The Poems of George Chapman*. Edited by Phyllis Brooks Bartlett. New York, 1962.

Church-Wardens' Accounts of Croscombe ... [and other parishes] ... 1349 to 1560. Somerset Record Society, vol. 4. Edited by Bishop Hobhouse. Taunton, 1890.

Clapham, John. *Elizabeth of England: Certain Observations Concerning the Life and Reign of Queen Elizabeth*. Edited by Evelyn Plummer Read and Conyers Read. Philadelphia, 1951.

Clifford, Anne. *The Diaries of Lady Anne Clifford*. Edited by D. J. H. Clifford. Stroud, 1990.

Cobbett's Complete Collection of State Trials. Edited by T. B. Howell. London, 1816.

Coignet, Matthieu. *Politique discourses upon trueth and lying An instruction to princes to keepe their faith and promise ... First composed by Sir Martyn Cognet*. Translated by Edward Hoby. 1586: STC 5486.

A Collection of national English airs: consisting of ancient song, ballad, & dance tunes, interspersed with remarks and anecdote, and preceded by an essay on English minstrelsy. Edited by W. Chappell. London, 1840.

Cranmer, Thomas. 'An Exhortation concerning good Order, and obedience to Rulers and Magistrates' in *Certaine sermons appoynted by the Queenes Maiestie, to be declared and readde, by al parsons, vicars, and curates, euery Sunday and holy daye in their churches: and by her graces aduice perused and ouerseene, for the better understanding of the simple people*. 1574: STC 13654.

Crawford, Patricia and Laura Gowing (eds). *Women's Worlds in Seventeenth Century England*. London and New York, 2000.

Crouch, John. *The man in the moon, discovering a world of knavery under the sunne; both in the Parliament, the Counsell of State, the army, the city, and the country. With intelligence from all parts of England, Scotland, and Ireland, 1649–50*.

The Diary of Thomas Crosfield M.A., B.D., Fellow of Queen's College, Oxford. Edited by F. S. Boas. London, 1935.

Dekker, Thomas. *The Shoemaker's Holiday*. Harvard Classics, Vol. 47, Pt. 1. Edited by Charles William Eliot. New York, 1909–14. Reissued by Bartleby.com, 2001: http://www.bartleby.com/47/1/, accessed 8 March 2016.

Dekker, Thomas and Thomas Middleton. *The Patient Man and the Honest Whore*. In *Middleton Works*, pp. 280–327.

D'Ewes, Simonds. *The Diary of Sir Simonds D'Ewes 1622–1624: Journal d'un étudiant londonien sous le règne de Jacques Ier*. Publications de la Sorbonne. Edited by Elizabeth Bourcier. Paris: Didier, 1974.

Dod, John and Robert Cleaver. *A Godly Forme of Householde Gouernement*. 1598: STC 5383.

Dorset Quarter Sessions Order Book 1625–1638: A Calendar. Dorset Record Society, vol. 14. Edited by Terry Hearing and Sarah Bridges. Dorchester, 2006.

Early Stuart Libels: An Edition of Poetry from Manuscript Sources. Edited by Alastair Bellany and Andrew McRae. Early Modern Literary Studies, Text Series I, 2005. http://www.earlystuartlibels.net/htdocs/index.html

The Egerton Papers, Camden Society, vol. 12. Edited by John Payne Collier. London, 1840.

Eglisham, George. *The Forerunner of Revenge Upon the Duke of Buckingham.* Franckfort [The Netherlands], 1626: STC 7548.

Elstrack, Renold. 'While maskinge in their folleis all doe passe, though all say nay yet all doe ride the asse'. British Museum, Prints and Drawings. 1855,0114.189, PRN PPA93995.

Emmison, F. G. (ed.). *Elizabethan Life: Morals and the Church Courts.* Chelmsford, 1973.

Ewen, C. L'Estrange. *Witch Hunting and Witch Trials: The Indictments for Witchcraft from the Records of 1373 Assizes held for the Home Circuit A.D. 1559–1736.* London, 1929.

Fairfax, Edward. *Daemonologia: A Discourse on Witchcraft, as it was acted in the family of Mr. Edward Fairfax.* Edited by William Grainge. Harrogate, 1882.

Field, Nathaniel. *Amends for Ladies*, in *Nero & Other Plays.* Edited, with introductions and notes, by Herbert P. Horne, Havelock Ellis, Arthur Symons and A. Wilson Verity. London, 1904.

Filmer, Robert. *Patriarcha and Other Writings.* Edited by Johann Somerville. Cambridge, 1991.

Fletcher, John. *The Woman's Prize, or The Tamer Tamed*, in *Three Shrew Plays.* Edited by Celia Daileader and Gary Taylor. Manchester, 2006.

Goodcole, Henry. *The Wonderfull Discouerie of Elizabeth Savvyer a Witch Late of Edmonton.* 1621: STC 12014.

Goodfellow, Robin. *Tarltons Newes out of Purgatorie: Onely such as iest as his Jigge, fit for Gentlemen to Laught at an Houre.* 1590: STC 23685.

Goodman, Godfrey. *The Court of King James the First; by Dr. Godfrey Goodman.* 2 vols. Edited by John S. Brewer. London, 1839.

Gouge, William. *Of Domesticall Duties: Eight Treatises.* 2nd edn. 1622: STC 12119.

Haec Vir; Or The Womanish-Man. 1620: STC 12599.

Harington, John. *Nugae Antiquae, being a Miscellaneous Collection of Prose and Verse.* London, 1792.

Hawarde, John. *Les reportes del cases in Camera stellata, 1593 to 1609 from the original ms. of John Hawarde.* Edited by W. Paley Baildon. London, 1894.

Heywood, Thomas. *A Woman Killed With Kindness.* http://www.luminarium.org/editions/womankilled.htm#491.3

Hic Mulier: Or, The Man-Woman. 1620: STC 13375.

Historical Manuscripts Commission, Reports:
 15th Report, Appendix 2: Hodgkin Mss. (1897).
 Dean and Chapter of Wells. Vol. 2. London, 1914.
 Earl of Mar and Kellie. Vol. 2. London, 1930.
 Marquess of Downshire. 5 vols. London, 1924–1995.

Holinshed, Raphael. *Chronicles of England, Scotland, and Ireland.* 1587: STC 135689. http://english.nsms.ox.ac.uk/holinshed/toc.php?edition=1587

Holland, Henry. *A Treatise against Witchcraft: or A Dialogue* ... Cambridge, 1590: STC 13590.

Hoskyns, John. *The Life, Letters and Writings of John Hoskyns, 1566–1638.* Edited by Louise B. Osborn. New Haven, 1937.

Hutchinson, Lucy. *Memoirs of the Life of Colonel Hutchinson, Governor of Nottingham, by his Widow Lucy.* Edited by Julius Hutchinson and C. H. Firth. London, 1906.

James VI and I. *Basilikon Doron.* In *King James VI and I: Political Writings.* Edited by Johann Somerville. Cambridge, 1994.

James VI and I. *The First Daemonologie.* Modern edition. London, 1924.

James VI and I. *Letters of King James VI and I.* Edited by G. P. V. Akrigg. Berkeley and Los Angeles, 1984.

Jonson, Ben. *Ben Jonson's Conversations with William Drummond of Hawthornden.* Edited by R. F. Patterson. London, 1924.

Jonson, Ben. *Bartholemew Fair.* In *The Cambridge Edition of the Works of Ben Jonson*, vol. 4. Edited by David Bevington, Martin Butler and Ian Donaldson. Cambridge, 2012.

Jonson, Ben. *Volpone, or The Fox.* In *The Cambridge Edition of the Works of Ben Jonson*, vol. 3. Edited by David Bevington, Martin Butler and Ian Donaldson. Cambridge, 2012.

Knolles, Richard. *The generall historie of the Turkes from the first beginning of that nation to the rising of the Othoman familie: with all the notable expeditions of the Christian princes against them.* 1603: STC 15051.

Laud, William. *Works of the Most Reverend Father in God, William Laud, D.D.* 7 vols. Edited by W. Scott and J. Bliss. Oxford, 1847–60.

Love in a Maze: / OR, / The young-man put to his dumps Discourse / on May-Day last between two witty Lovers. EBBA 30962: http://ebba.english.ucsb.edu/ballad/30962/image, accessed 4 April 2016.

McCormick, Ian (ed.). *Secret Sexualities: A Sourcebook of 17th and 18th Century Writing.* Oxford, 2003.

Machyn, Henry. *The Diary of Henry Machyn, Citizen and Merchant Taylor of London, From A.D. 1550–A.D. 1563.* Camden Society, vol. 42. Edited by John Gough Nichols. London, 1848.

Manningham, John. *Diary of John Manningham of the Middle Temple, 1602–1603.* Edited by Robert P. Sorlien. Hanover, NH, 1976.

Marston, John. *The Insatiate Countess.* Edited by Giorgio Melchiori. Manchester, 1984.

Mercurius Britanicus. 1643–44: TT E. 80 (9).

Middleton, Thomas. *The Collected Works.* Edited by Gary Taylor and John Lavagnino. Oxford, 2007.

Middleton, Thomas. *A Chast Maid in Cheapside.* In *Middleton Works*, pp. 907–57.

Middleton, Thomas. *The Revenger's Tragedy.* In *Middleton Works*, pp. 543–93.

Middleton, Thomas. *Women Beware Women: A Tragedy.* In *Middleton Works*, pp. 1488–1541.

Middleton, Thomas. *A Yorkshire Tragedy.* In *Middleton Works*, pp. 452–66.

Middleton, Thomas, and Thomas Dekker. *The Roaring Girl; or, Moll Cutpurse.* In *Middleton Works*, pp. 721–77.

The Most strange and admirable disoverie of the three Witches of Warboys, arraigned, convicted and executed at the last Assizes at Huntington. 1593: STC 25819.

Munda, Constantia. *The worming of a mad dogge: or, A soppe for Cerberus the iaylor of Hell No confutation but a sharpe redargution of the bayter of women.* 1617: STC 18257.

N., R. *Sir Thomas Overburies Vision.* 1616: STC 18524.

Nicholson, Samuel. *Acolastus his After-Witte.* 1600: STC 18546.

Now or Never: or, A New Parliament of Women Assembled and Met Together. 1656: Wing N1434.

O'Malley, Susan, Betty Travitsky and Patrick Cullen (eds). *Defenses of Women: Jane Anger, Rachel Speght, Ester Sowernam, and Constantia Munda.* New York: Scholar Press, 1996.

Osborne, Francis. *Historical Memoires on the Reigns of Q. Elisabeth and King James.* 1658: Wing O515.

Osborne, Francis. *A Miscellany of Sundry Essaies, Paradoxes, and Problematical discourses in The Works of Francis Osborn.* 1682: Wing O506.

Osborne, Francis. *The True Tragicomedy formerly acted at court.* Edited by John Pitcher and Lois Potter. New York, 1983.

Overbury, Thomas. *The 'Conceited Newes' Of Sir Thomas Overbury And His Friends: A Facsimile Reproduction of the 9th Impression of 1616 of Sir Thomas Overbury his wife.* Edited by James E. Savage. Gainesville, FL, 1968.

Overbury, Thomas. *The Miscellaneous Works in Prose and Verse of Sir Thomas Overbury, Knt.* Edited by Edward F. Rimbault. London, 1856.

Oxford Quarter Sessions Order Book, 1614–1637. Oxford Historical Society, NS 29. Edited by Robin Blades and Alan Crossley. Oxford, 2009.

The parlament of women. 1640: STC 19306.

Platter, Thomas and Horatio Busino. *The Journals of Two Travellers in Elizabethan and Early Stuart England: Thomas Platter and Horatio Busino.* Edited by Peter Razzell. London, 1995.

Poole, Elizabeth. *An Alarum of War, given to the Army, and to their High Court of Justice.* 1649: Wing P2809.

Poems and Songs Relating to George Villiers, Duke of Buckingham. Edited by F. W. Fairholt. London: Percy Society, 1850.

Proceedings in Parliament 1610. 2 vols. Edited by Elizabeth Read Foster. New Haven and London, 1966.

Proceedings in Parliament 1614 (House of Commons). Edited by Maija Jansson. Philadelphia, 1988.

Proceedings in Parliament 1626. 4 vols. Edited by William B. Bidwell and Maija Jansson. New Haven and London, 1991–96.

Perkins, William. *A golden chaine: or The description of theologie containing the order of the causes of salvation and damnation, according to Gods word.* 1600: STC 19646.

Poole, Elizabeth. *An alarum of war, given to the Army, and to their High Court of Justice (so called) revealed by the will of God in a vision to E. Poole.* 1649: Wing P2809.

Prynne, William. *The Unloveliness of Lovelocks.* 1628: STC 20477.

Quarter Session Records. North Riding Record Society, Vols 1–3. Edited by John Christopher Atkinson. 1884–85.

Quarter Sessions Records for the County of Somerset. Vol. 1: *James I, 1607–1625.* Somerset Record Society 23. Edited by E. H. Bates. Taunton, 1907.

Records of Early English Drama: Somerset. 2 vols. Edited by James Stokes. Toronto, 1996.

[Rhodes, John]. *The Spy: Discovering the Danger of Arminian Heresie and Spanish Trecherie.* Strasbourg, 1628: STC 20577.

R[owlands], S[amuel]. *The Bride.* 1617: STC 21315.5.

R[owlands], S[amuel]. *A Crew of Kind Gossips.* 1613: STC 21414.

Rowley, William, Thomas Dekker and John Ford. *The Witch of Edmonton.* In *Women on The Early Modern Stage.* Edited by Emma Smith. London, 2014.

Rural RECREATIONS: / OR, / The Young-Men and Maids Merriment at their Dancing round a / Country MAY-POLE. EBBA 21904: http://ebba.english.ucsb.edu/search_combined/?ss=21904

Scot, Reginald. *The Discoverie of Witchcraft.* 1584: STC 21864.

Scot, Thomas. *Philomythie or Philomythologie wherin outlandish birds, beasts, and fishes, are taught to speake true English plainely.* 1616: STC 21869; 2nd edn. 1616: STC 21870.

The Scottish Dove. No. 10, 15–22 Dec. 1643, E.79(5).

'Selections from the Delaval Papers'. Edited by Basil Anderton. In *Miscellanea.* Publications of the Newcastle Upon Tyne Records Committee, vol. 9. Newcastle, 1929 (1930).

Shakespeare, William. *As You Like It.* Edited by Juliet Dusinberre. Arden Shakespeare, 3rd series, 2006.

Shakespeare, William. *Merry Wives of Windsor.* Edited by Giorgio Melchiori. Arden Shakespeare, 3rd series, 1999.

Shakespeare, William. *The Taming of the Shrew.* Edited by Barbara Hodgdon. Arden Shakespeare, 3rd series, 2010.

Smith, Thomas. *De Republica Anglorum.* Edited by Leonard Alston. Cambridge, 1906.

Southampton Court Leet Records 1550–1624. 3 vols. Southampton Records Society 1, 2, 4. Edited by F. J. C. Hearnshaw and D. M. Hearnshaw. Southampton, 1905–08.

Sowernam, Esther. *Ester Hath Hang'd Haman: Or, an answer to a lewde pamphlet entituled, The Arraignment of Women, with the Arraignment of Lewd, Idle, Froward, and Unconstant Men, and Husbands.* 1617: STC 22974.

Speght, Rachel. *A Mouzell for Melastomus:, the Cynicall Bayter of, and foule mouthered Barker against Evahs Sex.* 1617: STC 23058.

Speght, Rachel. *The Poetics and Poems of Rachel Speght.* Edited by Barbara Kiefer Lewalski. Women Writers in English, 1350–1850. Oxford, 1996.

The Statutes of the Realm: Printed by command of his majesty King George the Third, Vol. 3 (Henry VIII) and Vol. 4 (Edward VI–James I). London, 1817–19.

Stuart, Arbella. *The Letters of Lady Arbella Stuart.* Edited by Sarah Jayne Steen. Women Writers in English, 1350–1850. Oxford, 1994.

Swetnam, Joseph. *The Araignment of Lewd, Idle, Froward, and unconstant women: Or the vanitie of them, choose you whether. With a Commendation of wise, vertous and honest women. Pleasant for married Men, profitable for young Men, and hurtfull to none.* 1615: STC 23534.

Swetnam, Joseph. *A critical edition of Joseph Swetnam's The araignment of lewd, idle, froward, and unconstant women (1615).* Edited by Cis van Heertum. Nijmegen, 1969.

Swetnam the Woman-Hater. 1620: STC 23544.

Swetnam the Woman-Hater: The Controversy and the Play. Edited by Coryl Crandall. Purdue, 1969.

The Taming of A Shrew. (1594). Reprinted in Shakespeare, *Taming of the Shrew,* Appendix 3.

Taylor, John. *A Juniper lecture. With the description of all sorts of women, good, and bad: from the modest to the maddest, from the most civil, to the scold rampant, their praise and dispraise compendiously related. Also the authors advice how to tame a shrew.* 1639: STC 23766.

Taylor, John. *Mad fashions, od fashions, all out fashions, or, The emblems of these distracted times.* 1642: TT E. 138[30].

Taylor, John. *A new discouery by sea, with a wherry from London to Salisbury.* 1623: STC 23778.

Taylor, John. [T.J.] *The World Turn'd Upside Down, or A briefe description of the ridiculous Fashions of these distracted Times.* 1647: Wing T532.

Tom Tell-Troath, or a A Free Discourse Touching the Manners of the Tyme. Holland, 1630: STC 23868.

A Transcript of the Registers of the Company of Stationers of London, 1554–1640 A.D. Edited by Edward Arber. 5 vols. London, 1875–77.

Tudor Royal Proclamations. 3 vols. Edited by Paul L. Hughes and James F. Larkin. New Haven, 1964–69.

Tuke, Thomas. *A Treatise Against Painting [sic] and Tincturing of Men and Women.* 1616: STC 24316.

Two most unnaturall and bloodie murthers the one by Maister Caverley, a Yorkeshire gentleman, practised upon his wife, and committed upon his two children, the

three and twentie of Aprill 1605. The other, by Mistris Browne, and her servant
Peter, upon her husband, who were executed in Lent last past at Bury in Suffolke.
1605: STC 18288.

Visitation Articles and Injunctions of the Early Stuart Church. Edited by Kenneth
Fincham. 2 vols. Church of England Record Society. Woodbridge, 1994, 1998.

Webster, John. *The Duchess of Malfi.* Edited by F. L. Lucas. New York, 1959.

Webster, John. *The Duchess of Malfi.* Edited by John Russell Brown. Cambridge,
MA, 1964.

Webster, John. *The Works of John Webster*, Vol. I. Edited by David Gunby, David
Carnegie and Antony Hammond. Cambridge, 1995.

Weldon, Anthony. *A Cat May Look Upon a King.* 1652: Wing W1271.

Weldon, Anthony. *The Court and Character of King James* (1650). Reprinted London,
1817. http://hdl.handle.net/2027/osu.32435003538725

Wells City Charters. Somerset Record Society 46. Edited by Dorothy O. Shilton and
Richard Holworthy. Taunton, 1932.

Wilson, Arthur. *The History of Great Britain, being the Life and Reign of King James the
First.* 1653: Wing W 2888.

Wiltshire County Records: Minutes of Proceedings in Sessions, 1563 and 1574 to 1592.
Wiltshire Archeological and Natural History Society, 4. Edited H. C. Johnson.
Devizes, 1948 and 1949.

Winwood, Ralph. *Memorials of Affairs of State in the Reigns of Q. Elizabeth and
K. James.* London, 1725.

The Wonderful Discoverie of the Witchcrafts of Margaret and Phillip Flower,
daughters of Ioan Flower neere Bever Castle: executed at Lincolne, March 11. 1618.
1619: STC 11107.

Worcestershire County Records. *Calendar of Quarter Sessions Papers.* 3 vols. Edited by
J. W. Willis Bund. Worcester, 1899–1900.

Secondary Sources

Akrigg, G. P. V. *Jacobean Pageant: The Court of King James I.* New York, 1967.

Allman, Eileen. *Jacobean Revenge Tragedy and the Politics of Virtue.* Newark, DE, 1999.

Almond, Philip. *The Witches of Warboys: An Extraordinary Story of Sorcery, Sadism and
Satanic Possession.* London, 2008.

Amussen, Susan D. 'Cuckold's Haven: Gender and Inversion in Popular Culture'. In
Smuts, *The Oxford Handbook of the Age of Shakespeare*, 528–42.

Amussen, Susan D. 'Elizabeth I and Alice Balstone: Gender, Class and the Exceptional
Woman in Early Modern England'. In *Attending to Women in Early Modern England*,
edited by Betty Travitsky and Adele Seeff, 219–40. Newark, DE, 1994.

Amussen, Susan D. *An Ordered Society: Gender and Class in Early Modern England.*
Oxford, 1988.

Amussen, Susan D. '"The Part of a Christian Man": The Cultural Politics of Manhood in Early Modern England'. In Amussen and Kishlansky, *Political Culture and Cultural Politics*, 213–33.

Amussen, Susan D. 'Punishment, Discipline, and Power: The Social Meanings of Violence in Early Modern England'. *JBS* 34, no. 1 (1995): 1–34.

Amussen, Susan D. 'Turning the World Upside Down: Gender and Inversion in the Work of David Underdown'. *History Compass* 11, no. 5 (2013): 394–404.

Amussen, Susan D. 'Social Hierarchies'. In *The Elizabethan World, edited by* Susan Doran and Norman Jones, 271–84. Abingdon, 2011.

Amussen, Susan and Mark Kishlansky (eds). *Political Culture and Cultural Politics in Early Modern England: Essays Presented to David Underdown*. Manchester, 1995.

Andrews, Jonathan. 'Napier, Richard (1559–1634)'. *ODNB*, accessed 24 February 2015.

Arnold, Thomas F. 'Fortifications and Statecraft of the Gonzaga, 1530–1630'. Ohio State University, PhD Dissertation, 1993.

Aughterson, Kate. 'Hatton, Elizabeth, Lady Hatton [*née* Lady Elizabeth Cecil; *other married name* Elizabeth Coke, Lady Coke] (1578–1646)', *ODNB*, accessed 28 July 2015.

Babcock, Barbara (ed.). *The Reversible World: Symbolic Inversion in Art and Society.* Ithaca, NY, 1978.

Baker, J. H. 'Egerton, Thomas, first Viscount Brackley (1540–1617)'. *ODNB*, accessed 15 October 2014.

Bakhtin, Mikhail. *Rabelais and His World*. Translated by Hélène Iswolsky. Bloomington, IN, 1984.

Bardsley, Sandy. *Venomous Tongues: Speech and Gender in Late Medieval England.* Philadelphia, 2006.

Barnes, A. W. *Post-Closet Masculinities in Early Modern England*. Lewisburg, PA, 2009.

Barnes, Thomas G. 'County Politics and a Puritan Cause Célèbre: Somerset Churchales, 1633'. *Transactions of the Royal Historical Society*, 5th series 9 (1959): 103–22.

Barnes, Thomas G. *Fines in the High Court of Star Chamber, 1590–1641*. Privately printed, 1971. (Copies available at TNA, Folger Shakespeare Library and Boalt Hall Library, Berkeley.)

Barroll, Leeds. 'The Court of the First Stuart Queen'. In *The Mental World of the Stuart Court*, edited by Linda Levy Peck, 191–208. Cambridge, 1991.

Batho, G. R. 'The Library of the "Wizard" Earl, Henry Percy, 9th Earl of Northumberland (1564–1632)'. *The Library* 15, no. 4 (1960): 246–61.

Bayman, Anna and George Southcombe. 'Shrews in Pamphlets and Plays.' In Wooton and Holderness, *Gender and Power*, 11–28.

Beier, A. L. '"A New Serfdom": Labor Laws, Vagrancy Statutes, and Labor Discipline in England, 1350–1800'. In *Cast Out: Vagrancy and Homelessness in Global and Historical Perspective*, edited by A. L. Beier and Paul R. Ocobock, 35–63. Athens, OH, 2008.

Bellany, Alastair. 'Mistress Turner's Deadly Sins: Sartorial Transgression, Court Scandal, and Politics in Early Stuart England'. *HLQ* 58, no. 2 (1995): 179–210.

Bellany, Alastair. 'The Murder of John Lambe: Crowd Violence, Court Scandal and Popular Politics in Early Seventeenth Century England'. *Past and Present* 200 (2008): 37–76.

Bellany, Alastair. *The Politics of Court Scandal in Early Modern England: News Culture and the Overbury Affair, 1603–1660.* Cambridge, 2002.

Bellany, Alastair. '"Rayling Rymes and Vaunting Verse": Libellous Politics in Early Stuart England'. In *Culture and Politics in Early Stuart England*, edited by Kevin Sharpe and Peter Lake, 285–310. Stanford, 1993.

Bellany, Alastair and Thomas Cogswell. *The Murder of King James I.* New Haven, 2015.

Bennett, Judith M. *Ale, Beer and Brewsters in England: Women's Work in a Changing World, 1300–1600.* New York, 1996.

Bennett, Judith M. 'Patriarchal Equilibrium'. In *History Matters: Patriarchy and the Challenge of Feminism*, 54–81. Philadelphia, 2006.

Bennett, Judith M. and Shannon McSheffry. 'Early, Erotic, and Alien: Women Dressed as Men in Late Medieval London'. *History Workshop Journal* 77 (2014): 1–25.

Bergeron, David M. *English Civic Pageantry 1558–1642.* Charleston, SC, 1971.

Boleyn, Deirdre. 'Because Women Are Not Women, Rather Might be a Fit Subject of an Ingenious Satyrist'. *Prose Studies* 32, no. 1 (2010): 38–56.

Bonzol, Judith. 'The Death of the Fifth Earl of Derby: Cunning Folk and Medicine in Early Modern England'. *Renaissance and Reformation* 33, no. 4 (2010): 73–106.

Boose, Lynda. 'Scolding Brides and Bridling Scolds: Taming the Woman's Unruly Member'. *Shakespeare Quarterly* 42, no. 2 (1991): 179–213.

Boys, Jayne E. E. *London's News Press and the Thirty Years War.* Woodbridge, Suff, 2011.

Braddick, Michael J. and John Walter. 'Introduction. Grids of Power: Order Hierarchy, and Subordination in Early Modern Society'. In *Negotiating Power in Early Modern Society: Order, Hierarchy, and Subordination in Britain and Ireland*, edited by Michael Braddick and John Walter, 1–42. Cambridge, 2001.

Braunmuller, A. R. and Michael Hattaway. *Cambridge Companion to English Renaissance Drama*, 2nd edn. Cambridge, 2003.

Bray, Alan. *Homosexuality in Renaissance England.* New York, 1995.

Breitenberg, Mark. *Anxious Masculinity in Early Modern England.* Cambridge, 1996.

Bruster, Douglas. 'The Horn of Plenty: Cuckoldry and Capital in the Drama of the Age of Shakespeare'. *Studies in English Literature* 30, no. 2 (1990): 195–216.

Bucholz, Robert and Joseph Ward. *London: A Social and Cultural History.* Cambridge, 2012.

Burke, Peter. *Popular Culture in Early Modern Europe*, 3rd edn. Farnham, Surrey, 2009.

Burrows, Montagu. *The Family of Brocas of Beaurepaire and Roche Court, hereditary Masters of the Royal Buckhounds, with some account of the English Rule in Aquitaine.* London, 1886.

Butler, Judith. *Gender Trouble: Feminism and the Subversion of Identity.* New York, 1999.

Callaghan, Dympna (ed.). *The Duchess of Malfi: Contemporary Critical Essays.* Basingstoke, 2000.

Callaghan, Dympna (ed.). 'The Duchess of Malfi and Early Modern Widows'. In *Early Modern English Drama: A Critical Companion*, edited by Garrett A. Sullivan Jr, Patrick Cheney and Andrew Hadfield, 272–86. New York, 2006.

Campbell, Douglas. *The Puritan in Holland, England and America: An Introduction to American History*. New York, 1893.

Capp, Bernard. 'English Youth Groups and *The Pinder of Wakefield'. Past and Present* 76 (1977): 127–33.

Capp, Bernard. *Puritan Reformation and Its Enemies in the Interregnum*. Oxford, 2012.

Capp, Bernard. *When Gossips Meet: Women, Family and Neighbourhood in Early Modern England*. Oxford, 2003.

Carnegie, David. *John Webster, The Duchess of Malfi*. London, 2014.

Carlson, Eric Josef. *Marriage and the English Reformation*. Oxford, 1994.

Carroll, Noël. *Humour: A Very Short Introduction*. Oxford, 2014.

Carroll, William. 'Vagrancy'. In Kinney, *Oxford Companion to Renaissance Drama*, 83–92.

Cave, Richard Cave. 'The Antipodes: Critical Introduction'. Richard Brome Online, (http://www.hrionline.ac.uk/brome), accessed 26 June 2016.

Chaytor, Miranda. 'Household and Kinship: Ryton in the Late 16th and Early 17th Centuries'. *History Workshop Journal* 10 (1980): 25–60.

Clark, Stuart. *Thinking with Demons: The Idea of Witchcraft in Early Modern Europe*. Oxford, 1997.

Cogswell, Thomas. 'John Felton, Popular Political Culture and the Assassination of the Duke of Buckingham'. *Historical Journal* 49, no. 2 (2006): 357–85.

Cogswell, Thomas. 'The People's Love: The Duke of Buckingham and Popularity'. In *Politics, Religion and Popularity in Early Stuart Britain: Essays in Honour of Conrad Russell*, edited by Richard Cust, Thomas Cogswell and Peter Lake, 211–34. Cambridge, 2002.

Cogswell, Thomas. '"Published by Authoritie": Newsbooks and the Duke of Buckingham's Expedition to the Île de Ré'. *HLQ* 67, no. 1 (2004): 1–25.

Cogswell, Thomas and Peter Lake. 'Buckingham Does the Globe: *Henry VIII* and the Politics of Popularity in the 1620s'. *Shakespeare Quarterly* 60, no. 3 (2009): 253–78.

Collinson, Patrick. 'The Shearmen's Tree and the Preacher: The Strange Death of Merry England in Shrewsbury and Beyond'. In *The Reformation in English Towns, 1500–1640*, edited by Patrick Collinson and John Craig, 205–20. Basingstoke, 1998.

Crawford, Patricia. *Parents of Poor Children in England, 1580–1800*. Oxford, 2010.

Cressy, David. *Birth, Marriage and Death: Ritual, Religion and the Life Cycle in Tudor and Stuart England*. Oxford, 1997.

Cressy, David. *Bonfires and Bells: National Memory and the Protestant Calendar in Elizabethan and Stuart England*. Berkeley, 1989.

Cressy, David. 'Gender Trouble and Cross-Dressing in Early Modern England'. *JBS* 35, no. 4 (1996): 438–65.

Croft, Pauline. 'Howard, Thomas, First Earl of Suffolk (1561–1626)'. *ODNB*, accessed 11 August 2016.

Curelly, Laurent. "'Ha, ha, ha": Modes of Satire in the Royalist Newsbook *The Man in the Moon'. Revue de la Société d'Études Anglo Americaines XVII–XVIII* 70 (2013): 73–91.

Cust, Richard. 'News and Politics in Early Seventeenth-Century England'. *Past and Present* 112 (1986): 60–90.

Cust, Richard and Peter Lake. 'Sir Richard Grosvenor and the Rhetoric of Magistracy'. *Bulletin of the Institute of Historical Research* 54 (1981): 40–53.

Cuttica, Cesare. *Sir Robert Filmer and the Patriotic Monarch: Patriarchalism in Seventeenth Century Political Thought.* Manchester, 2012.

Darr, Orna. *Marks of an Absolute Witch: Evidentiary Dilemmas in Early Modern England.* Farnham, Surrey, 2011.

Davies, Owen. *Popular Magic: Cunning Folk in English History.* Hambledon, 2007.

Davies, Simon. 'Superstition and Witchcraft'. In Hadfield, Dimmock and Shinn, *Ashgate Research Companion to Popular Culture*, 323–36.

Davis, Natalie Zemon. *Society and Culture in Early Modern France.* Stanford, 1975.

Dolan, Frances. '"Can This Be Certain?": The Duchess of Malfi's Secrets'. In Luckyj, *The Duchess of Malfi*, 119–35.

Dolan, Frances. *Dangerous Familiars: Representations of Domestic Crime in England 1550–1700.* Ithaca, NY, 1994.

Dolan, Frances. 'Introduction'. In *The Taming of the Shrew: Texts and Contexts* by William Shakespeare, edited by Frances Dolan, 1–38. New York, 1996.

Dolan, Frances. *True Relations: Reading, Literature, and Evidence in Seventeenth Century England.* Philadelphia, 2013.

Dolan, Frances. *Whores of Babylon: Catholicism, Gender, and Seventeenth Century Print Culture.* Ithaca, NY, 1999.

Donaldson, Ian. *Ben Jonson: A Life.* Oxford, 2011.

Donaldson, Ian. *The World Turned Upside Down: Comedy from Jonson to Fielding.* Oxford, 1970.

Doran, Susan and Norman Jones (eds). *The Elizabethan World.* London, 2011.

Duccini, Hélène. *Concini: Grandeur et misère du favori de Marie de Médicis.* Paris: Albin Michel, 1991.

Dutton, Richard (ed.). *The Oxford Handbook of Early Modern Theatre.* Oxford, 2009.

Dyson, Jessica. *Staging Authority in Caroline England: Prerogative, Law and Order in Drama, 1625–1642.* Farnham, Surrey, 2013.

Elmer, Peter. *Witchcraft, Witch-Hunting, and Politics in Early Modern England.* Oxford, 2016.

Estabrook, Carl. 'In the Mist of Ceremony: Cathedral and Community in Seventeenth-Century Wells'. In Amussen and Kishlansky, *Political Culture and Cultural Politics*, 133–61.

Ewen, C. L'Estrange. *Witchcraft and Demonianism: A Concise Account Derived from Sworn Depositions and Confessions in the Courts of England and Wales.* London, 1933.

Fletcher, Anthony. *Gender, Sex and Subordination in England, 1500–1800*. New Haven, 1995.

Forker, Charles R. *The Skull beneath the Skin: The Achievement of John Webster*. Carbondale, 1986.

Fox, Adam. 'Ballads, Libels, and Popular Ridicule in Jacobean England'. *Past and Present* 145 (1994): 47–83.

Fox, Adam. *Oral and Literate Culture in England, 1500–1700*. Oxford, 2000.

Fox, Adam. 'Rumour, News and Popular Political Opinion in Elizabethan and Early Stuart England'. *Historical Journal* 60 (1997): 597–620.

Foyster, Elizabeth. *Manhood in Early Modern England; Honour, Sex, and Marriage*. London, 1999.

Fraser, Antonia. *The Weaker Vessel*. New York, 1984.

Freeman, Thomas. 'Demons, Demoniacs, and Defiance: John Darrell and the Politics of Exorcism in Late Elizabethan England'. In Lake and Questier, *Conformity and Orthodoxy*, 34–63.

French, Anna. *Children of Wrath: Possession, Prophecy and the Young in Early Modern England*. Farnham, Surrey, 2015.

Froide, Amy. *Never Married: Singlewomen in Early Modern England*. Oxford, 2005.

Frye, Susan. *Elizabeth I: The Competition for Representation*. New York, 1993.

Fumerton, Patricia. *Unsettled: The Culture of Mobility and the Working Poor in Early Modern England*. Chicago, 2006.

García, Eva Cruz. *Secret Love and Public Service in El mayordomo de la duquesa de Amalfi, by Lope de Vega, and The Duchess of Malfi By John Webster*. Alcalá, 2003.

Gardiner, Samuel Rawson. *History of England, 1603–1616*. Vols 1–2 of *History of England, 1603–1660*. London, 1863.

Gaskill, Malcolm. 'Witchcraft Trials in England'. In Levack, *Oxford Handbook of Witchcraft*, 283–99.

Gibson, Marion. 'Applying the Act of 1604: Witches in Essex, Northamptonshire, and Lancashire'. In *Witchcraft and the Act of 1604*, edited by John Newton and Jo Bath, 115–28. Leiden, 2008.

Gibson, Marion. *Reading Witchcraft: Stories of Early English Witches*. London, 1999.

Gill, Pat. 'Gender, Sexuality, and Marriage'. In *The Cambridge Companion to English Restoration Theatre*, edited by Deborah Payne Fisk, 191–208. Cambridge, 2000.

Goldberg, Dena. *Between Worlds: A Study of the Plays of John Webster*. Waterloo, Ontario, 1987.

Goodchild, John. 'An Elizabethan Yeovil Festival'. *Somerset and Dorset Notes and Queries*, 17 (1921–23): 83–85.

Gossett, Suzanne. '"Best Men Are Molded Out of Faults": Marrying the Rapist in Jacobean Drama'. *English Literary Renaissance* 14, no. 3 (1984): 305–27.

Gowing, Laura. *Domestic Dangers: Women, Words and Sex in Early Modern London*. Oxford, 1996.

Gowing, Laura. 'Gender and Language of Insult in Early Modern London'. *History Workshop Journal* 35 (1993): 1–21.

Gowing, Laura, Michael Hunter and Miri Rubin (eds). *Love, Friendship and Faith in Europe, 1300–1800*. Basingstoke, 2005.

Greenblatt, Stephen. *Renaissance Self-Fashioning: From More to Shakespeare*. Chicago, 1980.

Greenfield, Peter H. "'The Actors Are Come Hither': Traveling Companies'. In Kinney, *A Companion to Renaissance Drama*, 212–22.

Greenfield, Peter H. 'Touring'. In Dutton, *Oxford Handbook of Early Modern Theatre*, 292–306.

Gregory, Anabel. *Rye Spirits: Faith, Faction and Fairies in a Seventeenth Century English Town*. London, 2013.

Gregory, Anabel. 'Witchcraft, Politics and "Good Neighbourhood" in Early Seventeenth-Century Rye'. *Past and Present* 133 (1991): 31–66.

Griffith, Eva. *A Jacobean Company and Its Playhouse*. Cambridge, 2013.

Griffiths, Antony. *The Print in Stuart Britain*. London, 1998.

Griffiths, Paul. 'Frith, Mary, (c.1584–1659)'. *ODNB*, accessed 30 December 2014.

Griffiths, Paul. *Lost Londons: Change, Crime and Control in the Capital City 1550–1660*. Cambridge, 2008.

Griffiths, Paul. 'Masterless Young People in Norwich, 1560–1645'. In *The Experience of Authority in Early Modern England*, edited by Paul Griffiths, Adam Fox and Steve Hindle, 146–86. New York, 1996.

Guynn, Noah. 'The Wisdom of Farts: Ethics and Politics, Carnival and Festive Drama in Late Medieval and Early Modern France'. Paper presented at Merced Centre for the Humanities, December 2013.

Hadfield, Andrew, Matthew Dimmock and Abigail Shinn (eds). *The Ashgate Research Companion to Popular Culture in Early Modern England*. Farnham, Surrey, 2014.

Hackett, Helen. *A Short History of English Renaissance Drama*. London, 2013.

Hajnal, J. H. 'European Marriage Patterns in Perspective'. In *Population in History: Essays in Historical Demography*, edited by D. V. Glass and D. E. C. Eversley, 101–43. London, 1965.

Harris, Tim. *Rebellion: Britain's First Stuart Kings*. Oxford, 2014.

Harris, Tim. *Restoration: Charles II and His Kingdoms, 1660–1685*. Oxford, 2005.

Hasler, P. W. and W. J. J. 'Egerton, Thomas I (1540–1617), of Lincoln's Inn, Islington, York House and Harefield, Mdx. and of Chester'. In *The History of Parliament: the House of Commons 1558–1603*, edited by P. W. Hasler, 1981, online at http://www.historyofparliamentonline.org/volume/1558–1603/member/egerton-thomas-i-1540-1617, accessed 11 December 2014.

Hattaway, Michael. 'Drama and Society'. In *Cambridge Companion to English Renaissance Drama*, 2nd edn, edited by A. R. Braunmuller and Michael Hattaway, 93–130. Cambridge, 2003.

Hayes, Tom. *The Birth of Popular Culture: Ben Jonson, Maid Marion and Robin Hood*. Pittsburgh, 1992.

Heal, Felicity. 'Reputation and Honour in Court and Country: Lady Elizabeth Russell and Sir Thomas Hoby'. *Transactions of the Royal Historical Society*, 6th Series 6 (1996): 161–78.

Heal, Felicity and Clive Holmes. *The Gentry in England and Wales, 1500–1700*. Stanford, 1994.

Heinemann, Margot. *Puritanism and Theatre: Thomas Middleton and Opposition Drama under the Early Stuarts*. Cambridge, 1980.

Hentschell, Roze. 'Treasonous Textiles: Foreign Cloth, and the Construction of Englishness'. In *The Culture of Cloth in Early Modern England: Textual Constructions of a National Identity*, 103–25. Burlington, VT, 2008.

Herford, C. H., Percy Simpson and Evelyn M. Simpson. *Ben Jonson: The Man and His Work*. 2 vols. Oxford, 1925–1952.

Herrup, Cynthia. *The Common Peace: Participation and the Criminal Law in Seventeenth Century England*. Cambridge, 1987.

Herrup, Cynthia. *A House in Gross Disorder: Sex, Law, and the Second Earl of Castlehaven*. Oxford, 1999.

Herrup, Cynthia. 'The King's Two Genders'. *JBS* 45, no. 3 (2006): 493–510.

Herrup, Cynthia. 'Touchet, Mervin, Second Earl of Castlehaven (1593–1631)'. *ODNB*, accessed 8 June 2016.

Hill, Christopher. *The World Turned Upside Down: Radical Ideas during the English Revolution*. London, 1972.

Hill, Tracey. '"On the most Eminent seate thereof is Gouernement Illustrated": staging power in the Lord Mayor's Show'. In *Staged Transgression in Shakespeare's England*, edited by Rory Loughnane and Edel Semple, 24–36. Basingstoke, 2013.

Hind, Arthur M. *Engraving in England in the Sixteenth and Seventeenth Centuries: A Descriptive Catalogue with Introductions*. Cambridge, 1952.

Hindle, Steve. 'Custom, Festival and Protest in Early Modern England: The Little Budworth Wakes, St Peter's Day, 1596'. *Rural History* 6 (1995): 166–71.

Hindle, Steve. 'Imagining Insurrection in Seventeenth Century England; Representations of the Midland Rising of 1607'. *History Workshop Journal* 66 (2008): 21–61.

Hindle, Steve. *The State and Social Change in Early Modern England, c. 1550–1640*. Basingstoke: Macmillan, 2000.

Holland, Peter. 'Shakespeare, William (1564–1616)'. *ODNB*, accessed 6 May 2015.

Holmes, Clive. 'Popular Culture? Witches, Magistrates, and Divines in Early Modern England'. In *Understanding Popular Culture: Europe from the Middle Ages to the Nineteenth Century*, edited by Steven L. Kaplan, 85–111. Berlin: Mouton, 1984.

Holmes, Clive. 'Women: Witnesses and Witches'. *Past and Present* 140 (1993): 45–78.

Horsman, E. A. (ed.). *The Pinder of Wakefield*. Liverpool, 1956.

Houston, R. A. *Bride Ales and Penny Weddings: Recreations, Reciprocity, and Regions in Britain from the Sixteenth to the Nineteenth Century*. Oxford, 2014.

Houston, S. J. *James I*, 2nd edn. London, 2014.

Howard, Jean E. 'Cross-Dressing, the Theatre, and Gender Struggle in Early Modern England', *Shakespeare Quarterly* 39, no. 4 (1988): 418–440.

Howard, Jean E. *Theatre of a City: The Places of London Comedy, 1598–1642*. Philadelphia, 2007.

Hoyle, R. W. 'Rural Economies under Stress: "A World So Altered." In Doran and Jones, *The Elizabethan World*, 439–57.

Hubbard, Eleanor. *City Women: Money, Sex and the Social Order in Early Modern London*. Oxford, 2012.

Hughes, Ann. 'The "Chalk" and the "Cheese": David Underdown, Regional Cultures and Popular Allegiance in the English Revolution'. *History Compass* 11, no. 5 (2013): 373–80.

Hughes, Ann. *Gender and the English Revolution*. London, 2012.

Hughes, Ann. 'Gender and Politics in Leveller Literature'. In Amussen and Kishlansky, *Political Culture and Cultural Politics*, 162–88.

Hume, Robert. 'The Socio-Politics of London Comedy from Jonson to Steele'. *HLQ* 74, no. 2 (2011): 187–217.

Hunter, Michael. 'Alchemy, Magic, and Moralism in the Thought of Robert Boyle'. *British Journal for the History of Science* 23, no. 4 (1990): 387–410.

Hutton, Ronald. *The Rise and Fall of Merry England: The Ritual Year 1400–1700*. Oxford, 1994.

Ingram, Martin. 'Charivari and Shame Punishments: Folk Justice and State Justice in Early Modern England'. In *Social Control in Europe: Vol. 1. 1500–1800*, edited by Herman Willem Roodenburg and Petrus Cornelis Spierenburg, 288–308. Columbus, 2004.

Ingram, Martin. *Church Courts, Sex and Marriage in England, 1570–1640*. Cambridge, 1987.

Ingram, Martin. 'Infanticide in Late Medieval and Early Modern England'. In *Childhood and Violence in the Western Tradition*, edited by Laurence W. B. Brockliss and Heather Montgomery, 67–73. Oxford, 2010.

Ingram, Martin. 'Juridical Folklore in England Illustrated by Rough Music'. In *Communities and Courts in Britain, 1150–1900*, edited by Christopher Brooks and Michael Lobban, 61–82. London, 1997.

Ingram, Martin. 'Ridings, Rough Music, and Mocking Rhymes in Early Modern England'. In *Popular Culture in Seventeenth-Century England*, edited by Barry Reay, 129–65. New York, 1985.

Ingram, Martin. 'Ridings, Rough Music, and the "Reform of Popular Culture" in Early Modern England'. *Past and Present* 105 (1984): 79–113.

Ingram, Martin. '"Scolding Women Cucked or Washed": A Crisis in Gender Relations in Early Modern England?' In *Women, Crime and the Courts in Early Modern England*, edited by Jenny Kermode and Garthine Walker, 48–80. Chapel Hill, 1994.

Ingram, Martin. 'Shame and Pain: Themes and Variations in Tudor Punishments'. In *Penal Practice and Culture,1500–1900: Punishing the English*, edited by Simon Devereaux and Paul Griffiths, 36–62. Basingstoke, 2004.

Ingram, Martin. 'Who Killed Robin Hood: Transformations in Popular Culture'. In Doran and Jones, *The Elizabethan World*, 461–81.

Jardine, Lisa. '*The Duchess of Malfi*: A Case Study in the Literary Representation of Women'. In *Modern Critical Interpretations: John Webster's The Duchess of Malfi*, edited by Harold Bloom, 115–27. New York, 1987.

Jardine, Lisa. *Still Harping on Daughters: Women and Drama in the Age of Shakespeare*. New York, 1989.

Johnston, Alexandra F. and Wim Hüsken (eds). *English Parish Drama*. Amsterdam: Rodopi, 1996.

Jones, Ann Rosalind and Peter Stallybrass. *Renaissance Clothing and the Materials of Memory*. Cambridge, 2000.

Jones, Karen. *Gender and Petty Crime in Late Medieval England: The Local Courts in Kent, 1460–1560*. Woodbridge, Suffolk, 2006.

Jowett, John. 'Textual Introduction: *Women Beware Women*'. In *Middleton Works*, 1488–92.

Kassell, Lauren. 'Forman, Simon (1552–1611)'. *ODNB*, accessed 24 February 2015.

Kelly, Joan. 'Early Feminist Theory and the *Querelle des Femmes*, 1400–1789'. In *Women, History and Theory: The Essays of Joan Kelly*, 65–109. Chicago, 1984.

Kelsey, Sean. 'Scott, Thomas (*d.* 1626)'. *ODNB*, accessed 22 December 2015.

Kent, E. J. *Cases of Male Witchcraft in Old and New England, 1592–1692*. Turnhout, Belgium, 2013.

King, Helen. *The One Sex Body on Trial: The Classical and Early Modern Evidence*. Farnham, Surrey, 2013.

Kinney, Arthur. *A Companion to Renaissance Drama*. Oxford, 2004.

Kishlansky, Mark. *A Monarchy Transformed: Britain, 1603–1714*. London, 1996.

Kishlansky, Mark. 'A Whipper Whipped: The Sedition of William Prynne'. *Historical Journal* 56, no. 3 (2013): 603–27.

Knapp, Robert S. 'The Academic Drama'. In Kinney, *Companion to Renaissance Drama*, 257–65.

Knight, Stephen. *Robin Hood: A Complete Study of the English Outlaw*. Oxford, 1994.

Knowles, James. '"To Enlight the Darksome Night, Pale Cinthia Doth Arise": Anna of Denmark, Elizabeth I and the Images of Royalty'. In *Women and Culture at the Courts of the Stuart Queens*, edited by Clare McManus, 21–48. Basingstoke, 2003.

Kowaleski, Maryanne. 'Singlewomen in Medieval and Early Modern Europe: The Demographic Perspective'. In *Singlewomen in the European Past, 1250–1800*, edited by Judith Bennett and Amy Froide, 38–81. Philadelphia, 1999.

Korda, Natasha. 'The Case of Moll Frith: Women's Work and the "All-Male stage."' In *Women Players in England, 1500–1660: Beyond the All Male Stage*, edited by Pamela Allen Brown and Peter Parolin, 71–87. Burlington, VT, 2005.

Kövecses, Zoltán. *Metaphor: A Practical Introduction*, 2nd edn. Oxford, 2010.

Lake, Peter. *The Antichrist's Lewd Hat: Protestants, Papists and Players in Post-Reformation England*. New Haven, 2002.

Lake, Peter. *The Boxmaker's Revenge: 'Orthodoxy', 'Heteredoxy' and the Politics of the Parish in Early Stuart London*. Stanford, 2001.

Lake, Peter and Michael Questier (eds). *Conformity and Orthodoxy in the English Church, 1560–1660*. Woodbridge, 2000.

Lakoff, George and Mark Johnson. *Metaphors We Live By*, 2nd edn. Chicago, 2003.

Lamont, William. *Marginal Prynne, 1600–1669*. London, 1963.

Laqueur, Thomas. *Making Sex: The Body and Gender from the Greeks to Freud*. Cambridge, 1990.

Lee, Patricia-Ann. 'A Bodye Politique to Governe: Aylmer, Knox and the Debate on Queenship'. *The Historian* 52 (1990): 242–61.

LeRoy, Ladurie, Emanuel. *Carnival in Romans*. New York, 1979.

Levack, Brian (ed.). *The Oxford Handbook of Witchcraft in Early Modern Europe and Colonial America*. Oxford, 2013.

Lewalski, Barbara Kiefer. 'Enacting Opposition: Queen Anne and the Subversions of Masquing'. In *Writing Women in Jacobean England*, 15–43. Cambridge, MA, 1993.

Lewalski, Barbara Kiefer. 'Old Renaissance Canons, New Women's Texts: Some Jacobean Examples'. *Proceedings of the American Philosophical Society* 138, no. 3 (1994): 397–406.

Levine, Laura. *Men in Women's Clothing: Anti-Theatricality and Effeminization, 1579–1642*. Cambridge, 1994.

Lindley, David. *The Trials of Frances Howard: Fact and Fiction at the Court of King James*. London, 1993.

Lockyer, Roger. 'Villiers, George, First Duke of Buckingham (1592–1628)'. *ODNB*, accessed 30 June 2016.

Lockyer, Roger. *Buckingham: The Life and Political Career of George Villiers, First Duke of Buckingham*. London, 1981.

[Longueville, Thomas.] *The Curious Case of Lady Purbeck: A Scandal of the Seventeenth Century*. London, 1909.

Loomis, Catherine. *The Death of Elizabeth I: Remembering and Reconstructing the Virgin Queen*. New York, 2010.

Luckyj, Christina (ed.). *The Duchess of Malfi: A Critical Guide*. London, 2011.

Luckyj, Christina. '"Great Women of Pleasure": Main Plot and Subplot in *The Duchess of Malfi*'. *Studies in English Literature 1500–1900* 27, no. 2 (1987): 267–83.

Luckyj, Christina. 'A Mouzell for Melastomus in Context: Rereading the Swetnam-Speght Debate'. *English Literary Renaissance* 40, no. 1 (2010): 113–31.

M., JE. 'Brocas, Pexall (1563–1630)'. In *The History of Parliament: The House of Commons, 1558–1603*, edited by P. W. Hasler, http://www.historyofparliamentonline.org/volume/1558–1603/member/brocas-pexall-1563–1630, accessed 28 October 2014.

MacCulloch, Diarmaid. *Reformation: Europe's House Divided*. London, 2003.

Macdonald, Michael. *Mystical Bedlam: Madness, Anxiety, and Healing in Seventeenth-Century England*. Cambridge, 1981.

Macdonald, Michael (ed.). *Witchcraft and Hysteria in Elizabethan London: Edward Jorden and the Mary Glover Case*. London, 1991.

Macfarlane, Alan. *Marriage and Love in England:1300–1840*. Oxford, 1986.

Macfarlane, Alan. *Witchcraft in Tudor and Stuart England: A Regional and Comparative Study*. London, 1970.

McClendon, Muriel. 'A Moveable Feast: St. George's Day Celebrations and Religious Change in Early Modern England'. *JBS* 38, no.1 (1999): 1–27.

McConnell, Anita. 'Lambe, John (1545/6–1628)'. *ODNB*, accessed 7 December 2015.

McEachern, Claire. 'Why Do Cuckolds Have Horns?' *HLQ* 71, no. 4 (2008): 607–31.

McElligott, Jason. 'The Politics of Sexual Libel: Royalist Propaganda in the 1640s'. *HLQ* 67, no. 1 (2004): 75–99.

McGee, J. Sears. *An Industrious Mind: The Worlds of Sir Simonds D'Ewes*. Stanford, 2015.

McIntosh, Marjorie Keniston. *Controlling Misbehavior in England, 1370–1600*. Cambridge, 1998.

Mack, Phyllis. *Visionary Women: Ecstatic Prophecy in Seventeenth Century England*. Berkeley, 1992.

Malcolmson, Cristina and Mihoko Suzuki (eds). *Debating Gender in Early Modern England, 1500–1700*. London, 2002.

Manley, Lawrence. *Literature and Culture in Early Modern London*. Cambridge, 1995.

Manning, Roger B. *Village Revolts: Social Protest and Popular Disturbances in England, 1509–1640*. Oxford, 1988.

Marcus, Leah. 'The Duchess's Marriage in Contemporary Contexts'. In Luckyj, *Duchess of Malfi*, 107–18.

Marcus, Leah. *Puzzling Shakespeare: Local Reading and Its Discontents*. Berkeley, 1988.

Marcus, Leah. 'The Shrew as Editor/Editing Shrew'. In Wooton and Holderness, *Gender and Power*, 84–100.

Marsh, Christopher. 'Order and Place in England: The View from the Pew'. *JBS* 44, no. 1 (2005): 3–26.

Mendelson, Sara and Patricia Crawford. *Women in Early Modern England*. Oxford, 1998.

Mikalachki, Jodi. 'Taking the Measure of England: The Poetics of Antiquarianism in the English Renaissance'. Yale University PhD Dissertation, 1990.

Mikalachki, Jodi. 'Women's Networks and the Female Vagrant: A Hard Case'. In *Maids and Mistresses, Cousins and Queens: Women's Alliances in Early Modern England*, edited by Susan Frye and Karen Robertson, 52–69. Oxford, 1998.

Mossman, Judith. 'Holinshed and the Classics'. In *Oxford Handbook to Holinshed's Chronicles*, edited by Felicity Heal, Ian Archer and Paulina Kewes, 303–17. Oxford, 2012.

Muir, Edward. *Ritual in Early Modern Europe*. Cambridge, 1997.

Muldrew, Craig. 'Interpreting the Market: The Ethics of Credit and Community Relations in Early Modern England'. *Social History* 18, no. 2 (1993): 163–83.

Munro, Ian. *The Figure of the Crowd in Early Modern London: The City and Its Double.* Basingstoke, 2005.

Murphy, Gwendolen. *A Bibliography of English Character-Books, 1608–1700.* Bibliographical Society Transactions, Supplement 4, 1925.

Neale, John E. *Elizabeth I and Her Parliaments, 1584–1601.* New York, 1966.

Nichols, John. *The Progresses, Processions, and Magnificent Festivities, of King James the First, His Royal Consort, Family and Court.* 4 vols. London, 1828.

Nicholls, Mark. 'Markham, Sir Griffin (*b. c.*1565, *d.* in or after 1644)'. *ODNB*, accessed 12 August 2016.

Nicholls, Mark. 'Percy, Henry, Ninth Earl of Northumberland (1564–1632)'. *ODNB*, accessed 12 March 2015.

Notestein, Wallace. *Four Worthies: John Chamberlain, Anne Clifford, John Taylor, Oliver Heywood.* London, 1956.

Notestein, Wallace. *A History of Witchcraft in England from 1558–1718.* New York, 1968.

O'Connor, Marion. 'Introduction: *The Witch*'. In *Middleton Works*, 1124–28.

Orlin, Lena Cowen. *Private Matters and Public Culture in Post-Reformation England.* Ithaca, NY, 1994.

Ortman, Scott G. *Winds from the North: Tewa Origins and Historical Anthropology.* Salt Lake City, 2012.

Ostovich, Helen, Holger Schott Syme and Andrew Griffin (eds). *Locating the Queen's Men, 1583–1603: Material Practices and Conditions of Playing.* Farnham, Surrey, 2009.

Oxford Dictionary of National Biography. Oxford, 2004; online edn 2005. www.oxforddnb.com

Panek, Jennifer. *Widows and Suitors in Early Modern English Comedy.* Cambridge, 2004.

Panek, Jennifer. '"A Wittall Cannot Be a Cookold": Reading the Contented Cuckold in Early Modern English Drama and Culture'. *Journal for Early Modern Cultural Studies* 1, no. 2 (2001): 66–92.

Parish, Helen. *Clerical Marriage and the English Reformation: Precedent, Policy and Practice.* Aldershot, 2000.

Patterson, Annabel. 'Introduction: *The Changeling*'. In *Middleton Works*, 1632–36.

Payne, Helen. 'Howard, Katherine, Countess of Suffolk (*b.* in or after 1564, *d.* 1638)'. *ODNB*, accessed 11 August 2016.

Peck, Linda Levy. *Court Patronage and Corruption in Early Stuart England.* Boston, 1990.

Peck, Linda Levy. *Northampton: Patronage and Policy at the Court of James I.* London, 1982.

Perks, Lisa Glebatis. 'The Ancient Roots of Humor Theory'. *Humor: International Journal of Humor Research* 25, no. 2 (2012): 119–32.

Perry, Ruth. 'Brother Trouble: Incest Ballads of the British Isles'. *The Eighteenth Century* 47, no. 2/3 (2006): 289–307.

Peters, Christine. 'Religion, Household-State Authority, and the Defense of "Collapsed Ladies" in Early Jacobean England'. *Sixteenth Century Journal* 45, no. 3 (2014): 631–57.

Peterson, Joyce E. *Curs'd Example: The Duchess of Malfi and Commonweal Tragedy*. Columbia, MO, 1978.

Phythian-Adams, Charles. 'Ceremony and the Citizen: The Communal Year at Coventry, 1450–1550'. In *Crisis and Order in English Towns, 1500–1700*, edited by Peter Clark and Paul Slack, 57–85. London, 1972.

Phythian-Adams, Charles. *Desolation of a City: Coventry and the Urban Crisis of the Late Middle Ages*. Cambridge, 1979.

Pope, F. J. 'Roman Catholics at Bewill, Dorset'. *Somerset and Dorset Notes and Queries* 13 (1912–13): 348–9.

Purkiss, Diane. *Literature, Gender and Politics during the English Civil War*. Cambridge, 2005.

Purkiss, Diane. *The Witch in History: Early Modern and Twentieth Century Representations*. London, 1996.

Quaife, G. R. 'The Consenting Spinster in a Peasant Society: Aspects of Premarital Sex in "Puritan" Somerset 1645–1660'. *Journal of Social History* 11, no. 2 (1977): 228–44.

Questier, Michael. 'Conformity, Catholicism, and the Law'. In Lake and Questier, *Conformity and Orthodoxy*, 237–61.

Ranald, Margaret Loftus. *John Webster*. Boston, 1989.

Randall, David. 'Joseph Mead, Novellante: News, Sociability, and Credibility in Early Stuart England'. *JBS* 45, no. 2 (2006): 293–312.

Raymond, Joad. *The Invention of the Newspaper: English Newsbooks 1641–1649*. Oxford, 1996.

Richardson, Ralph. *Household Servants in Early Modern England*. Manchester, 2010.

Rickman, Johanna. *Love, Lust and License in Early Modern England: Illicit Sex and the Nobility*. Farnham, Surrey, 2008.

Roberts, R. Julian. 'Dee, John (1527–1609)'. *ODNB*, accessed 24 February 2015.

Roper, Lyndal. *Oedipus and the Devil: Witchcraft, Sexuality and Religion in Early Modern Europe*. London, 1994.

Roper, Lyndal. *Witchcraft in the Western Imagination*. Charlottesville, 2012.

Royer, Katherine. *The English Execution Narrative 1200–1700*. London, 2014.

Rubin, Gayle. 'The Traffic in Women: Notes on the "Political Economy" of Sex'. In *Toward an Anthropology of Women*, edited by Rayna R. Reiter, 157–210. New York, 1975.

Sacks, David Harris. *The Widening Gate: Bristol and the Atlantic Economy, 1450–1700*. Berkeley, 1991.

Scott, James. *Domination and the Arts of Resistance: Hidden Transcripts*. New Haven, 1992.

Serel, Thomas. *Historical Notes on the Church of St Cuthbert, in Wells*. Wells, 1875.

Sharp, Buchanan. *In Contempt of All Authority: Rural Artisans and Riot in the West of England, 1586–1660*. Berkeley, 1980.

Sharpe, James. *The Bewitching of Anne Gunter: A Horrible and True Story of Deception, Witchcraft, Murder, and the King of England*. New York, 2000.

Sharpe, James. *Instruments of Darkness: Witchcraft in England, 1550–1750*. London, 1997.

Sharpe, James. *Remember, Remember: A Cultural History of Guy Fawkes Day*. Cambridge, MA, 2005.

Sharpe, James. *Witchcraft in Early Modern England*. Edinburgh, 2001.

Sharpe, James. *Witchcraft in Seventeenth Century Yorkshire: Accusations and Counter Measures*. Borthwick Papers, 81, 1992.

Shepard, Alexandra. 'Family and Household'. In Doran and Jones, *Elizabethan World*, 352–71.

Shepard, Alexandra. 'From Anxious Patriarchs to Refined Gentlemen? Manhood in Britain, circa 1500–1700'. *JBS* 44, no. 2 (2005): 281–95.

Shepard, Alexandra. 'Manhood, Credit and Patriarchy in Early Modern England'. *Past and Present* 167 (2000): 75–106.

Shepard, Alexandra. *Meanings of Manhood in Early Modern England*. Oxford, 2003.

Shepard, Alexandra. ' "Swil-bols and Tos-pots": Drink Culture and Male Bonding in England, c. 1560–1640'. In Gowing et al., *Love, Friendship and Faith*, 110–30.

Shepherd, Simon. *The Woman's Sharp Revenge: Five Women's Pamphlets from the Renaissance*. New York, 1985.

Sherlock, Peter. 'The Monuments of Elizabeth Tudor and Mary Stuart: King James and the Manipulation of Memory'. *JBS* 46, no. 2 (2007): 263–89.

Sherman, William. *Used Books: Marking Readers in Early Modern England*. Philadelphia, 2009.

Singman, Jeffrey L. *Robin Hood: The Shaping of the Legend*. Westbrook, CT: Greenwood Press, 1998.

Sisson, C. J. *Lost Plays of Shakespeare's Age*. Cambridge, 1936.

Smuts, Malcolm (ed.). *The Oxford Handbook of the Age of Shakespeare*. Oxford, 2016.

Spence, Richard T. 'Clifford, Anne, Countess of Pembroke, Dorset, and Montgomery (1590–1676)'. *ODNB*, accessed 22 June 2011.

Stanivukovic, Goran. 'Between Men in Early Modern England'. In *Queer Masculinities, 1550–1800: Siting Same-Sex Desire in the Early Modern World*, edited by Katherine O'Donnell and Michael O'Rourke, 232–51. Basingstoke, 2006.

Stater, Victor. 'Radcliffe, Robert, Fifth Earl of Sussex (1573–1629)'. *ODNB*, accessed 5 May 2015.

Steen, Sara Jayne. 'The Crime of Marriage: Arbella Stuart and *The Duchess of Malfi*'. *Sixteenth Century Journal* 22 (1991): 61–73.

Stephens, Frederick George. *Catalogue of Political and Personal Satires ... in the British Museum*, Vol. I, *1320–1689*. London, 1978, reprint of 1870 edn.

Stewart, Alan. 'A Society of Sodomites: Religion and Homosexuality in Renaissance England'. In Gowing et al., *Love, Friendship and Faith*, 88–109.

Stock, Angela. '"Something Done in Honour of the City": Ritual, Theatre and Satire in Jacobean Civic Pageantry'. In *Plotting Early Modern London: New Essays on Jacobean City Comedy*, edited by Dieter Mehl, Angela Stock and Anne-Julia Zwierlein, 125–44. Aldershot, 2004.

Stokes, James. 'Robin Hood and the Churchwardens in Yeovil'. *Medieval and Renaissance Drama in England* 3 (1986): 1–25.

Stokes, James. 'Women and Mimesis in Medieval and Renaissance Somerset'. *Comparative Drama* 27 (1993–94): 176–96.

Stone, Lawrence. *The Crisis of the Aristocracy 1558–1641*. Oxford, 1965.

Stone, Lawrence. *Family and Fortune: Studies in Aristocratic Finance in the Sixteenth and Seventeenth Centuries*. Oxford, 1973.

Stone, Lawrence. *The Road to Divorce: England, 1530–1987*. Oxford, 1990.

Stretton, Tim. 'Women'. In Doran and Jones, *Elizabethan World*, 335–51.

Strong, Roy. *The Cult of Elizabeth: Elizabethan Portraiture and Pageantry*. Berkeley, 1986.

Sugden, Edward. *A Topographical Dictionary to the Works of Shakespeare and His fellow Dramatists*. Manchester, 1925.

Taylor, Gary. 'Introduction: *A Game at Chess*, A Later Form'. In *Middleton Works*, 1825–29.

Thomas, Keith. *Religion and the Decline of Magic*. New York, 1971.

Thompson, Edward. '"Rough Music": Le Charivari Anglais'. *Annales: ESC*, 27 (1972): 285–312.

Thompson, Edward. 'Rough Music'. In *Customs in Common: Studies in Traditional Popular Culture*, 467–531. London, 1991.

Tittler, Robert. *Townspeople and Nation: English Urban Experiences*. Stanford, 2001.

Traub, Valerie. *Thinking Sex with the Early Moderns*. Philadelphia, 2016.

Trotman, E. E. 'The Church Ale and the Robin Hood Legend'. *Somerset and Dorset Notes and Queries* 28 (1961–67): 37–8.

Underdown, David. '"But the Shows of Their Street": Civic Pageantry and Charivari in a Somerset Town, 1607'. *JBS* 50, no. 1 (2011) 4–23.

Underdown, David. *Fire from Heaven: Life in an English Town in the Seventeenth Century*. London, 1992.

Underdown, David. *A Freeborn People: Politics and the Nation in Seventeenth-Century England*. Oxford, 1996.

Underdown, David. 'The Language of Popular Politics in the English Revolution'. In *Place and Displacement in the Renaissance*, edited by Alvin Vos, 107–31. Binghamton, 1995.

Underdown, David. *Revel, Riot and Rebellion: Popular Politics and Culture in England, 1603–1660*. Oxford, 1985.

Underdown, David. 'The Taming of the Scold: The Enforcement of Patriarchal Authority in Early Modern England'. In *Order and Disorder in Early Modern England*, edited by Anthony Fletcher and John Stevenson, 116–36. Cambridge, 1985.

Underdown, David. 'Yellow Ruffs and Poisoned Possets: Placing Women in Early Stuart Political Debate'. In *Attending to Early Modern Women*, edited by Susan D. Amussen and Adele Seeff, 230–43. Newark, DE, 1998.

Ungerer, Gustav. 'Mary Frith, Alias Moll Cutpurse, in Life and Literature'. *Shakespeare Studies* 28 (2000): 42–84.

Wales, Tim. '"Living at Their Own Hands": Policing Poor Households and the Young in Early Modern Rural England'. *Agricultural History Review* 61, no. 1 (2013): 19–39.

Walker, J. W. *Wakefield: Its History and People*. Wakefield, 1934.

Wall, Alison. 'Rich, Penelope, Lady Rich (1563–1607)'. *ODNB*, accessed 16 February 2016.

Walsham, Alexandra. 'The Godly and Popular Culture'. In *The Cambridge Companion to Puritanism*, edited by John Coffey and Paul Chang-Ha Lim, 277–93. Cambridge, 2008.

Walter, John. '"The Pooremans Joy and the Gentlemans Plague": A Lincolnshire Libel and the Politics of Sedition in Early Modern England'. *Past and Present* 203 (2009): 29–67.

Watt, Tessa. *Cheap Print and Popular Piety, 1550–1640*. Cambridge, 1991.

Weil, Rachel. *Political Passions: Gender, the Family and Political Argument in England, 1680–1714*. Manchester, 1999.

Weil, Rachel. 'Politics and Gender in Crisis in David Underdown's "The Taming of the Scold."' *History Compass* 11, no. 5 (2013): 381–88.

Weiser, Brian. 'The Shamings of Falstaff'. In Smuts, *Oxford Handbook of the Age of Shakespeare*, 512–27.

Wells, Stanley. 'Introduction: A Yorkshire Tragedy'. In *Middleton Works*, 452–55.

Whittle, Jane. 'Housewives and Servants in Rural England, 1440–1650: Evidence of Women's Work from Probate Documents'. *Transactions of the Royal Historical Society*, 6th Series 15 (2005): 51–74.

Whittle, Jane (ed.). *Landlords and Tenants in Britain, 1440–1660*. Woodbridge, 2013.

Wilby, Emma. *Cunning Folk and Familiar Spirits: Shamanistic Visionary Traditions in Early Modern British Witchcraft and Magic*. Brighton, 2005.

Wiles, David. *The Early Plays of Robin Hood*. Ipswich, 1981.

'The Will of John Hole, 1618'. *Somerset and Dorset Notes and Queries* 15 (1916–17): 214–15.

Willis, Deborah. *Malevolent Nurture: Witch-Hunting and Maternal Power in Early Modern England*. Ithaca, NY, 1995.

Winston, Jessica. 'Literary Associations of the Middle Temple'. In *History of the Middle Temple*, edited by Richard O. Havery, 147–71. Oxford, 2011.

Woodbridge, Linda. 'Introduction: *A Chaste Maid in Cheapside*'. In *Middleton Works*, 907–11.

Woodbridge, Linda. *Women and the English Renaissance: Literature and the Nature of Womankind, 1540–1620*. Urbana, 1986.

Wooton, David and Graham Holderness (eds). *Gender and Power in Shrew Taming Narratives 1500–1700*. Basingstoke, 2010.

Wrightson, Keith. *Earthly Necessities: Economic Lives in Early Modern Britain*. New Haven, 2000.

Wrightson, Keith and David Levine. *Poverty and Piety in an English Village: Terling 1525–1700*. New York, 1979.

Wrigley, E. A. and R. S. Schofield. *The Population History of England 1541–1871: A Reconstruction*. Cambridge, 1989.

Young, Michael. *James I and the History of Homosexuality*. Basingstoke: Macmillan 2000.

Young, Michael. 'James VI and I: Time for a Reconsideration?' *JBS* 51, no. 3 (2012).

Young, Michael. 'Queen Anna Bites Back: Protest, Effeminacy and Manliness at the Jacobean Court'. In *Gender Power and Privilege in Early Modern Europe*, edited by Jessica Munns and Penny Richards, 108–22. Harlow, 2003.

Zwicker, Stephen. '"What Every Literate Man Once Knew": Tracing Readers in Early Modern England'. In *Owners, Annotators, and Signs of Reading*, edited by Robin Myers, Michael Harris and Giles Mandelbrote, 75–90. London, 2005.

Index

A Mouzell for Melastomus 25–6, 47, 93
Munda, Constantia 27

Napier, Richard 131, 154
news 12, 32, 33, 65–6, 82, 158, 159
North Moreton, Berkshire 141, 142
Norwich 68, 110

order 1–2, 3, 9, 11, 46, 52, 58, 93, 101, 105,
    124, 129–30
    gender order 2–3, 5, 6, 7, 15, 16, 19, 24,
        27, 30, 41, 43, 48–9, 50, 58, 81, 92, 93,
        95, 100, 111, 132, 145, 151, 159, 160,
        160–1, 161, 162
    ideas about 1–2, 10–11, 125, 127
    political 2, 3, 8, 43, 81, 93, 158
    social order 2, 8–9, 11, 13, 17, 71, 89–90,
        113, 145, 161
Osborne, Francis 53, 57
Overbury, Sir Thomas 34, 35–6, 39, 43–4,
    45–6, 48, 54, 55, 57, 66, 150–1, 161
    and Webster 77, 81–2
    A Wife 43–4, 82
Oxford 28
Oxford University 141–2

pageants and plays 110, 112, 118–21, 135
Palmer, Humphrey 103
Parlament of Women 157
parliament 8, 11, 84, 152, 157–8, 159
*The Patient Man and the Honest
    Whore* 14–15
patriarchs 53, 91
    failed 4, 5, 7, 18, 50, 51, 58, 62, 64–5,
        66, 69, 71, 75, 80, 87, 88, 98, 102, 143,
        157, 160, 162
patriarchal equilibrium 18, 27, 161
Perkins, William 14, 131
Platter, Thomas 106, 135
poison 32–5, 36, 39, 42, 46, 57, 62, 73, 76,
    80, 84, 86, 88, 91, 137, 151–2
politics 1, 2, 4, 7, 12, 19, 25, 76, 85, 89, 105,
    111, 119, 125, 156, 160–1
Poole, Elizabeth 159
popular culture 8, 98, 128, 129
    witchcraft in 131–2, 134
possession 139–45
Prideaux, John 142
printing and print culture 8, 12, 13, 76, 142

Protestantism 6, 8, 9, 11, 12, 22, 65, 109, 113
    culture 9, 11, 109, 111, 113
Prynne, William 50
Purbeck; *see* Villiers, Frances; Villiers, John
puritans 11, 50, 55, 57, 109, 111–12, 113,
    115, 117–20 passim, 123, 124, 125,
    126, 127, 137

Quakers 4
queens 2, 6, 13
Quemerford, Wiltshire 69–70

Radcliffe, Bridget 59, 151–2
Radcliffe, Robert 59, 65, 151–2
Ranters 4
rape 63, 64–5, 74, 86–7, 88, 153
Red Bull theatre 25, 78, 94
Reformation 8, 9, 10, 105
Restoration 161–2
revenge tragedy 73, 77, 85–9, 161
The Revenger's Tragedy 86–7
Rich, Penelope 40
ritual inversion 3, 7, 8–9, 15, 16–17, 18, 23,
    67, 108, 110, 111, 113–14, 126, 133
    shaming 30, 69–70, 105, 106, 108, 120,
        123, 126
The Roaring Girl 40, 98–100, 102
Robin Hood 8–9, 78, 112–14, 118, 119, 128
Rodney, Sir John 114, 119, 121, 123
Romans, carnival in 9, 17
Rosyer, Nicholas 30, 106
Rowlands, Samuel 2, 22, 47

Samuel, Alice 140
scolds 5, 6, 7, 15, 17, 19, 27–9, 38, 49, 70,
    75, 96, 137, 155, 160
Scot, Reginald 137
Scot, Thomas 35–6, 47
Scottish Dove 158
Scots, dislike of 54, 84
separation, *a menso et thoro* 66–7, 70–1
servants 2, 7, 15, 27, 31, 51, 52–3, 54, 56,
    58, 60, 61, 64–5, 71–2, 73, 74, 76, 101
    unruly 74, 129, 149, 155
Seymour, William 124
sex and money 90–1, 98
Shakespeare, William 12, 77–8
shrew plays 22, 36
Shrove Tuesday 9, 109

9 781350 090057